Switzerland: A Village History

Also by David Birmingham

THE AKAN OF GHANA (*editor*)

CENTRAL AFRICA TO 1870: Zambezia, Zaire and the South Atlantic

A CONCISE HISTORY OF PORTUGAL

THE DECOLONIZATION OF AFRICA

L'EUROPE ET L'AFRIQUE (*with M. Chamberlain and C. Metzger*)

FRONTLINE NATIONALISM IN ANGOLA AND MOZAMBIQUE

HISTORY OF CENTRAL AFRICA (*editor with Phyllis M. Martin*)
Volume One: The Early Years to 1870
Volume Two: The Colonial Era, 1870–1960
Volume Three: The Contemporary Years, since 1960

KWAME NKRUMAH: The Father of African Nationalism

THE MAKING OF MODERN ANGOLA (*with Jill R. Dias, forthcoming*)

PORTUGAL AND AFRICA

THE PORTUGUESE CONQUEST OF ANGOLA

PRE-COLONIAL AFRICAN TRADE (*editor with Richard Gray*)

TRADE AND CONFLICT IN ANGOLA: The Mbundu and their Neighbours

TRADE AND EMPIRE IN THE ATLANTIC, 1400–1600

WHITE PRESENCE AND POWER IN AFRICA (*editor*)

Switzerland: A Village History

David Birmingham
Professor of Modern History
University of Kent at Canterbury

First published in Great Britain 2000 by
MACMILLAN PRESS LTD
Houndmills, Basingstoke, Hampshire RG21 6XS and London
Companies and representatives throughout the world

A catalogue record for this book is available from the British Library.

ISBN 0–333–80014–1

 First published in the United States of America 2000 by
ST. MARTIN'S PRESS, INC.,
Scholarly and Reference Division,
175 Fifth Avenue, New York, N.Y. 10010

ISBN 0–312–23076–1

Library of Congress Cataloging-in-Publication Data
Birmingham, David.
Switzerland : a village history / David Birmingham.
p.   cm.
Includes bibliographical references and index.
ISBN 0–312–23076–1 (cloth)
1. Château d'Oex (Switzerland)—History. 2. Villages—Switzerland—Gruyáre
Region—Rural conditions. I. Title.

DQ851.C355 B57   2000
949.4'53—dc21
99–051698

This book is printed on paper suitable for recycling and made from fully managed and sustained
forest sources.

10   9   8   7   6   5   4   3   2   1
09   08   07   06   05   04   03   02   01   00

Printed and bound in Great Britain by
Antony Rowe Ltd, Chippenham, Wiltshire

To
Marcel Bernasconi
Raoul de Pesters
Paul Dubuis
Marcelle Gétaz
Nelly Menoud
Michel Perrier

Contents

List of Plates		viii
List of Sketch Maps and Figures		ix
Preface		x
Glossary and Chronology		xiv
Acknowledgements		xvii
1	The Valley of the Cranes	1
2	Under the Paw of the Bear	19
3	Tradition and Reformation	36
4	The Milk of the Land	57
5	Fairs and Markets	81
6	The Green Flag of Liberty	101
7	Butchers, Bakers and Candlestick-Makers	119
8	Education and Social Change	143
9	The Romance of the Alps	159
10	Patriotism and the Shadow of War	176
Sources		201
Index		218

List of Plates

1   Market square (Château-d'Oex museum collection)
2   Castle motte (Museum old postcard)
3   Rossinière old chalet (drawing by E. Gladbach in E. Henchoz, *Revue Historique Vaudoise*, March 1964)
4   Wooden interior (Museum collection)
5   Pack-mule (M. Henchoz and G. Morier-Genoud, *Château-d'Oex*, 1990)
6   Cheese porter (G. Fleury, Villars-sur-Glâne)
7   Cowmen at play (Museum old postcard)
8   Seventeenth-century cow bells (DBB)
9   Cheese dairy (Siegfried Eigstler, Thun)
10 Lumberjacks on the river (André Jacot, *Chroniques*, n.d. [1996])
11 Hay-carrying (Museum old postcard)
12 Alpine dairymen (Museum old postcard)
13 Winter sports (Museum old postcard)
14 Luxury rail travel (M.O.B. railway company)
15 Paper cut-out art (Château-d'Oex museum exhibit by J.J. Hauswirth)
16 Barn decoration (G. Fleury, Villars-sur-Glâne, from Bulle museum exhibit by Silvestre Pidoux)

List of Sketch Maps and Figures

Sketch map 1   The principality of Gruyère and the
                    old Swiss republics   xix
Sketch map 1.1 The five military mandates of the
                    principality of Gruyère   2
Sketch map 4.1 Streams and alps around Château-d'Oex   58
Sketch map 5.1 Trade paths out of Château-d'Oex   83
Sketch map 7.1 Château-d'Oex cart tracks before the
                    railway   121

Figure 1.1   The House of Gruyère 1157–1554   5
Figure 9.1   Diagram of railway politics   161

Preface

Switzerland is a complex country. The Swiss 'nation' was founded 150 years ago – in 1848 – by the union of two dozen small republics. The essential components of Switzerland, however, are the 3000 boroughs to which Swiss people feel that they truly belong. This is a study of one such borough, Château-d'Oex (pronounced Chateau-Day), and the book's aim is to illuminate the central themes of Switzerland's history from a local, rural perspective. The story begins 1000 years ago when pioneers began to clear the alpine woodland and drain the glacial marshes. In the Swiss mountains, peasant societies learned how to tame the wilderness and raise dairy cattle while, on the plain, lake-side towns developed cheese markets. Swiss society, however, was not simply divided between the highland and the plain. It was also divided by language and religion. In the early modern period the lords-bailiff of Château-d'Oex spoke German, the clerks and schoolmasters wrote in French, and the farmers spoke a local Romanic *patois* based on Latin interspersed with Celtic words from the Helvetian past. Until 1555 the Château-d'Oex highland was Roman Catholic but in that year the Protestant Reformation was imposed on the parish, much to the dismay of the faithful.

In the heyday of the Holy Roman Empire most Swiss principalities were poor and precarious. Among them, however, the princes of Gruyère – to whom Château-d'Oex belonged – were more successful than most in building up their estates in clusters of castles, towns and alpine villages. They reached out into France and Italy and established diplomatic ties with the great duchies of Burgundy and Savoy which surrounded them. While Gruyère prospered as a principality many other Swiss states turned to republican forms of government. In 1291 the death of the most powerful of the Swiss aristocrats, the prince of Habsburg, compelled the lake-side dwellers of central Switzerland to adopt a self-reliant form of high justice. They had a Latin charter drawn up in which wealthy local burghers became the guarantors of imperial law and economic order. In the wake of this republican initiative a kaleidoscope of villages, valleys and markets made and unmade hundreds of local pacts and treaties which gradually coalesced into the Swiss system of military alliances.

The rise of Swiss republicanism did not immediately affect the aristocratic tradition in Château-d'Oex, but by the fifteenth century one of the newest and most thrusting of the Swiss republics, the city-state of Bern, had begun to send its regiments of militia into the Gruyère highlands in search of wealth and influence. By 1554 the last reigning prince of western Switzerland was driven to bankruptcy and Gruyère county was partitioned among republican neighbours belonging to the Swiss alliance. The village of Château-d'Oex became a borough of the Bernese Oberland, albeit one whose peasants spoke Romanic rather than the Alemannic *patois* of their neighbours.

The Reformation brought new disputes to Switzerland and over three centuries was the cause of many local wars, culminating in the civil war of 1847. In Château-d'Oex church government was influenced by the ideas of Zwingli of Zürich while church practice was affected by the puritanical doctrines of Calvin of Geneva. Highland farmers fiercely resisted change and resented the puritan proscription of their festivals, funerals and feast days. Young men who had served abroad in the mercenary armies which enriched the 'red economy' of the Swiss states particularly resented moral restraint after their years of drinking and whoring in France and the Low Countries.

The eighteenth century saw the rise of unaccustomed alpine prosperity as the dairy industry became a source of wealth. In our own post-agricultural age, when farming is carried out by a mere 2 per cent of the population, the detailed emphasis of Chapter 4 on daily life and practice is a deliberate reminder that farming was the all-encompassing experience of most alpine people for most of their working careers until at least the mid-twentieth century. Cattle which migrated into the mountains each summer produced Gruyère cheeses of ever-growing size, quality and value. Cheesemongers became landowners, merchants and moneylenders in the highland and alpine cheeses were headloaded down to the lakes for sale to wholesalers from across half of Europe. Some of the Château-d'Oex cheeses were destined for overseas consumption by West Indian planters and Ottoman courtiers.

Wealth was replaced by poverty in the wake of Bonaparte's invasion of Switzerland in 1798. The *ancien régime* collapsed in Bern and in its Oberland boroughs. The new craft industries of Switzerland, fine metals and the watch industry around Geneva, and embroidered ribbons and the textile industry around Zürich, did not reach the Alps and chronic poverty spread through many rural communities. Child beggars preyed on the conscience of the first generation of tourists seeking pure air, mountain scenery and escape from the grime of industrialisation in England. Alongside the poverty there grew a community of wealthy expatriates to whom the Alps were the romantic playground celebrated by Rousseau.

Modern politics began very slowly to rescue Switzerland from a post-Napoleonic recession. The state of Vaud, to which Bonaparte had given Château-d'Oex in 1803, retained its hold on the highland borough in 1815, thanks to the intervention of Tsar Alexander of Russia. It was he who stemmed the enthusiasm of some European powers anxious to restore pre-revolutionary political systems to the Swiss republics and bring the *ancien régime* of Bern back to Château-d'Oex. Fifteen years later the revolution of 1830 brought cautious liberals some political influence, but by 1848 the more ambitious radicals had gained the power to create a Swiss federal union.

The first generation of democratic Swiss politicians, in Château-d'Oex as elsewhere, encouraged state services which would revive prosperity. The unification of the private and provincial postal services, the creation of a single currency, the standardisation of weights and measures, the dismantling of the inter-community customs posts and the encouragement of universal primary education all paved the way for a slow economic revival among highland peasants who lived off stock-raising, timber-felling and subsistence agriculture. A second generation of politicians favoured greater private initiative when stage-coaches brought the first big wave of vacationers to the hotels of the mountains. Investors sponsored the building of electric railways and by the outbreak of the Great War a gravel motor-road was in use across the mountains from the Rhône.

In 1914 the tourist industry collapsed, bringing hardship to many. Farmers were conscripted to man the frontiers far away from Château-d'Oex while women and children milked the beasts and harvested the crops. As food scarcity bit into urban Switzerland farm prices began to rise, causing butchers and buttermaids to witness a modest return to prosperity. Hardship soon returned, however, with a postwar pandemic of influenza which killed many demobilised young farmers. Recovery had hardly begun when the world depression again brought poverty to Swiss farming, a poverty which still prevailed when the Second World War broke out and the country was besieged by Fascist Italy, Nazi Germany and Vichy France. Survival owed much to a shrewd and charismatic leader, General Guisan, who became the public face of Swiss independence. More privately the Swiss hosted bankers from all the combatant nations in the castle of the old Château-d'Oex lords-bailiff at Rougement and Swiss business tried to maintain commercial normality throughout the hostilities.

For 50 years after the collapse of Germany in 1945 Switzerland prospered. Agriculture, even small-scale mountain agriculture, was subsidised and mechanised by state governments while the confederation funded new infrastructure and support services. By 1990 this miracle had begun to falter, and narrow rural self-interest prevented the federal government from taking Switzerland into the European Union. At the same time the collapse of the Soviet Union deprived Switzerland of its recognised role as one of the West's bastions against communism. The United States rounded on its former ally and threatened to cut off banking relations if the wartime records of dormant Swiss accounts were not opened to investigation. A convulsion of self-doubt caused the Swiss to throw themselves into the commemoration of past patriotism. The charter of 1291 gave cause to the celebrations of 1991, while 1998 witnessed the bicentenary of the Napoleonic revolution. As an afterthought the Swiss also celebrated the 150th anniversary of their modern constitutional union.

This book takes a new look at the thousand-year span of Switzerland's history. It not only depicts the major changes which took place over the centuries, but also evokes in intimate detail the daily life of a peasant community preserved for posterity in the private and public archives rediscovered by the author in his childhood village of Château-d'Oex.

Glossary and Chronology

Note: The text uses popularised English terminology with the Swiss originals glossed below.

Helvetia	(i) Roman province of the Swiss Celts
	(ii) Napoleonic Switzerland
	(iii) The Confederation of Helvetia, CH, modern Switzerland
Romanic Switzerland	*Suisse Romande*, Franco-Provençal Switzerland (later French-speaking and not to be confused with Romanche Switzerland in the Engadine or Latin Switzerland in Tessin)
Alemannic Switzerland	Swiss German regions, peoples and dialects
Gruyère	(i) Holy Roman principality and castle symbolised by an heraldic crane
	(ii) Alpine valley crossing three Swiss states and containing Château-d'Oex
	(iii) Highland of the upper Sarine river
	(iv) Mature full-fat cheese widely exported
Simmental	(i) Alpine valley disputed between Gruyère and Bern
	(ii) Breed of cattle favoured for meat
Ormont	(i) Alpine valley disputed between Gruyère and Savoy
	(ii) Highland district conquered by Bern in 1476 and by Vaud in 1798
Bern	(i) Alemannic Swiss city-state founded in AD 1191 with the bear as its emblem
	(ii) Oligarchic republic which dominated Château-d'Oex 1403–1554 and ruled it till 1798
	(iii) Capital of the Swiss confederation after the unification of 1848
Lord-bailiff	*Bailli* commander of a rural bailliwick belonging to the city of Bern

Vaud (state)	(i) Autonomous Swiss republic with a green and white flag from 1803
	(ii) Federated Swiss *canton* from 1848
Moudon	(i) Capital of Vaud under Savoy rule
	(ii) Codified common law granted to the highland boroughs by the counts of Gruyère
Lausanne	(i) Seat of a Catholic bishop (until 1536) and later Protestant cathedral chapter governing the highland deanery of Ogo and the castle church of Oex
	(ii) Academy (later university) founded in 1537
	(iii) Capital of Vaud from the Swiss Revolution of 1798
Vevey	Industrial and viticultural centre on Lake Geneva and cheese-market for the highland
Bulle	Corn market of the Fribourg plain once owned by the bishops of Lausanne
Highland (district)	*Pays-d'Enhaut* (or *Oberland*), one of 21 districts of the state of Vaud
Governor/ vice-governor	*Préfet/sous-préfet* representative of the state of Vaud in the highland from 1798
Château-d'Oex (borough)	Largest of three municipal *communes* of the Highland district (between Rougemont and Rossinière)
Mayor	*Syndic* (chief executive, burgomaster, formerly *châtelain*) of the borough of Château-d'Oex
Etivaz	(i) Mountain parish of Château-d'Oex
	(ii) Brand-name for highland Gruyère cheese

Rough guide to eighteenth-century: money and coinage

Kreutzer or cruche	Small copper coin of Bern, a quarter Batz, farthing
Schilling or sol	Coin also called sou, a half Batz, a twentieth of a livre, a ha'penny
Batz or bache	Copper coin of *ancien régime* Bern, large penny
Gulden of florin	Money of account based on German book-keeping, four Batzen

Pfund or livre   Money of account based on French book-
                       keeping, two-and-a-half florins, later a franc
                       of twenty sous or 100 cents
Krone or écu   Silver crown (or half-crown) of varying size,
                       minted by the bishop of Lausanne and others
Louis d'or   Gold sovereign of varying size, eight small
                       crowns.

Acknowledgements

Among my colleagues at the University of Kent, Andrew Butcher has, over many years, provided me with clues about how to think imaginatively about small-scale medieval societies and, although I shall never be a medieval historian, I hope that my introductory chapters will provide at least an adequate frame of reference. Chapter 1 was kindly read by Bruce Webster who checked my use of feudal terminology and raised unanswerable questions about the philanthropic motivation of crusaders who bequeathed meadows to the highland church. David Potter, the leading specialist both on Burgundy and on the early modern nobility of Europe, generously read a long early draft of Chapter 2 which subsequently had to be pared down rather than give full treatment of the Gruyère principality and its relationship with the city–state of Bern. Clive Church, Britain's expert on Swiss politics, advised me over an article on the unification of Switzerland which originally appeared in *History Today* and has now been cannibalised here. In Chapter 3 I had to recognize that I was only semi-literate in matters of theology and asked Doreen Rosman for advice on the treatment of the Reformation. She willingly did much more than that and read the entire typescript both in an early draft and in its shortened form. Without her incisive suggestions for restructuring the work, and for reshaping many of its chapters, this village history would never have been completed.

This book has been made possible by the generous help given to me by many Swiss curators of museums and archives. Marcel Henchoz, the curator of the Highland Museum in Château-d'Oex, gradually introduced me over several years to the wealth of historical records that are invisibly locked away in all the wardrobes, chests and cupboards on display in a museum initiated by his father in 1921. Gabriel Morier-Genoud, who succeeded to the museum curatorship, as well as being clerk to the village parliament, was able to find for me extensive collections of private papers that were housed in the attic of the Hôtel de Ville, among them records originally found in the great chalet at Rossinière. Jean-Claude Rosat, the town clerk of Château-d'Oex, gave me every facility in consulting the borough's municipal archives stored in the cellar underneath the annexe to the village hall. Samuel Henchoz, the district *préfet*, showed me some of the records kept by his legendary predecessor, Auguste Cottier. Madame Favez generously lent me her private deed box whose records date back to 1551 and are now in the possession of the museum.

In Bern, Lucienne Hubler, whose maternal family comes from Château-d'Oex, took time off from her encyclopaedic editing to give me constant encouragement and advice. In Lausanne, Ghislaine Vautier and her family provided gracious hospitality while stimulating my wider interest in Swiss culture and facilitating my researches in the university library. In Geneva, Edouard and Bridget Dommen read the whole manuscript and gave me encouragement as well as detailed advice based on their familiarity with Switzerland in general and the highland in particular. In the Jura, Claudine Roulet's literary imagination constantly inspired me to keep writing. In Basel, Paul and Jennifer Jenkins took an enthusiastic interest in the work and introduced me to their colleagues in the field of local history. Last but not least my fellow Africanist, the late Robert Netting, supplied the classic study of Swiss history, *Balancing on an Alp*, which kept my own aspirations suitably humble.

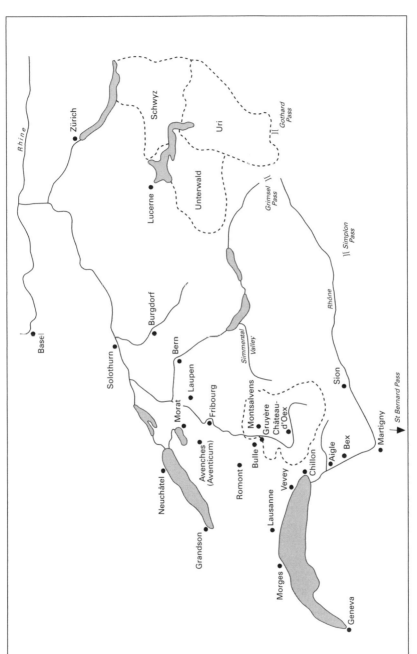

Sketch map 1 The Principality of Gruyère and the old Swiss republics

1
The Valley of the Cranes

The village of Château-d'Oex lies in the highland of Gruyère in the western Alps of Switzerland. The principality of Gruyère took shape during the eleventh century and ruled over the highland throughout the Middle Ages. Its prince was a one-time forest warden who obtained authority over the region with the imperial title of count – *comes* in Latin, *Graf* in German and *comte* in French – granted by the Holy Roman Emperor. The county, or earldom, adopted the crane as its emblem, a bird called 'Grue' in French and therefore symbolically appropriate for a territory called 'Gruyère'. The valley of the cranes was predominantly forested before the eleventh century and there is no particular evidence that cranes ever nested there on their seasonal migrations through Switzerland. Ever since the Middle Ages, however, the heraldic crane has flown on the military banners and civic flags of Château-d'Oex and of the neighbouring villages of Saanen, Rougemont and Rossinière. In Saanen the crane was granted a golden beak and gold claws by Pope Julius II in gratitude for military services rendered to the Vatican. In Château-d'Oex the heraldic bird strode fiercely across the ramparts of the castle which gave the village its name.

The first piecemeal colonisation of forest clearings in the highland began before the establishment of an imperial county in Gruyère. A tradition of northern colonisation made its impact on Switzerland after the decline of the Roman empire when Alemannic shepherds from the Rhine settled in vacant niches on the frontiers of the old Celtic farming communities of the Swiss plain. The immigrants gradually penetrated the forests and entered the mountains on the edge of the Alps. By the eighth century these foresters and pastoralists had began to explore and exploit pastures and woodlands in the Simmental valley, less than a day's walk across the mountains north of Château-d'Oex.

1

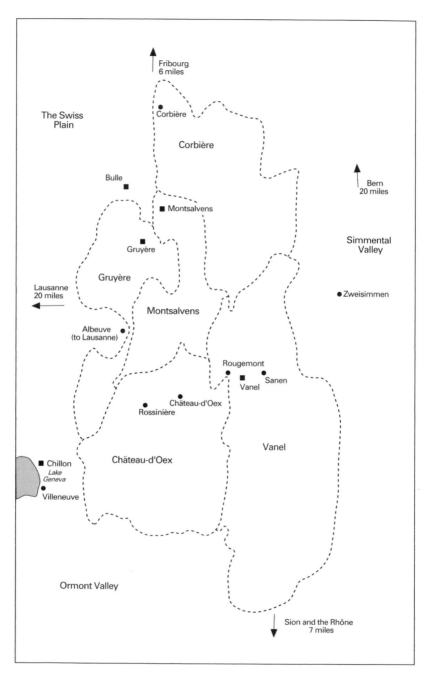

Sketch map 1.1   The five military mandates of the principality of Gruyère

By the tenth century the Alemannic immigrants had crossed the mountain and scattered through the uppermost reach of the Gruyère valley. The early pioneers generally preferred the security of isolation in far-flung homesteads to the protection of community in clustered hamlets. The tradition of isolation enabled them to retain their Alemannic language and their Germanic customs though it probably did not deter them, when opportunity arose, from raiding their lowland neighbours for livestock and for young women. The tenth-century Alemannic colonisation of the eastern Gruyère highland never reached Château-d'Oex but stopped at the gorge on the Sarine river called Vanel.

In the centuries following the Alemannic invasions a second influx of northern immigration brought rather different traditions from Germany to Switzerland during the 'dark ages'. These new traditions were to become the traditions of Château-d'Oex. The later waves of migrants across the Rhine chose to associate themselves with the Helvetian farmers of the Swiss plain and with the post-Roman patricians who ruled over them. As they settled down the migrants lost their Germanic dialects and adopted the Romanic dialects of the Romanised Celts who had become their hosts. The Romanic-speakers of western Switzerland adopted a pattern of village-based farming as they set about clearing and tilling vacant land on the plain. Only when new soils became scarce did farmers start to seek virgin territory in the Alpine foothills. Romanic-speaking pioneers made clearings in the forests at the western end of the valley of Gruyère, gradually moving into the highland until they encountered the Alemannic frontier at the gorge of Vanel. By the year 1040 monks in the ancient Roman monastery of St Maurice, far below the highland on the banks of the Rhône, had heard that people were living in the mountains above them in a territory called 'Ogo'.

The name Ogo, alternatively Oex as in Château-d'Oex, probably meant highland or *hoch gau*. Indeed the first feudal princes of Gruyère called themselves the counts of Ogo, the earls of the highland. Gaining possession of the recently-settled highland may not have required any great military effort by the newly-enobled counts. If given a choice farming peoples naturally preferred to cultivate the richer, warmer soils of the plain and population remained rather sparse in the cold, stony highland. The young principality probably met little resistance and was able to extend its sovereign authority beyond Château-d'Oex and to cross the great linguistic divide which separated Switzerland into its two distinct cultural halves, one Romanic and the other Alemannic.

In order to rule over a valley containing different cultural traditions the counts of Gruyère adjusted their administrative practices to the varying judicial customs of their peoples.

Once the highland had been conquered, the feudal lords of Gruyère had to devise a means to hold on to it. As population pressure increased in the lowland, mountain farming became a less unattractive economic option and competition for access to highland pastures began to develop. Some lowland princes in the Rhône valley and on the Swiss plain made seasonal agreements to rent highland grazing for their transhumant cattle. In exchange the plains dwellers offered temperate produce such as fruit and wine which porters carried up to the mountain on their backs. The complex seasonal migrations were carefully supervised by officials appointed to control the pastures and protect the forests. As modest mountain prosperity grew the counts built a series of fortresses to protect their highland domains.

The oldest and eventually most commodious castle of the princes of Gruyère was the Home Castle. It was built in the mild climate at the lower end of the valley where wheat grew reasonably well and some fruit could ripen in benign weather. The castle occupied a hill from which vantage point the ruler could watch over seasonal migrations of livestock between the plain and the highland. Only herdsmen who owed him allegiance, or paid him appropriate dues, could take their beasts up to the highland during the summer season. The castle could also ensure that all deliveries of goods carried up the mountain would be subjected to appropriate levies. Produce travelling down to the plain, flax, wool, leather and cheese, could also be supervised and taxed. In the early years of the principality the count held a licence from the Holy Roman Emperor to hold a market in his castle town at Gruyère. This imperial licence entitled him to levy taxes on stallholders, cobblers, wine-porters, tinkers and all other merchants and artisans who visited the fair. The revenue contributed to the cost of administering and protecting the highland from which the count's wealth flowed. Over time the income from Gruyère market became so great that fierce competition broke out over the right to host it. In the ensuing conflict the prince of Gruyère lost imperial favour and the market franchise was transferred to the more powerful prince-bishop of Lausanne. The bishop moved the lucrative fair-ground away from Gruyère town to establish it three miles out into the plain beside his own castle of Bulle.

The second most important castle of the Gruyère principality was the castle of Montsalvens. This castle, now ruined, occupied the eastern side of the valley almost within cannon shot of the Gruyère home

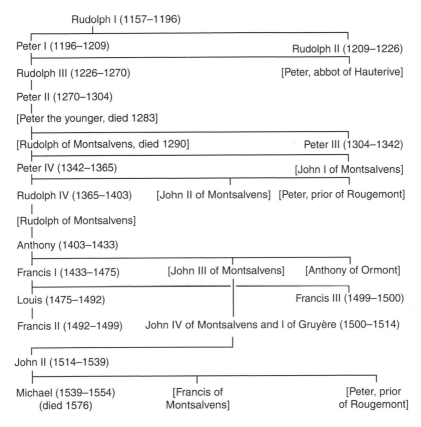

Figure 1.1 The House of Gruyère 1154–1554

castle. Montsalvens was held by a viscount who headed a junior branch of the Gruyère family. This viscount was the feudal lord who owned the village of Château-d'Oex. His castle controlled entry to the valley of Jaun which ran into the highland on a line parallel to the valley of Château-d'Oex. The Jaun valley, like the Château-d'Oex valley, had been colonised by Romanic-speaking farmers along its lower stretch and by Alemannic-speaking pastoralists on its upper reaches. The two valleys were linked in summer by a long and arduous cattle trail across the mountains. The crossing was so steep that in places steps had been carved from the living rock to enable the holder of Montsalvens castle to reach his highland pastures at Château-d'Oex without having to trespass over meadows in the lower reaches of the main Gruyère valley. Some of these meadows, at Albeuve, were owned by the hostile prince-bishop of Lausanne while others were directly held by Montsalvens' suzerain, the count of Gruyère.

The third of the great castles of the principality was the castle of Vanel located on the boundary between Gruyère's Alemannic-speaking and Romanic-speaking subjects. Like Montsalvens it was governed by a junior branch of the reigning family to which political responsibility had been delegated. The prime purpose of Vanel appears to have been the protection of the eastern marches of the state against foreign invaders and mountain raiders. The castle was securely built on a hill dominating the upper gorge of the Sarine. The keep, in which cattle, children and women could be protected, allegedly had subterranean access to the river enabling it to survive sieges even when the springs were dry and the cisterns empty. In addition to its rôle in international defence the castle served domestic policy by supervising any commercial movement along the valley. The main trade path for porters and pack animals passed through the castle courtyard. At night the great doors were barred and no movement of people or goods was permitted lest smugglers evade the reach of the aristocratic tax collectors. It was alleged by Dean Bridel, a latter-day romantic novelist, that Vanel castle was surrounded not only by a high wall but also by a dry moat patrolled by huge mastiffs which terrified any traveller trying to pass unobserved.

In addition to the three great residential castles occupied by the prince and his two viscounts, Gruyère had a number of more or less heavily fortified positions along the valley floor. Some may have served primarily as places of refuge in time of war. Lesser castles may also have been havens to which the nobility and its clients could retreat when the agricultural peasantry rebelled in protest at the unequal terms of the feudalism to which it was subjected. The most prominent of the lesser castles was the one built on a green motte beside the village of Château-d'Oex. Much speculation has been devoted to the relationship between the *castrum*, the château of Oex, and the village, the Villa-d'Oex located on the facing hillside. Although the castle was a very visible focus for the community, the bailey apparently contained neither wells nor cisterns to enable those who lived or hid within it to withstand long sieges. Since Château-d'Oex lay at the heart of the Gruyère highland, rather than on one of the frontiers, major sieges may not have been expected. Despite this relatively remote and safe location, foreign armies did attack the village on several occasions during the five centuries of Gruyère sovereignty over the highland.

The defence of the territory of Gruyère was the responsibility of five regiments of local militiamen one of which was based at Château-d'Oex. The military commander of the regiment was the custodian of the regimental banner and bore the prestigious title of bannaret. It was he who carried the banner into war and made sure that his followers could see him in the throng of battle and rally to him amid the noise, the dust and the confusion. The great war banner of Château-d'Oex bore a most distinctive coat-of-arms. On a red field the castle was drawn in gold and surmounted by a rampant silver crane. The custodian of the Château-d'Oex coat-of-arms was also the village master-of-ceremonies. It was he who received oaths of loyalty from the citizens at the coronation of each new prince. In addition to his military and ceremonial roles he was responsible for auditing the accounts of the administration, for supervising civic officers, and later for chairing a borough council. As the guardian of law and order the bannaret supervised civil magistrates who resolved community disputes, checked weights and measures and prosecuted traders who bought long and sold short. Outside the village the bannaret was assisted by a forest warden who patrolled the borough's countryside and by a marshal who supervised its toll bridge across the Sarine river.

The civil representative of the prince in Château-d'Oex was the chatelain, the keeper of the castle and the president of the assize court of justice. While holding office a chatelain was a man of considerable power. He had the right to arrest and torture suspected criminals, always provided that they were not foreigners whose protests might involve the county in war. The chatelain had some latitude in deciding on the appropriate rigour of the punishments he meted out but had to take constant care lest excessive penalties cause social turbulence. A felon convicted of a serious crime could only be sentenced to bodily mutilation after the bannaret had summoned the militia to quell any public sympathy for the convict or repress any disorder the sentence might cause. Sentences of death could not be carried out at the sole discretion of the chatelain but required confirmation by the count and the appointment of approved witnesses to observe the execution. The office of chatelain was held for three years at a time and at the end of each period of judicial service the holder was required to submit his account-book to the count's auditors and swear on the gospels that he had been faithful to his lord and master.

By the sixteenth century the judicial power of the counts and of their chatelains began to be curbed as highland subjects won new rights and freedoms. In 1500 John I of Gruyère was compelled to grant the people of Saanen the right to object to any chatelain who was not familiar with Alemannic legal custom. The people of Château-d'Oex immediately demanded a similar right to be consulted over the choice of their chatelain. Their case was a more difficult one to argue since Château-d'Oex was governed by the same Romanic legal codes as those used at the prince's court. The Château-d'Oex burghers nevertheless argued that a 'stranger' from outside the highland might hand down ignorant or grievous rulings from the judicial bench. Their plea was initially rejected but the dispute went to higher feudal arbitration and the count was reprimanded for having improperly used the lucrative office of chatelain of Château-d'Oex to reward the gentlemen of his court for their loyalty to his person. He was ordered to choose in future a chatelain acceptable to his highland subjects. He was also instructed to limit each appointment to a single three-year term. Thereafter the position of chatelain of Château-d'Oex rotated among the leaders of the highland community. Senior burghers gained the opportunity to earn the chatelain's salary of twenty imperial florins a year and to apportion to themselves some of the fines which they imposed.

The establishment and maintenance of Gruyère princely authority with its network of castles, its system of militia defence and its hierarchy of justice was costly, and the farming peoples of Château-d'Oex came to resent the feudal price they paid for incorporation into the principality. Over the course of the Middle Ages no less than 28 different types of taxation were imposed, albeit partially in exchange for protection and arbitration. The pleas of the princes for full and prompt payment and the protests of the peasants that noblemen used extortion to enhance their personal wealth, present a confrontational picture of medieval Swiss society. One of the highland taxes in dispute was a pelt tax to be paid on the skins and furs of wild animals caught in the forest. As the wilderness receded, and animals became scarce, lord and vassal agreed to convert the giving of animal pelts into the payment of farm produce such as poultry and barley. In 1372 the subjects of Château-d'Oex drove the bargain even further and were able to buy themselves out of any liability for the pelt tax in exchange for a down payment in ready coin. To prove their exemption they received a valuable Latin charter which was granted in perpetuity. Such charters of tax exemption were carefully preserved and produced in court every time a new prince tried to restore hereditary revenues. In the near-by village of Rougemont a long-running dispute broke out over the pelt tax when the citizens failed to produce a parchment proving that they had been granted an exemption similar to that accorded to Château-d'Oex. It was eventually determined that no such exemption had ever been awarded and Rougemont therefore continued to be liable for the archaic tax, though it usually chose to settle it in labour service rather than in animal skins.

The tax which may have had the most serious consequences for the history of Château-d'Oex was the house tax. This tax apparently began as a poll-tax paid by each member of the family, then became a hearth-tax paid by each household and finally a roof tax, paid on each dwelling regardless of the number of households sheltering in it. Under this arrangement tax liability could be minimised by building one large roof which spread over the living space of two or more families. The carpenters of Château-d'Oex built ever larger houses, clustered on the motte where building sites had been exempted from land taxes. Each house was subdivided among siblings and children, or even partitioned into sections for strangers to occupy. This tax-induced pattern of construction had many social and legal disadvantages. It led to frequent disputes over noise and smell, over access and sanitation, and over repairs and maintenance. The greatest disadvantage of multiple occupancy, however, was that it increased the serious risk of fire. All houses were built of timber, were lit with candles and were heated by kitchen hearths beneath great open chimneys of smoke-stained wood. All roofs were clad in wooden shingles which in dry weather could be ignited by sparks, and floors were carpeted with straw which could be set alight by falling brands. The risk of fire was always acute and although it is not known how often Château-d'Oex caught fire in medieval times, between 1664 and 1800 the village was comprehensively burnt down on no less than three occasions. Despite this great risk of fire the fiscal advantage of crowding under one roof meant that struggling peasant families continued to huddle together on the Château-d'Oex motte to reduce their tax liability.

The highland subjects of the prince of Gruyère were not only required to pay in kind and in cash for their right to belong to the principality; they also had to contribute their time to the service of the community and to the well-being of its rulers. Police duty was a form of labour service that was widely imposed and reluctantly accepted. Farm servants could be recruited as watchmen to give warning of fire or of brigand attack. Loyal land-owners were posted to the frontiers as sentinels, though for a fee of twelve pence a year the well-to-do could buy exemption from watch-duty. A more burdensome liability than the watch was the obligation to serve the prince in times of war. Although none of Gruyère's foreign borders was more than one day's march from any of the castles in which the regiments of militia mustered, campaigns could last several days and thus seriously disrupt the cycle of agricultural duties. The counts of Gruyère regularly took their armies abroad on raids, or on mercenary campaigns that earned them a foreign income. The farmers naturally tried to resist such demands for military service and one charter of 1448 granted an exemption from service abroad to all citizens in the village of Saanen. Normally, however, a militiaman could be called-up to serve for eight days at a time. He was required to follow the banner at his own expense to any territory within western Switzerland. Only when the count led his men beyond the frontiers of the three bishoprics of Sion, Lausanne and Geneva was he required to pay for their maintenance.

Highland vassals who did not bear arms for the prince did other work. Château-d'Oex was expected to plough its sovereign's land in the spring or else pay an indemnity of three shillings in good Lausanne coin. The village was also assessed for six shillings' worth of summer mowing. In winter labour service involved much carting, carrying and sledging to bring timber out of the prince's forests for delivery at his castle door. The lords of the lesser castles were entitled to receive free firewood from their subjects, a heavy burden in a land with long cold winters, draughty stone apartments and huge open fireplaces. When the nobility travelled through their estates their roadside subjects were also required to provide them with free board and lodging. It was specified in the statutes that hospitality at the guest table was to include good quality meat and wine, foods rarely indulged in by peasants accustomed to living on bean stew and barley meal.

The never-ending ways in which the nobility raised revenue included the confiscation of stray animals and bee-swarms, the charging of tolls along trade paths, the right to receive the property of deceased aliens and the levying of fees on water mills. The count had a right to all wild game in the highland but could sell to those who could afford it a licence to fish or to hunt. He also held monopolies on the threshing and milling of corn, on the building of public bread ovens, and on the operating of saw-mills. He licensed the butchers and controlled the fulling and dyeing of cloth. He could raise gratuitous contributions to finance the wedding of each princess of the court. In emergencies he could expect his subjects to ransom him should he be kidnapped on a crusade to the Holy Land. The plethora of duties that the nobility could impose on the working population of Château-d'Oex made feudalism seem very burdensome even if it did provide an over-arching framework of security in a world of violence and uncertainty.

The taxes imposed on agricultural land, on agricultural produce and most especially on agricultural labour, were the ones which brought the greatest grief to Gruyère's Château-d'Oex vassals. Before 1300, during the first two centuries of Alpine colonisation, labour on the highland farms was often serf labour. Conquerors of virgin territory found that labour was scarce and they therefore wanted workers whom they could tie to their land and who could not readily decamp to offer their services to a higher bidder. Highland landlords tried covertly to attract and hold runaway serfs from the baronial estates on the plain. By attaching fugitive serfs to their mountain holdings, however, highland noblemen sometimes sparked serious conflicts with their lowland neighbours. Aggrieved landowners mounted armed campaigns to recapture fugitive serfs who had absconded in search of a less exacting master. They also tried to recover married serfs who escaped out of a natural desire to join their partners on distant estates. In order to minimise the incidence of labour wars the count of Gruyère and the dean of Lausanne cathedral signed an accord in 1210 in which they agreed not to pursue women fugitives who had escaped across the strip of land which separated their border fortresses. Despite this concession, however, male serfs continued to flee from their owners and in 1237 a new treaty was signed which outlawed all forms of serf-hunting in the district. The treaty was a step towards the concept of personal freedom for farm labour in the principality of Gruyère, though the disabilities and taxes imposed on serfs, and on former serfs, continued to be heavy.

In addition to being tied to the land, serfs had to pay a tax on their produce to the sovereign. This serf tax, the *taille*, was not only a financial burden but also a stigma of servitude branded on any peasant compelled to pay it. Highland farm labourers went to great lengths, and considerable expense, to achieve an abolition of this badge of feudal dependency. The serfs of Château-d'Oex finally succeeded in overcoming the great legal disability and financial burden represented by the *taille* when in 1341 they were able to buy themselves out of any responsibility for paying the serf tax. The historic exemption which they won enhanced their social status though it did not reduce their liability to other produce taxes such as the tithe which had once financed the church but was now a tax paid to the prince. In Château-d'Oex this tithe represented the eleventh part of the harvest as each farmer retained ten sheaves of his barley, wheat, oats, hemp or flax for every one that he or she paid to the feudal tax collector. Lesser taxes were also paid on wool, leather, fruit, poultry, new-born livestock, and the staple foods of broad beans and cooking butter.

Once Château-d'Oex had freed itself from the serf tax its next aspiration was to free itself from a peculiarly burdensome form of inheritance tax. A modified law of *mainmorte* decreed that former serfs with no direct heirs were forbidden from bequeathing their land to relatives by will and testament but were compelled, as of old, to surrender their property to their sovereign when they died. As a result of this law families had difficulty in building up their wealth, diversifying their holdings, or planning their estates in an economically rational manner. The transfer of land dependent on accidents of birth and death and on the archaic sequestration of property. Even the recognized legal heir to a farm was required to give his prince a portion of his chattels and the best of his cows. In 1388 the citizens of Château-d'Oex succeeded in challenging this inheritance custom. They compelled Rudolph IV of Gruyère to confess that the law had been illegitimately applied in Château-d'Oex. He admitted that his ancestors had committed sins against Jesus Christ and brought suffering to impoverished highland subjects. In order to rescue the endangered souls of these former princes, and to make amends for past errors, Rudolph relinquished his right to inherit the farms of former serfs. The people of Château-d'Oex had shrewdly sweetened their demand for a tax exemption with a cash payment of 1600 imperial florins of gold. The ready money may have done as much to influence the count as his anguish over the souls of his ancestors languishing in purgatory. The bargain, although expensive, was deemed by highland farmers to be a good one. As freed subjects they had now acquired new incentives to stay on the land and invest skill and time to improve its productivity.

By securing better land rights the people of Château-d'Oex significantly diminished the sovereign authority of the count of Gruyère and accelerated the decline in his economic fortunes. One-off payments received from subjects to satisfy the pressing demands of the court's creditors were no substitute for long-term inheritance taxes to maintain the viability of the county. The shift in the balance of power between suzerain and vassal formed part of a tide of change affecting late fourteenth-century Switzerland. In most areas this sea-change brought the decline of the Swiss aristocracies and the rise of republican oligarchies. Although Château-d'Oex, and the other rural boroughs of Gruyère, continued to wring concessions from their sovereign after 1388, the principality nevertheless survived better than many of the neighbouring Swiss counties. The Gruyère princes, however, were always short of gold to sustain their opulent life style and maintain the lavish households which they kept in Paris and in Turin and in

Brussels. They still expected their highland subjects to pay taxes with which to service the expensive debts which they had accumulated among the great moneylenders of the Swiss republics. As the civic rights of citizens became more entrenched, however, the leverage of the count diminished and Rudolph IV was forced to abandon the practice of demanding that taxes be paid in advance. Henceforth Château-d'Oex would not pay its feudal dues until sun-down on the appointed day of settlement.

The concessions in matters of taxation which were granted after 1388 were followed in the fifteenth century by the awarding of new legal privileges. In 1436 the burghers of Château-d'Oex won from Count Francis I the right to be governed according to written legal custom. The village adopted as its customary laws the statutes that had been granted over the course of centuries to the citizens of Moudon, a small burgh of the Swiss plain 15 miles west of Gruyère castle. Moudon custom derived from early medieval charters which the German family of Zähringen had granted to its followers while colonising the Black Forest in south Germany. Zähringen noblemen later crossed the Rhine in search of vacant Swiss land and might have become the royal family of Switzerland had the line not died out in 1218. The grants of legal rights which they had made to their Swiss subjects nevertheless continued to be cherished in many small towns including Moudon. An early transcript of Moudon custom was made in 1285 when Amadeus V of Savoy, the then ruler of western Switzerland, took an oath to defend the rights of his citizens as handed down by oral tradition. These rights circumscribed absolute sovereignty and granted townspeople, if not country folk, an element of consent in borough affairs. Moudon civic rights encouraged the growth of trade and prosperity by guaranteeing an immunity from arbitrary arrest to merchants who travelled to local markets and visited regional fairs. In Moudon, citizenship was a jealously guarded privilege and in 1359 the count of Gruyère was compelled to grant similar privileges to the citizens of Gruyère town. Less than a century later highland citizens won the same rights and Moudon custom became the common law of Château-d'Oex.

The law was a matter of great importance to the feudal people of Château-d'Oex. As settlers cut the forests, drained the marshes, cleared the meadows and broke the soils, land became ever more valuable and disputes over land use and land ownership became increasingly protracted. Laws of land tenure were couched in Latin and farmers needed licensed notaries to interpret their rights and obligations. Lawyers became a constant and much resented source of expense for the people of Château-d'Oex. No land could be bought or sold, bequeathed or inherited, given or received, parcelled out or consolidated, without a certificate drafted in Latin and sealed by feudal authority. Fees on land transactions became a major source of noble revenue as each deed was authenticated with the great seal, or the small seal, or the counter-seal. The cost of obtaining these seals generated great bitterness, but sometimes debt-ridden princes agreed to waive prospective fees in exchange for down payments. In 1448, for instance, the citizens of Saanen paid 24 733 silver coins to buy a permanent exemption from the stamp duty of one shilling in the pound hitherto levied on property transfers. In Château-d'Oex partial exemptions of property taxes on buildings, on fields and on mountain pastures were negotiated, though the concessions caused endless litigation over boundary stones and title records. Some of the legal disputes concerned land owned by the church.

In the eleventh-century colonisation of the Alps the church had played an important rôle. The head of the highland church of Gruyère was the dean of Ogo, a member of the Lausanne cathedral chapter. Unlike his civic counterpart the dean did not change the title of his office from Ogo to Gruyère. As the population of the highland grew parishes proliferated and by the thirteenth century the dean of Ogo ruled over 23 churches, almost as many as those controlled by his northern neighbour, the dean of Bern. As the prosperity of the deanery increased more prestigious churches were built including the castle church on the Château-d'Oex motte. It was dedicated to an early medieval Irish monk, St Donat, who had helped to revive Christianity in Switzerland and had been elected bishop of Lausanne. The Château-d'Oex church eventually housed five shrines and was served by three priests. Its original graveyard, and possibly a chapel as well, probably lay 200 metres north of the motte, beside an ancient oak tree at the Villa-d'Oex where bones have occasionally been excavated. As the complex of stone buildings and fortifications on the summit of the motte was remodelled and rebuilt over the course of time the church grew larger and eventually the great castle dungeon became the church tower.

The principality of Gruyère maintained not only 23 parish churches but also half a dozen monasteries. Most of these were built by communities of Cistercians, Augustinians and Carthusians in the mild lowland parts of the principality. The oldest and smallest, however, was a priory established in the eleventh century at Rougemont, a village in the heart of the highland four miles upstream from Château-d'Oex. The tiny priory was endowed with land and serfs and was dedicated to St Nicholas. It was maintained by two or three Benedictine monks sent into the Alpine wilderness by the great Burgundian monastery at Cluny. In 1096, some years after the priory's establishment, William of Gruyère, accompanied by two hundred of his subjects, planned to set off for Jerusalem to take part in the first crusade. The priory of Rougemont benefited by the acquisition of several of their little plots of highland territory, and Redboldus of Gruyère sold the prior 105 shillings-worth of male and female serfs. Ulrick of Gruyère, a young canon in charge of the Château-d'Oex church, transferred half of his parish tithes to the priory before leaving for the Holy Land.

Members of the ruling family of Gruyère were not the only benefactors of the monastery at Rougemont. William of Corbière, wishing to ensure the salvation of his soul, gave the prior a valuable drinking pond at the summit of the pass linking Château-d'Oex to Montsalvens castle. Others gave the prior roods of land, hogsheads of grain, and even a small lowland vineyard belonging to Oudorico-the-German, a member of the Lausanne cathedral chapter. This enthusiasm for monasticism did not last long among highland settlers, however, and by the year 1115 those who had solemnly promised to support the monastery were being sternly reminded of their obligations. A draconian parchment signed and sealed on the eighth Sunday after Whitsun by Gerald, bishop of Lausanne, Christian, prior of Rougemont, and William, count of Gruyère, warned donors suffering from short memories that an anathema would be pronounced against any who failed in their obligations towards the priory however trivial the sum of pennies which they had promised might seem to be.

The priority of Rougemont was so small that the rule of St Benedict could not be regularly observed. The monks were fully occupied with their hay meadows and cattle-herds, the monastic buildings were not always in good repair, and inspectors from Cluny were reluctant to brave highland snowstorms to supervise them. Despite their relative penury the monks did raise a loan to replace a broken chapel bell with one of such good quality that it rang out across the valley for centuries. When the prior was away his ill-educated monks sometimes consorted indecorously with local folk and were accused of trafficking in monastic produce, or even of embezzling funeral fees. The priory served its patrons rather well, however, building prestigious tombs for the Gruyère nobility and singing masses for the souls of those who could afford the expense of the necessary sponsorship. The count put forward the names of his protégés when vacancies occurred in the priory establishment. In 1371 the countess of Gruyère was granted custody of the monastic estates when no prior could be appointed, perhaps as a consequence of the plague. Spasmodic neglect did not mean that the Rougemont priory was insignificant to the medieval Swiss church and one absentee prior became chamberlain to Pope Clement VII at Avignon, thereby earning for himself a cardinal's hat. In 1481 Rougemont established one of the first printing presses in the Alps and Henry Wirczburg, using carved wooden letters probably brought from Geneva, printed several dozen copies of a history of the world which he annotated with snippets of Swiss history. In particular he recorded the devastations of a great storm which swept through Château-d'Oex and Rougemont during his sojourn in the highland. Despite its remote location the little monastery survived such vicissitudes for five hundred years.

The medieval opening up of the Gruyère highland gradually attracted a growing foreign interest. In Roman times the Château-d'Oex valley had rarely, if ever, been used by travellers and traders who sought the least difficult footpaths through the Alps. In medieval times, as trade between Germany and Italy grew, every crossing of the mountains was explored for its viability. The great Swiss family of Habsburg took an early interest in the possibility of using the banks of the Sarine river as a route for long-distance trade caravans. Traders from the Habsburg market cities of the Swiss plain wanted in particular to find a way of by-passing the Savoy fortress of Chillon, at the head of Lake Geneva, which controlled and taxed the old Roman highway to Turin, Piedmont and Genoa via the St Bernard pass. A possible alternative route would have passed through Château-d'Oex to Sion, on the upper Rhône, and then over the then little-used Simplon pass to Milan, Lombardy and Venice. Habsburg aspirations to investigate such a prospective highway naturally met with fierce Savoy opposition and the principality of Gruyère was drawn into a confrontation between two of Europe's rising dynasties.

In 1268 Château-d'Oex suddenly found itself at the centre of a European controversy. Rudolph III of Gruyère was threatened by the armies of Peter of Savoy coming from the south and the armies of Rudolph of Habsburg coming from the north. While the sabres rattled, however, Rudolph of Gruyère suddenly died leaving the principality's foreign policy in the hands of his son Peter II of Gruyère. The new prince decided that his first hope of survival depended on making peace with his bitter enemy, the prince-bishop of Lausanne. Even an alliance of Gruyère and Lausanne was not powerful enough, however, to forestall a Habsburg invasion from the north and the frontier castle of the marcher lord of Corbière, a mere eight kms from Gruyère castle, fell to the Habsburgs. In the face of such military pressure Peter of Gruyère conceded feudal rights over his highland to Savoy rather than allow his territory to be overrun by the Habsburgs. In exchange he received from Savoy an immediate payment of 1000 French *livres* to strengthen his northern defences. In the longer term, however, Savoy's price was control over Château-d'Oex. Such control would ensure that no trail could be opened through the western Swiss Alps to rival the Savoy highroad to Italy via Chillon castle. Before the peace could be sealed, however, Savoy soldiers appear to have entered the highland and sacked Château-d'Oex in 1270. It has also been alleged that the invaders compelled the people of Château-d'Oex to dismantle their castle fortifications, though walls and a dungeon continued to adorn the summit of the motte for centuries to come.

In Château-d'Oex the political situation remained tense but in 1273 it changed abruptly. In that year Rudolph of Habsburg was unexpectedly elected ruler of the Holy Roman Empire. Habsburg world strategy changed in scale and the family's immediate interest in the comparatively small principality of Gruyère waned. When Rudolph next visited western Switzerland, two years later, he came with all the pomp and ceremony of an emperor. At Lausanne he met the pope and together they attended the consecration of Switzerland's most magnificent gothic cathedral. Despite the new eminence of their patrons, however, the Swiss client towns of the Habsburgs had not forgotten the potential strategic and economic value of the principality of Gruyère. In a renewed attack forces loyal to the Habsburgs were able to seize the castle of Montsalvens, seat of the suzerain lord of Château-d'Oex. Château-d'Oex thus found itself under Savoy military occupation while the castle of its overlord was in the hands of the Habsburgs. This Habsburg assault on the western ramparts of the Alps proved ephemeral, however, and peace was soon restored, albeit on down-to-earth peasant terms. The raiding party was bought off in 1277 with meadows producing 17 waggon-loads of hay plus a few small plots of arable land.

By the end of the thirteenth century Alpine colonisers had reached the ecological limits of viable farming all round Château-d'Oex and no further margins of the wilderness could be brought into production. In order to increase their wealth the princes of Gruyère therefore sought to expand beyond the frontiers of their original highland domain. Their first target for territorial conquest lay to the south of Château-d'Oex.

On the far side of the watershed, beyond the high butter farms of the Etivaz summer pastures, lay the secluded Romanic-speaking valley of Ormont high above the Rhône floor. The mixture of woodland, small arable fields and extensive mountain pasture closely resembled the ecological make-up of the Gruyère highland itself. It was therefore economically logical that when Château-d'Oex ran out of grazing for its cattle Count Peter III should attempt to conquer the Ormont valley and create new living space for his highland subjects. His campaign, however, ran into stern opposition from his new suzerain, the count of Savoy. Although Savoy accepted the legitimacy of some of Gruyère's expansionist claims, it nevertheless preferred to pay Peter III compensation for loss of territory rather than permit his cowmen to trespass on the Rhône side of the mountain. In 1321 a treaty was signed after which Gruyère withdrew from Ormont while Savoy built a powerful castle to dominate the valley and discourage future incursions from Château-d'Oex.

As an alternative to capturing new grazing lands in the south, Peter III turned Gruyère's military and strategic energies towards the northeast. He set his sights on gaining control of the Alemannic-speaking valley of the Simmental. The long Simmental valley contained a farm acreage comparable to that of highland Gruyère and was farmed by almost as many people, with almost as many cattle and almost as many goats. In attempting to double the size of his pastoral principality Peter III showed that he was not only a great war leader but also a shrewd diplomat. He negotiated a dynastic marriage with a powerful Simmental family and thereby significantly increased his wealth and influence on the northern side of his mountain frontier. Territorial aspirations in the Simmental, however, soon brought him into conflict with the most militant of his northern neighbours, the young city–state of Bern. Conflict and competition between Gruyère and Bern were to dominate the history of Château-d'Oex for the next two centuries. In the process the highland village was gradually detached from the aristocratic traditions of the nobility which ruled western Switzerland to become linked to the republican traditions of the oligarchies which ruled central Switzerland.

2
Under the Paw of the Bear

The city of Bern was to become a foremost military power among the Swiss during the course of the fourteenth century. By 1403 its influence had reached Château-d'Oex and its oligarchic rulers replaced the nobility of Gruyère as the protecting power over the highland villages. A century later, in 1555, the city senate was able to purchase full property rights over Château-d'Oex and the surrounding highland. Bern was not an ancient city, like the Swiss towns with Roman roots; it did not have a lake-side port, like those which traditionally dominated much of Switzerland's trade and industry; and it was never the seat of a bishop, like Lausanne to which city the bishop of Aventicum had moved after the fall of the Roman empire. The founders of Bern had only arrived in Switzerland, so legend tells, from the Black Forest of Germany in 1191. They settled 50 km north of Château-d'Oex in a forested area which they cleared and farmed. To improve their defence against hostile local inhabitants the immigrants built a fortified post on a cliff high above a triple bend in the Aar river. To give this town-in-the-woods a classical status the founders called their settlement New Verona. Their neighbours, however, soon corrupted 'Verona' to 'Berona' and then to 'Bern', the Alemannic word for bears. As a consequence the new city adopted a carnivorous black bear as its heraldic beast. On the city's banner the fearsome bear marched across a field of red and gold. In a bear pit beside the river tame brown bears became the city mascots.

Bern consolidated its military position between the plain and the mountain by forming and re-forming pacts with its neighbours. After each local war peacebrokers and village diplomats arranged for plundered loot and stolen cattle to be retained by the victors or restored to the losers in whatever manner had been agreed. Each local treaty was 'perpetual' and had no fixed term but held good until a better treaty could be negotiated. During the thirteenth century this kaleidoscope of ever-changing village pacts evolved throughout central Switzerland. In these conditions Bern, a small but aggressive warrior town, proved particularly successful in furthering its expansionist ambitions. It did so at a time of agricultural innovation and rising prosperity. The development of iron-tipped plough-shares facilitated land reclamation from the forest and concepts of crop rotation improved productivity on the new farms. Agricultural success coincided with a temporary improvement in the harsh Swiss climate. As cereal cropping and dairy farming became more specialised, market-oriented trade supplemented subsistence-oriented trade to generate new wealth. Bern market became particularly famous for its onions and the onion fair became a lasting occasion of civic celebration. As the city's achievements grew the immigrant aristocracy was replaced by a town corporation of free citizens. Some members of the new oligarchy were minor landlords of the rural nobility who joined a city corporation which had proved its capacity to manage agrarian change and modernise farming.

It was the agricultural base of Bern's prosperity which initially caused its war leaders to cast covetous eyes on the city's southern marches and the panoramic highland at the heart of which lay Château-d'Oex. The increasing value of mountain pasture had tempted Peter III of Gruyère to invade the Simmental valley in the 1330s. Bern also aspired to control the Simmental and war between Gruyère and Bern would have broken out in 1339 had the local cattle barons not succeeded in brokering a truce between the old principality and the new city-republic. Peace, however, did not last long. In 1342 a newly-enthroned prince of Gruyère, formerly the lord of the eastern fortress at Vanel castle, aspired once more to lay hands on the Simmental cattle pastures. He attacked with such ferocity that a Bern regiment of militia was driven right out of the valley and down to Lake Thun. The city's fleeing soldiers almost suffered the ultimate feudal humiliation of losing their regimental war-banner to the enemy. Bern's rising reputation as a warrior-city was in danger of being destroyed by an old-fashioned prince of the Swiss nobility. The city's retaliation, although delayed until 1349, was agressive. Bern not only returned to ransack the villages of the Simmental, but also unexpectedly crossed the mountains in midwinter and plundered isolated homesteads in the eastern Gruyère highland. Bern raiders almost reached the village of Saanen, a mere ten kms from Château-d'Oex, before the farmers were able to buy them off with bribes of money. When the raiders withdrew, however, they left a deadly legacy which delayed the expansion of the mountain dairy industry; it was they, apparently, who brought the first epidemic of plague to the farming peoples of the Château-d'Oex highland.

While Bern was establishing claims to the highland it was simultaneously spreading its diplomatic and military influence across the Swiss plain. In 1339, the very same year in which its first raid on the Simmental took place, Bern strikingly demonstrated its growing military capacity on the plain. It did so by boldly challenging the united power of the Swiss nobility. The battlefield on which the confrontation took place was at Laupen, 32 kms down the Sarine river from Gruyère castle. The lords of the plain, among them the count of Gruyère who held several lowland castles as well as his highland domain in Château-d'Oex, mustered an army of one thousand mounted knights and several thousand foot-followers. They were led by the Holy Roman Emperor himself, Louis IV of Bavaria, and were supported by the Habsburgs. Against this show of imperial strength the citizen-militia of Bern demonstrated, in a way that was to have momentous repercussions, that a well-drilled, well-equipped, city infantry could resist a cavalry charge and defeat an imperial army. Eighty members of Switzerland's nobility fell on the battlefield and hundreds of their subjects were killed. Bern had made its most decisive mark on the history of Switzerland.

Once Bern had defeated the Swiss nobility it set about negotiating a treaty of friendship with the Swiss republics which clustered round Lake Lucerne. In these republics shifting alliances between rich merchants, small towns and large monasteries had created a system of local justice to enhance the security of property owners. Although the right of borough citizens to be free-citizens of the Holy Roman Empire had been recognized in a charter drawn up in 1231, the effective provision of justice by the empire was on the wane. The decline in the authority of the emperor had been particularly acutely felt in 1291 when Rudolph of Habsburg, the local overlord who had been elected emperor in 1273, unexpectedly died. In the temporary absence of a Swiss feudal suzerain to settle conflicts, the men from three of the local village polities, in Uri, in Schwytz and in Lower Unterwald, swore an oath to support one another in times of trouble. Their Latin treaty of mutual assistance may have been drawn up for them by scribes from the Habsburg chancery; it was certainly authenticated with the appropriate seals.

The Swiss treaty of 1291 was no charter of rights, like the English Magna Carta, but was a loyal vow to honour the laws of the empire and appoint local magistrates to enforce them. Far from instituting democracy, as later patriots liked to believe, the pact of 1291 legitimised wealth, order and hierarchy, when recourse to outside justice was not immediately available. Soon after the pact had been sealed, however, two of the states made a separate treaty between themselves which bore no seals, was written in Alemannic dialect rather than in Latin, and was personally signed by powerful burghers who wished to link their republics to the free city of Zürich rather than to the Habsburg market town of Lucerne. Zürich was a major commercial centre for the republics of central Switzerland and its currency was common tender in many Alpine villages and monasteries. The city's dictator-for-life became one of the arbiters of relations between the declining Swiss nobility and the rising Swiss republics.

As their wealth and autonomy grew the Swiss republics anxiously watched the rising influence of Bern at the western end of the Swiss plain. The lake-side merchants of Zürich became particularly worried when Bern, having destroyed an army of noble plainsmen, turned its military attention to the republics in the central Alps in an apparent search for a route across the mountains into Italy. When Bern conquered the southern half of the republic of Unterwald and won access to an Alpine trail over the Grimsel pass, the Swiss republics felt compelled to swallow their distaste for the thrusting upstart city and negotiate an alliance with it. The merchants of Uri, whose control of the Gothard pass had given them a growing influence in trans-alpine trade since the early thirteenth century, persuaded their allies that Bern would be less dangerous as a commercial associate than as a rival. They also argued that the city of Bern could act as a counterbalance to the city of Zürich which had been formally enrolled into the Swiss system of alliances in 1351. Equally significantly Uri and its allies recognised that Bern might provide effective military resistance to any attempt by the Habsburgs to restore their traditional authority over central Switzerland. Thus it was that in 1353, 14 years after it had proved its military prowess by defeating the Swiss nobility at Laupen, the western city–state of Bern was reluctantly accepted into an enlarged Swiss pact of eight jealously sovereign republics. Once this pact was sealed, Bern could turn its military energies once more to the conquest of the agricultural highland. In so doing it brought the republican concepts of late medieval Switzerland to Château-d'Oex.

By the end of the fourteenth century the Bern militias had conquered four great Alpine valleys, including the Simmental, to create the Bernese Oberland. The city's Alpine ambitions, however, were still not satisfied and Bern next proceeded to challenge the ascendancy of the counts of Gruyère on the upper Sarine river. Although Bern's traditional wealth had been based on the artisanship of the town and on the farm trade of the plain, the Gruyère highland held three attractions for the prospective invaders. The first attraction was the quality of its cheeses and the skill of its cheesemakers. Bern aspired not only to trade in Gruyère highland cheese, but also to improve the quality and profitability of its Emmental dairy farms by bringing cheesemakers down from Château-d'Oex to the lowland. Although the migrant dairymen did eventually make cheeses similar in size and firmness to Gruyère cheeses, the lowland cheeses of the Emmental never achieved the distinctive flavour of mountain cheeses. The second and perhaps more immediate advantage, as far as Bern was concerned, of conquering more highland territory was that it enlarged the pool of youths of military age whom Bern could train for the defence of its rural boroughs, for aggression in its Alpine campaigns and subsequently for foreign export as paid mercenaries. A third reason why Bern cast covetous eyes on the highland beyond the Simmental was that if the soldiers of Gruyère's overlord Savoy could be driven out of Château-d'Oex, Bern might succeed in opening a passage through the mountains to reach the Rhône valley and the busy mule-track over the St Bernard pass into Italy. Challenging the might of Savoy, however, was a daunting prospect and Bern therefore moved into the Gruyère highland with stealth, using the Alemannic-speaking farmers of Saanen as a fifth column.

In 1398 the burghers of Saanen succeeded in emulating the bid for freedom which Château-d'Oex had made in 1388 and bought themselves an exemption from the old inheritance tax on the properties of former serfs. The price of the franchise was the handsome sum of 5200 imperial florins which they paid to the count of Gruyère. Not satisfied with this liberation from fiscal servitude, the men of Saanen apparently sought to go further and to shake off Gruyère suzerainty altogether. They allegedly appealed to Bern for help, though the story of their appeal is suspect since it derives from the Bern interpretation of events. Bern, responding to the appeal with alacrity, offered the men of Saanen citizenship rights similar to those accorded to the free citizens of the Simmental. Troops were sent to impose a 'protectorate' over Saanen to shield its people from the wrath of their Gruyère prince. The citizens were given a dual nationality, with rights and obligations both to Bern and to Gruyère, though the senators of the Bern oligarchy had not deigned to consult the courtiers of Gruyère over the matter but had simply confronted the count with a military *fait accompli*. Bern replaced Savoy as the overlord of the Alemannic-speaking section of the Gruyère highland. In future judicial appeals against Gruyère judgements would no longer be heard by Savoy tribunals in Turin but by the senate of Bern.

The imposition of Bern jurisprudence in Saanen might have had some logic in terms of shared Alemannic custom and language. The *coup* had not, however, satisfied the long-range strategic requirements of Bern. The city was still anxious to push its sphere of influence towards the Rhône and therefore into Romanic-speaking territory. In 1403 Bern unilaterally extended its protectorate over the eastern Gruyère highland to include Château-d'Oex and the adjacent boroughs of Rougemont and Rossinière. Bern proclaimed, in spurious self-justification, that it was protecting free highland citizens from the oppressive nobility on the plain. The burghers of Château-d'Oex were granted dual nationality whether they sought it or not. The 'privilege' they had been offered was, moreover, expensive. Bern insisted that Château-d'Oex should pay one eight-ounce mark of silver as a fee for becoming an incorporated borough of the Bernese Oberland. Château-d'Oex refused the payment and bitter litigation ensued. Eventually the village lost the suit and was compelled both to surrender the silver bullion which Bern demanded and also to pay 60 French *livres* in judicial costs. The bear of Bern appeared to have put its paw firmly on Château-d'Oex.

Château-d'Oex legends tell of the fierce resistance which the village mounted on being incorporated into the Bern sphere of military influence. The burghers appealed to Anthony of Gruyère for help. The youthful prince ordered his regent to march on Château-d'Oex immediately, outrageously offending against civil custom by carrying weapons on a market day. In the Château-d'Oex cattle market the prince's armed band accused traders from Saanen of being traitors who had encouraged Bern to capture Château-d'Oex. In the ensuing skirmish the 'sovereign' forces of Gruyère were routed by the 'protectorate' forces of Bern. To discourage any further protest against its military occupation of the highland, Bern insisted that the count's great castle of Vanel be destroyed lest it be used to shelter rebels and insurgents. The dominant symbol of nobility, of feudalism and of Gruyère sovereignty in the highland was vandalised in 1407.

When the counts of Gruyère partially lost control over Château-d'Oex and the eastern half of their highland territory they concentrated on building new careers for themselves as international statesmen and as generals with soldiers whom they could hire out to the highest bidder. Gruyère noblemen resident at the court of Savoy in Turin travelled widely as a diplomats. A particularly difficult episode in Alpine politics occurred in 1467 when Bern signed an agreement with Savoy which gave the city its long-sought access to Italy over the St Bernard pass. Bern's Swiss allies, whose wealth derived from the rival St Gothard route to Italy, were dismayed. The senate of Bern sent Francis of Gruyère to central Switzerland with a gift of 60 000 golden écus to pacify its angry Swiss allies and more especially to satisfy the merchant republic of Uri. The sum, however, was quite inadequate to compensate Uri for the potential loss of trade. Gruyère was therefore invited to help mobilise an army which could march on Milan and destroy Uri's Italian trading partner to the benefit of the rival city of Turin. Bern offered to supply some of its own troops for the expedition but only on the prudent condition that Gruyère should guarantee their remuneration out of any booty captured from Milan. A war in which rival members of the Swiss pact were ranged against each other seemed imminent, but before a shot was fired Milan capitulated. As a broker in Alpine affairs the principality of Gruyère had reached the height of its diplomatic prowess.

The international interests of their rulers had significant implications for the lives of the people of Château-d'Oex. The right of the prince to levy troops from the highland was burdensome for men of military age, and this burden was augmented rather than eased as Bern enhanced its influence in the highland. No detailed account exists of the Gruyère army setting out to war, but in 1490 the Zürich army marched out of the city to attack the neighbouring town of St Gallen and a description provided by an Italian witness gives the flavour of an age in which the men of Château-d'Oex marched under the colours of Gruyère.

Then they all set off in order of march. First came twelve well-dressed noblemen on horses, armed with crossbows, then two knights and some pioneers with axes, and some drummers. A company of 500 long pikes followed, well armed, led by the sons of knights and marching three abreast in orderly ranks. These were followed on foot by 200 arquebuses and 200 halbardiers, a drum major and the pipers, followed by the banner carried on foot by a striking looking man. With the flag bearer were two court ushers, carrying their staffs of office, and each with the authority to commit an offender to prison without argument. Then followed the executioner with three helpers, and six prostitutes chosen and paid by the town. Another 400 halbardiers followed, the strongest and best armed, for these had the task of guarding the flags; their weapons looked like a thick forest. Four hundred crossbowmen, including the sons of gentlemen drawn from all classes of the people, next stepped proudly past. They in turn were followed by many pikemen. All in all, the force numbered 4000 men and included participants from many surrounding districts, as well as more than twenty drummers. Following the main force came three trumpeters on horseback dressed in the colours of Zürich. Immediately behind was the Captain and Knight, Konrad Schwend, on horseback, well equipped with arms decorated with gold insignia, carrying the ceremonial staff of office and with a garland of flowers on his head. Following him, all on horseback, were a valet, whose lance and shield carried the captain's gold coat of arms, six bodyguards with lances on their thighs and twelve crossbowmen.

> John McCormack, *One Million Mercenaries*
> (London, 1993), p.17, citing in translation
> J. Häne, *Zum Wehr-und Kriegswesen in der Blütezeit der Alten*
> *Eidgenossenschaft* (Zürich, 1900), p.29.

The young highlanders who were trained for service in the Gruyère army placed great value on their honour. They were sensitive to any insult that might be cast upon themselves, their courage, their family, or their highland 'tribe'. The epitome of this honour was the banner of the crane which they fought to protect and which could not be insulted, sullied or surrendered to enemy hands. Adolescents took part in martial competitions and a teenage soldier could handle an eight-foot war axe with a spearhead for lunging at infantrymen and an iron crook for unseating cavalrymen. The Swiss went into battle without shields, wielding their halberds with both hands and persistently keeping up the offensive since they had no defensive armour to protect a retreat. The Swiss armies included runners equipped with 6 metre pikes made of ash wood and tipped with iron which they tilted at the enemy as they ran. The pikemen could also be formed up in ranks serried four deep and able to hold a heavy cavalry charge by impaling both riders and horses. From the core of such a hedgehog formation bowmen could fire volleys of arrows over the heads of pikemen. The elite of a fifteenth-century Swiss army consisted of crossbow archers who could fire two or even three bolts per minute and could hit an enemy at 300 paces. The performance of Swiss crossbows was superior to that of early matchlocks, arquebuses, or other firearms.

In an elegant montage of slides and music put together in 1994 to publicise the virtue of Château-d'Oex cheese, an historical commentator made the customary but controversial statement that the peasants of Château-d'Oex liked nothing better that to set off on armed adventures in foreign service. The concept of the Swiss joyously tumbling out of their mountains to go to war is an old one as recognized by Thomas More when, in 1516, he described a people presumed to be the Swiss whose only interests were raising cattle and seeking opportunities for warfare. The men of Château-d'Oex did leave their mountains as military conscripts, and some did survive to return home with a small purse of savings or a little war booty. But whether they enjoyed military service is quite another matter.

The record suggests that the conscripts suppressed their loneliness in the ardent, if poxy, embraces of foreign women and spent their wages on gutrotting liquor. Glory and camaraderie may have had some appeal to adolescents wanting to escape the loneliness of herding goats in the wilderness or milking cows in freezing dark byres, but two out of three never came home and many died a gangrenous death in some foreign ditch. When Château-d'Oex cheese farmers went to war the experience was more akin to being press-ganged than to volunteering for a life of adventures. Any voluntary incentive to go to war was prosaically related to the fact that military wages on the plain were 30 per cent higher than the farm wages in the highland. Even when the cost of uniforms and weapons had been deducted from the monthly pay packet, military service appeared a viable career to some highland men.

The impact of mobilisation on a small farming community can be well illustrated by the events of the 1470s. Soon after the threat of war with Milan had receded, the Gruyère army was called out again. This time it marched northward to Alsace where the Habsburgs had attacked the then-Swiss town of Mulhouse. This mobilisation called for the services of 130 men from Château-d'Oex. The conscription was ordered in the month of May and must have been exceedingly unpopular, coming as it did on the eve of the great annual cattle migration to the highest Alpine pastures. Worse was to follow in June, however, when the recruiting sergeants returned to demand a second Château-d'Oex levy for the war in Alsace. June was the peak of the haymaking season on the Château-d'Oex meadows and a second call to arms would severely disrupt the harvesting of fodder for the long winter. Such disruptions became more frequent and more severe as Gruyère witnessed the war fever which threatened to engulf the European powers. The men of Château-d'Oex were called-up on at least three further occasions to serve the military ambitions, not only of their prince in Gruyère castle but also of the republic of Bern, the protecting power in the highland.

In 1472 Bern sent a regiment of 500 men across the Château-d'Oex highland to the Rhône, allegedly to collect a debt of 20 000 florins from the town of Bex, but also no doubt to explore any prospects for further territorial expansion. Two years later Bern troops, including members of the Château-d'Oex militia, were again sent down to the Rhône valley, this time to prevent mercenaries recruited in Italy from passing through western Switzerland to join the armies of Burgundy. These mercenaries, however, had been recruited by none other than Francis of Gruyère who had given them a safe conduct to cross Swiss territory. To honour his commitment, and to safeguard his revenue as a mercenary contractor, Francis sent a force of his own down to the Rhône to protect his Italian recruits and to drive off the Bern expedition sent to waylay them. Both Bern and Gruyère protested to their allies about the incident, Bern accusing Gruyère of supplying mercenaries to its enemies and Gruyère complaining that Bern was frustrating its legitimate commercial activities, but the conflict was not resolved and Francis died soon afterwards.

In a third Château-d'Oex foray down to the Rhône the highlanders seized and fired the great castle of Aigle, killing five of its defenders, plundering the town, and scattering another column of Italian mercenaries that were in transit. The new count of Gruyère, Louis, protested to a Diet of Swiss ambassadors then assembled in Lucerne about Bern's continued and unwarranted interference with his business affairs. The Diet, which was supposed to regulate disputes between members of the Swiss pact and their neighbours, chose to ignore Louis' appeal for retribution. Bern calmly sent envoys to Château-d'Oex to claim two thirds of the booty which the highlanders had won at Aigle. By now, however, the continuous disruption of the passage of Italian mercenaries, and the constant plundering of the towns along the Rhône, had become intolerable to Burgundy. Charles the Bold therefore commissioned an expedition to destroy Château-d'Oex. Despite the force which it could have mustered, Burgundy's assault on the highland proved ineffectual. One Burgundian company allegedly succeeded in setting fire to the priory village of Rougemont but it failed to establish any hold on the highland. Instead the expedition withdrew with the loss of 30 men and of several valuable war horses. Highland raids on the plain continued and in their next attack the men of Château-d'Oex fired the great castle of Chatelard and spent eight days looting the market of Vevey on Lake Geneva. When men from Saanen arrived to claim a share of the spoils they found Vevey deserted. Burgundy had meanwhile decided to embark on a fateful attempt to conquer western Switzerland.

The ambiguous political loyalities of the fighting men of Château-d'Oex, and the confused rights of Gruyère and Bern to levy troops in the highland, were illustrated by the great war between Bern and Burgundy. In 1475 the war was preceded by a hasty realignment of Europe's military forces. Bern made an alliance with France and Burgundy made an alliance with Austria. Louis of Gruyère hovered anxiously in the middle. He was a vassal of Burgundy's ally Savoy, but also a neighbour of Bern to whom half his subjects were attached by bonds of joint citizenship. Louis hoped that war could be averted and that the old Swiss republics, which had no stomach for a war in the west, would refuse to support Bern. Gruyère's diplomacy failed, however, and the dynamism of Bern's city army drew most of the Swiss republics into its wake. At the first battle, fought at Grandson in March 1476, men of Château-d'Oex fought victoriously on the side of Bern, and took home to the highland their small share of one of the most fabulous treasure collections that any army had ever won on the field of battle. At the second battle, fought at Morat in June 1476, Louis abandoned his neutrality and joined the 90 citizens of Château-d'Oex fighting on behalf of Bern. Louis's local army of 31 horsemen and 143 foot soldiers entitled him to some share in the new spoils before Charles the Bold was driven back into Burgundy where he died after a third defeat at Nancy. The remains of Charles' empire fell into the hands of the Austrian Habsburgs while the Swiss, including the Château-d'Oex highlanders, plundered his allies.

Immediately after the battle of Morat, Louis of Gruyère and his men rode to Lausanne to punish the bishop, who was believed to have supported Charles of Burgundy and to have provided his army with hospitality during the previous winter. The episcopal city was briskly pillaged for three days and even the great Dominican and Franciscan churches were plundered. Bern followed in Gruyère's steps and ransacked the vineyards of the lake-side towns around Lausanne. By the time the men of Château-d'Oex returned to the highland they had acquired for the borough a magnificent silver goblet decorated with gold and for the church a fine communion cup which served the congregation until it was eventually lost, presumed melted, in the great fire of 1800. One tragic sequel to the war was a fierce craze of witch-hunting which seized the Swiss plain. It was orchestrated by the tribunal of the inquisition which the Dominican order of monks had introduced to Lausanne 30 years earlier. Accusations of witchcraft, and the cruel treatment of those convicted of it, became notorious both in the lowland and in the highland for the next two-and-a-half centuries.

The defeat of Burgundy gave the highlanders an opportunity to plunder the plain and the cathedral city of Lausanne. It also gave Bern an opportunity to seize the towns which Savoy controlled along the Rhône above Lake Geneva. The castle of Aigle, which Château-d'Oex had so recently plundered and fired, was restored as a fortress and became the seat of a Bern governor. The conquered Rhône territory was divided into four military mandates, one of which included the highland valley of Ormont on Château-d'Oex's southern flank. These four mandates, although Romanic-speaking, were integrated into the home provinces of Alemannic-speaking Bern. The most direct access to them remained via Château-d'Oex and Bern's protectorate over the highland therefore became strategically more important than ever. The new governor of Aigle castle not only secured for Bern a strong point on the trail which brought oriental textiles and spices from Italy to western Switzerland, but also supplied the city with good Rhône wines.

In the late fifteenth century demographic growth in the Alps once more led to pressure of people on the tilled land of livestock on the pasture. Fourteenth-century Château-d'Oex farmers had failed to win access to the southern pastures of the Ormont valley, before the Black Death decimated highland populations and eased the pressure to expand. A century later the restored population once more needed access to new grazing to enhance the Alpine dairy industry. As border struggles over land resources intensified, war broke out between Château-d'Oex and Ormont in 1502. Three hundred armed men from Château-d'Oex invaded the disputed pastures, killed six cowmen, robbed the corpses of their personal possessions, butchered their animals and drove the survivors down the valley towards the Rhône. For good measure they hurled abuse at the new Bern overlords who had seized Ormont from Savoy. Bern took the insults against its sovereign dignity seriously and immediately declared war on Château-d'Oex. It ignored the rights of the count of Gruyère, and accused the marauders not only of committing atrocities, but also of insulting the honour of a proud city. A brutal village skirmish became an international incident. The strategic reliability of Château-d'Oex as a military dependency guarding the highland route between Bern and the Rhône seemed in doubt.

To avenge the insults of 1502 Bern sent a large army of 2000 men up the Simmental to invade Château-d'Oex. The neighbouring states tried to take rapid action to avoid another war in the Alps. Matthew Schinner, the bishop of Sion who later became one of Switzerland's foremost cardinals, hastily climbed the mountain by a stony footpath to try to mediate a peace agreement. Members of the parliaments of both Basel, which had not yet joined the Swiss pact, and Fribourg, which had very recently been admitted to it, also asked Bern to find a peaceful solution to the conflict. The price which Bern exacted from Château-d'Oex, and from its hapless prince in Gruyère castle, was a heavy one. The count of Gruyère lost all his surviving territorial rights over the valley of Ormont, including his nominal title to a castle there. At the same time his Ormont subjects were released from their oath of loyalty to him, a loyalty which he had hitherto been able to use to raise much needed taxation. Bern partially moderated the penalty by insisting that some of the count's loss of revenue in Ormont should be made good by the farmers of Château-d'Oex since it was they who had perpetrated the outrage against the Ormont cattle-farmers. Bern also demanded for itself a sum of 4000 Rhine florins to meet the expenses it had incurred in mobilisation for war. Three quarters of the indemnity was to be levied on the farmers who had conducted the invasion of Ormont and proffered insults against Bern. The remaining quarter of the fine was to be paid by the people of Château-d'Oex as a whole to symbolise their 'gratitude' to Bern for its 'magnanimity' in sparing the borough the rigours of an armed invasion. The ringleader of the raid on Ormont was handed over to Bern for exemplary punishment. Almost as an afterthought the wronged Ormont farmers were given permission to recover compensation for property they had lost. By then, however, these farmers had almost caused a new conflict by taking the law into their own hands and helping themselves abundantly to cheeses from Château-d'Oex homesteads which they raided.

Bern had made it clear that it was now in control of the Oberland, including the sections of the highland which were still owned by the count of Gruyère. Although highland farming was firmly under Bern domination, the protectorate over Château-d'Oex still did not provide the city with adequate access to the Rhône trade route to Italy. It also gave Bern control over only a small part of the vineyards of western Switzerland. In 1536, therefore, Bern attacked the remaining Savoy territories on the north side of Lake Geneva. It captured the fortress of Chillon, seized the great vineyards between Vevey and Geneva, and drove the prince-bishop and his canons out of the wealthy cathedral city of Lausanne. Bern had now gained a more direct access to the highway over the St Bernard pass. It no longer needed to negotiate steep, and poorly maintained, trails through Château-d'Oex either for long-distance commerce or for the strategic reinforcement of its garrisons on the Rhône. But although Château-d'Oex was no longer of strategic importance for communications, it was becoming increasingly important for military recruitment.

After the defeat of Burgundy the armies of Bern and of the associated Swiss republics were among the most feared in Europe. For a time it seemed that Bern might become a great territorial power in its own right. Instead, however, the city–state made its fortune by renting out Swiss soldiers to other nations as mercenaries. The growth of Swiss mercenary service was partly related to demographic pressure in the over-exploited Alpine pastures, where human fertility continued to exceed population mortality in the fifteenth century. At the same time the transformation of mountain economies from labour-intensive crop farming to animal-intensive dairy farming reduced employment opportunities and drove many labourers out from all of the Swiss highlands. Bern, like other members of the Swiss pact, raised levies of men from its villages who could be incorporated into regiments and hired out to foreign governments according to long-term contracts.

The mercenary tradition took on a particular importance for Château-d'Oex in 1516 when the Bern army, then fighting in Italy, was comprehensively defeated by Francis I of France at the battle of Marignano. Thereafter Bern signed a peace treaty with France that was to last for nearly 300 years. Henceforth France gave international protection to Bern, but in exchange Bern agreed to allow the recruitment of mercenaries for France. Under the terms of the perpetual treaty between Bern and France Château-d'Oex was able to claim an annual fee of 200 *livres* in return for the French rights to conscript mercenaries. France also granted a regular purse to the boroughs of the highland with which to pay disability pensions to men who had been injured and repatriated. Thereafter Château-d'Oex always had its share of lame war veterans, pensioners with timber toes and shoulder crutches who helped out on the farms as best they could.

Little is known of the manner in which Bern raised mercenary levies in Château-d'Oex, but the business was probably as agonising and corrupt as it was in other Swiss republics. In Uri, for instance, the recruiting sergeants built a chain of prisons across the Alps in which mercenaries hired out to Italian princes and republics were securely locked at night to hinder desertion by men desperate to get home to their children and their cattle. Those who did escape from the forced marches were swiftly replaced in savage reprisals on their home villages. In Solothurn mercenary recruitment depended on the fees and bribes which the French embassy gave to local officials, including bursaries to Paris university for their sons. Innkeepers frequently provided the premises in which innocent lads were persuaded to surrender their freedom in exchange for financial and alcoholic inducements. The deluded 16-year-olds who then struggled over the Jura mountains to France carrying heavy pikes or flintlocks were promised a mere four-and-a-half *livres* per month if they survived the wars in which they were deployed.

The success of the Swiss as hired soldiers depended not only on their numerical strength, as tens of thousands of them were drilled for service in royal guards and foreign infantries, but also on their superior handling of the changing weaponry which was being adopted by Bern's own regiments. By 1500 the crossbow began to be supplemented by firearms: first the arquebus, then the heavy flintlock and later the lighter musket that could be carried on long marches. The training of marksmen by retired veterans began young and from the age of eight Château-d'Oex children learnt to shoot with the crossbow before they had the strength needed to pull a longbow. Archery long remained the popular sport and Bern had to offer cash inducements to persuade the men of Château-d'Oex to adopt competitive firearm shooting, but gradually musketeers outnumbered bowmen and pikemen. In Château-d'Oex firearms were manufactured by local blacksmiths who took great pride in their work. They tried to ensured that their clients, who were commonly also their relatives, would go to war with the safest and most effective guns that craftsmen could fashion. The families Rosat, Turrian and Favrod all boasted gunsmiths of repute, while the farrier Lenoir, and the nailmaker Morier, forged excellent bayonettes which could be fitted to the gunbarrels.

Château-d'Oex played an unquantified part in the 'red economy' of Switzerland by contributing the blood of very young men to the overseas agreements which Bern contracted. France was not the only country to rent Château-d'Oex soldiers from Bern. Over the centuries men from the village died in every corner of Europe: Jean-Philippe Pilet died of pulmonary phthisis in Bavaria when aged 18; Pierre David Raymond fell in Spain at 17; a fife-player, Jean-Jacques Desquartiers, died of a French fever while still in his teens. Josué Pilet was considered lucky when permitted a Protestant burial while fighting for the king of Sardinia. David Jornayvaz, unlike the others, survived his service and was given a safe conduct in the Netherlands by his Bern colonel; it enabled him to take home leave without being pressganged or charged with desertion.

While Bern developed as one of the leading merchants of mercenary regiments in Europe, its old rival Gruyère declined. Gruyère had possessed a strong military tradition, with extensive contacts in Italy, France and the Netherlands, and a good Gruyère commander and business entrepreneur might have been able to gain both wealth and status for the principality on the sixteenth-century arms circuit. The last counts of Gruyère, however, possessed none of the skills of their forbears and in two generations they lost both their status and their wealth. A particularly severe crisis hit the principality in 1544 when the last count, Michael of Gruyère, supplied Francis I, the now elderly king of France, with a contingent of 4000 mercenaries for a campaign in Italy. The recruits Gruyère had raised were inexperienced, their performance at the battle of Ceresole was abysmal, and France refused to pay for the poor military service rendered. Michael had equipped this large mercenary force at his own expense, but he never received any reimbursement of his costs let alone any payment for his men or profit for himself. His debt to the moneylenders of the Swiss republics deepened. He tried to solve his financial crisis by minting his own gold coin, as an ancient licence from the Holy Roman Emperor entitled him to do, but he fell victim to the deceptions of crooks from the French underworld. The feckless prince simultaneously failed to make his fortune with a successful marriage into his European network of aristocratic relatives. In 1554 Michael of Gruyère fled to Brussels, where he had once been a courtier at the imperial court of Emperor Charles V. He died there in 1576. A mausoleum was built in his honour in the Netherlands but back in his Alpine highland his creditors plundered his princely estate.

Bern's authority over Château-d'Oex had expanded steadily while sovereignty was still held by the declining nobility of Gruyère. When in 1554 Michael of Gruyère was declared bankrupt, deposed and forced to flee into exile, the future of Bern's influence in the borough was called into doubt. The principality's main creditors were the Swiss republics. The Swiss Diet met to resolve the debt problem and decided that as an interim measure it would invite two of its member-states to administer the county jointly as a 'communal bailliwick'. One of these trustees was to be Bern. The other was to be Bern's great rival, the city–state of Fribourg. One solution to Gruyère's future would have been to declare the principality a republic and convert the honorary membership of the Swiss pact which had been granted to the prince in 1549 into full membership with a seat in the Diet. Such a solution, however, would not have generated the income needed to pay off the deposed prince's debts. A permanent condominium under Bern and Fribourg would also not have released the capital sums required by the central Swiss republics. The Diet therefore resolved to sell Gruyère to the highest bidder. The property was financially attractive since the dairy industry continued to thrive on the Alpine pastures and the related production of hides and skins supplied the famous tanneries and leather workshops of Fribourg with their necessary raw materials. Fribourg, which had also grown wealthy from textile weaving, seemed to be the obvious candidate to purchase the whole of Gruyère from the count's creditors. The city was only 20 kms from Gruyère castle.

The sale of Gruyère county to Fribourg city was vigorously opposed by Bern which had been entrenched as the protecting power over Château-d'Oex for the past century-and-a-half. The Diet therefore decided to partition Gruyère and sell only the lower, if larger and richer, part to Fribourg. The price received was 53 518 *écus*, 18 *Groschen* and 6 pence. The smaller, highland, section of the county, including Château-d'Oex, was sold to Bern for 16 981 *écus*, 43 *Groschen* and 6 pence. Once the purchase was finalised Bern united the Romanic and Alemannic sections of the highland into a single bailliwick. Since the great castle of Vanel had been destroyed in 1407 there was no suitable residence for a highland governor and the first lord-bailiff appointed by Bern lived in Saanen. At a later date Bern built a suitable castle for its lord-bailiff at Rougemont, on the site of the now-abandoned Benedictine priory. Château-d'Oex remained a self-governing borough with its own chatelain but it did not become the centre of the new highland administration. It did, however, come to adopt as its own the republican laws of Bern, although the neighbouring boroughs retained the customary Moudon laws which they had inherited from Gruyère. Integration into the legal, fiscal and military tradition of Bern was to last for more than two centuries. Equally significantly Château-d'Oex was now compelled to adopt the reformed religion of Bern.

3
Tradition and Reformation

In Château-d'Oex the church dominated many walks of life. The church building stood tall over the village as church traditions stood pre-eminent in highland culture. During the first half of the sixteenth century the church remained staunchly Roman Catholic. In the second half of the century, however, the congregation was abruptly transformed into a Protestant community. This reluctant 'reformation' of religious custom was not inspired by local protests at church abuse, or by highland demands for a change in tradition. On the contrary the Château-d'Oex farmers were extremely loath to give up their accustomed source of spiritual security. The religious transformation of the highland was brought about by the political change of sovereignty. When the holders of the credit notes of the bankrupt count of Gruyère wanted to recover money rashly lent to the incompetent prince, debt recuperation was more important to them than religious solidarity. Whatever ecclesiastical sympathy Catholic creditors may have had for their fiscal hostages in Château-d'Oex was outweighed by financial considerations. When they sold the village, and the surrounding Gruyère highland, to the Protestant city–republic of Bern they acknowledged that all the inhabitants would be required to become Protestants.

The traditional highland congregation of Château-d'Oex was generally in good standing with the Catholic Church in the century before Reformation fever suddenly began to take a hold of northern Switzerland. The old Château-d'Oex priests, for instance, had succeeded in getting the Catholic hierarchy to recognize that the highlands were a bleak place in which to live. As a result the people of Château-d'Oex gradually won concessions to make daily life more comfortable. The church acknowledged that the Sarine river contained few fish and so when necessary parishioners were given a dispensation to eat meat on Fridays. They were also permitted to eat cheese and eggs on fast days when the people of the plain were forbidden to do so. In 1462 the church recognized that the highlands had no olive trees to supply cooking oil and the people of Château-d'Oex were therefore given permission to cook in butter during Lent, though they were still expected to refrain from eating cheese during their forty days of Lenten fasting. Like people throughout Europe the highlanders were pleased to be able to buy from the church indulgences which absolved them from sin. In 1519 the people of Rossinière welcomed an indulgence-peddler from Milan. In exchange for a contribution towards the cost of building St Peter's Cathedral in Rome they received a papal indulgence. Their consciences were apparently not perturbed by the disquiet which this trade had caused to Luther, in the previous year, as no Protestant sympathies had yet reached the highland.

The first awareness of the stirrings of the Reformation was recorded in Château-d'Oex in 1530. The local response was strongly antipathetic to new religious ideas. In that year the treaty of protection that linked the Gruyère highland to the city of Bern was due for renewal. Two years before, however, Bern had decided to emulate Zürich and adopt a Protestant form for the city's national church. As a result Bern no longer recognized the legitimacy of the Catholic saints who were so highly honoured in Château-d'Oex. Bern proposed a new oath of loyalty to bond the highland to the city omitting the names of the saints who had traditionally sanctified the legitimacy of the treaty. The highlanders refused to accept the new oath and the treaty of protection would have lapsed had Bern not eventually given way and allowed its Catholic protegés to retain the customary use of saints for the swearing of oaths. Four years later a new confrontation over religion broke out when Bern called-up its armies in order to invade Geneva and impose the Reformation on the then still Catholic city. It expected the highland regiments to take part in the campaign, but Château-d'Oex refused to participate in a war against fellow Catholics. Even greater stress was caused to the treaty of protection in 1536 when Bern tried to mobilise its highland regiments again, this time to attack Lausanne. Lausanne was the seat of the bishop who held ecclesiastical authority over Château-d'Oex and was the site of the cathedral to which the dean of the highland was responsible. As in the case of Geneva, Château-d'Oex would not allow its troops to be used to spread the Reformation and attack a Catholic city.

Château-d'Oex's loyal Catholic refusal to take part in the Protestant attack on Lausanne did little to protect the episcopal city from the ravages of Bern. The cathedral treasure, to which the highland churches had contributed in their small way over the course of five centuries, was systematically looted by the Protestant armies. The great Madonna, coated in 250 ounces of gold, was removed to Bern and melted down into bars of bullion for the city treasury. The cathedral organ was ripped out and sold to the Catholic cathedral of Sion for 6000 imperial florins. Cathedral canons who succeeded in escaping across the lake to Savoy allegedly took with them the most valuable relics, the rib of St Lawrence, the hair of the Virgin, the wooden splinter from the true cross. The count of Gruyère was forced to accept the imposition of the Reformation on most of his properties around Lausanne though he did temporarily succeed in protecting one of his Catholic churches on the plain and installing in it an image of St Pancras which became a lucrative focus for clandestine pilgrimage. In the Gruyère highland Catholicism was even more staunchly preserved and the people of Château-d'Oex continued to cherish their shrines and their relics.

In the church of St Donat one of the oldest venerated objects was a small wooden statuette which was probably associated with the church's Irish patron. The old saint had conducted his journeys through Switzerland four centuries before any church was founded at Château-d'Oex, but the memory of his mission and his election as bishop by the see of Lausanne, was still alive. When the Reformation finally reached Château-d'Oex, and ardent Protestant preachers tried to have the holy objects thrown out of the church, the statue of St Donat was so securely walled into a niche that it survived not only the Reformation but also four centuries of recurrent damage and restoration before it was finally rediscovered. Another prized object of veneration was the great Château-d'Oex Madonna which also survived the Protestant upheavals. The carved and heavily painted statue of the Virgin was probably smuggled out of the church by a pious family called Geneyne who presumably took it when later emigrating out of the highland to go down to the lower valley of Gruyère where Catholic traditions survived under the sovereignty of the city–republic of Fribourg. For nearly three centuries the statue disappeared from view, but in 1822 the descendants of its rescuers gave it to their local church at Grandvillars, near the castle of Montsalvens. They had found it, they claimed, beside the Sarine where it had been beached, miraculously intact, after the Protestants had thrown it into the river.

The crisis of the Reformation which led to the hiding or destroying of Catholic objects of veneration reached the highland on

22 December 1555, the day on which the Bern purchase of the high-land was confirmed. The Alemannic burghers of Saanen immediately took the initiative in trying to prevent Bern from imposing the Reformation on the newly-bought territory. They sent a diplomatic envoy over the mountains to the ancestral Swiss republic of Unterwald to ask for help in protecting their Catholic faith. Unterwald, although a member of the Diet which regulated the Swiss military pacts was no friend of Bern, a city which had usurped many of its highland posses-sions, and no friend of the Protestants who challenged its strongly held Catholic traditions. But Unterwald was no military match for Bern. The speaker of the Bern senate, in his capacity of head-of-state, summoned the leaders of the Gruyère highland communities and imposed upon them a Protestant oath of loyalty. Enforcing that loyalty, however, proved difficult. No civic officer in Bern had courage enough to take up office as lord-bailiff of the highland. The people up there were known to be ferocious 'idolaters' and no one dared to venture into the hostile territory upon which Bern wished to impose the Reformation. Eventually an old, corpulent, citizen and former bannaret, Hans-Rudolph von Graffenried, accepted nomination to the highland. He took on the responsibility of governing both Saanen and Château-d'Oex. After two years in the mountains the grateful senate allowed him to return to the city and tend his frail health.

The first people of the Château-d'Oex valley to feel the theological wind of change were the Benedictine monks of Rougemont priory. They left the valley in hasty disarray on Christmas Day 1555. The pop-ulation at large had no option of fleeing and so determined to mount the strongest possible resistance to the threatened religious changes. The common people could not accept that their friends, neighbours and relatives-by-marriage in the adjacent villages of Valais and Fribourg were suddenly declared to be damned while they themselves were compelled to accept erstwhile heresy as true religion. Saanen suffered a particularly brusque Protestant initiation. Its first reformed preacher was Jean Haller, a disciple of Zwingli who had been the great Alemannic pioneer of the Swiss Reformation in the church of Zürich. Haller was a distinguished theologian attached to Bern cathedral, but he was a townsman who was terrified of the rustic highland natives. He described what he saw as their murderous customs and their phi-landering absence of morals in the most vituperative terms. He drove out the people's much-loved priests and within a fortnight had destroyed all the shrines, altars, crosses, crucifixes, Madonnas, saints and relics that he could find. When, soon afterwards, Haller returned to Bern he was rewarded with a barrel of wine and his student assistant was given a new coat and a pair of trousers. His report to his mentors in Zürich that he had eradicated the old beliefs was, however, premature. In a tiny chapel in the woods at Gstaad the *Ave Maria* was still being sung two years after Haller's whirlwind visitation. Even more surprisingly the magnificent wall paintings in the Saanen parish church continued to be cherished and admired as a traditional pictorial cathechism. Only in 1604, half-a-century after Haller's desecrations, did the Protestant taste for decorative simplicity cause the paintings to be covered over with whitewash.

Bringing the Reformation to Château-d'Oex was more difficult than bringing the Reformation to Saanen since the parishioners of Château-d'Oex did not understand the Alemannic dialects spoken by Protestant preachers in Bern and Zürich. The reforming politicians had to look for a Romanic preacher with the ability and courage to challenge the Catholic traditions of Château-d'Oex. The lords of Bern wasted no time in their endeavour to stamp their own beliefs on the village. On 30 December 1555, three days after Haller was appointed to break the Catholic spirit of Saanen, Bern invited Pierre Viret to carry the word of God to Château-d'Oex. Viret was a disciple of Guillaume Farel, the old preacher who had helped to persuade the young John Calvin to leave France and settle at Geneva. Viret was asked, in Latin, if he could preach to the people of Château-d'Oex in the 'gallica lingua', the Gaullish tongue of Romanic Switzerland. Viret was a man of quite different character from the fearful and violent Haller. He made a quiet visit to the highland and found one potential convert, a man who had heard Farel preach some 30 years earlier. In the spring 1556 the gentle Viret returned to the highland bringing with him the old thunderer, Farel himself. They spread the message of the Reformation throughout the highland valley. On 10 May Viret wrote to Calvin, in Latin, reporting that although they were very foot sore they had been successful in their mission.

The success of Calvin's preachers in Château-d'Oex, like the success of Zwingli's followers in Saanen, was only partial. In the first year of the Reformation 40 mutinous men were charged with having listened to a Mass. The ensuing riot had to be quelled by forces from Bern. The covertly Catholic Château-d'Oex families thereafter learnt to be more discreet and to keep their favourite religious images well hidden in private homes. For all their apparent quiescence the forced converts were often immobilised by depression when they could no longer watch mystery plays or sing hymns. Cases of farmers committing suicide were reported and some women became so angry that they stoned the new Protestant clergymen. Further trouble broke out in September 1556 when the preacher appointed at Rougemont sought to gain possession of the revenues of the dissolved monastery. The exiled prior, Peter of Gruyère, refused to supply documentary evidence relating to the monastic estates which Bern wished to expropriate and an exchange of vituperative slander ensued. The dispute escalated to involve the governments of both Fribourg and Bern and was referred for arbitration to Solothurn, the seat of the French ambassador to the Swiss republics and the *de facto* headquarters of the Swiss pact. The Protestant preacher refused to retract the anti-Catholic tirade which had landed him in a Fribourg gaol, but Bern agreed to restrain him for the sake of peace and even paid Fribourg compensation for its legal and diplomatic expenditure.

The difficulty in imposing the Reformation on Château-d'Oex did not only derive from traditional resistance to political transformation. It also involved the choice of a theological structure for the church in the new highland territory. The Alemannic tradition of Zwingli accepted that the state would be paramount in society and would govern the affairs of the church. The Romanic tradition of Calvin, by contrast, gave greater authority to the church in many matters of public life. Because the Romanic highlanders were better able to read French than German it was Calvin's religious writing which influenced the Château-d'Oex pastors and came to inform local patterns of behaviour and belief. The Church of Bern, however, was unwilling to accept Calvinist administrative practice and adopted a more Zwinglian approach to church–state relations both in the city and in its new highland parishes. Authority was put into the hands of a powerful consistory tribunal made up both of representatives of the state and of elders appointed by the local congregations. The Château-d'Oex religious court was supervised by a supreme consistory which met in Bern. Although the national senate of Bern controlled the highland congregations, the Château-d'Oex church elders normally hired ministers from the Romanic-speaking towns of the Swiss plain, or even from France. Many of these preachers espoused the strict views on social morality associated with Calvin.

After the Reformation Protestant life in Château-d'Oex became more subdued than Catholic life had ever been. Regular attempts were made, though not always successfully, to stamp out the old tradition of carnivals, processions and feast days, and to turn the valley into a place of quiet, almost puritanical, sobriety. One of the changes most painfully felt was the church's attempt to terminate the community celebration of funerals. In the eyes of highland worshippers the neglect of traditional burial customs was especially perplexing and caused much grief. Mourners continued to insist that they wanted their dead to benefit from a grave in consecrated ground. The people of Etivaz, who had no chapel or graveyard of their own at the time of the Reformation, were particularly incensed to be told that they should bury their dead locally in wayside graves. Despite the remonstrations of the Protestant pastors these remote farmers insisted on tying the corpses of their loved ones to sledges and hauling them across the mountain in midwinter for burial in the graveyard at Château-d'Oex. Eventually the church gave way to public demand but retained the right to refuse burial to anyone who had taken his or her own life. The consistory tribunal was charged with determining which deaths had been accidental and which had been deliberate suicide. One old widow who had been given permission to collect riverside firewood to heat her cabin had fallen through the ice and drowned. The rope she used for hauling her sticks was found on the bank and it was decided likely that she had died accidentally while trying to reach a branch. Jean Byrde, on the other hand, who was found drowned at the age of 84, was deemed to have led a less than blameless life and it was decided that he should not be permitted an honourable burial. In such cases families sometimes tried to avoid humiliation and disgrace by appealing to Bern against the harsh decisions of the local church elders.

The honour of deceased persons had traditionally been measured by the number of people who followed their funeral procession. Those anxious to have a grand funeral often included in their will a provision which said that anyone who came to the door of the house on the day of the funeral should be given copper coins as alms. The Protestant church tried to ban this ostentatious practice, but to no avail. Alms continued to be given out and people flocked from near and far to attend a good funeral and partake of the feast afterwards. Although funeral processions and feasts were retained the Catholic view of an after life that had to be permanently catered for was apparently eradicated. Graves in the Château-d'Oex cemetery ceased to be permanent resting places for the departed and became municipal plots that grieving families could rent and tend for 30 years after which they reverted to the borough to become available for a new occupant.

Château-d'Oex's reluctance to accept the new transformations and abandon the old traditions continued to be felt both in matters of worship and in matters of social behaviour. At the end of the sixteenth century one brave farmer declared that he would gladly give up his entire herd of cattle to see the Mass restored. Others were more discreet in clinging to tradition and walked stealthily through the woods, avoiding police patrols, in order to worship in the unreformed village chapels of the neighbouring valleys. Five of the old church sacraments had been abandoned by the reformers as unscriptural. Baptism, a Biblical practice, was retained, as was the celebration of the Lord's Supper; in the reformed era, however, the bread and the wine were no longer deemed to be transubstantiated into the body and blood of Christ. Although attendance at the new Protestant services was supervised with increased rigidity, traditionalists still managed to steal away from the village to have their children baptised in what they saw as genuine Catholic christening services. In an attempt to root out such practices men who failed to be accounted for at Sunday worship could be fined ten *livres* by the consistory court. Women were also subject to penalties for absence, though the fine was only five *livres*. Rigid supervision of church attendance almost turned Château-d'Oex into a police state in which neighbours were encouraged to spy on one another and gossip could be sold to the authorities for a reward.

One feature of the reformed church which led to great confrontations was the preservation of the sabbath as a day set aside primarily for worship. The Protestant church was particularly keen to ensure that Sunday was observed and respected as a day of prayer and sobriety. Anyone seen ploughing, planting, scything, harvesting, hedging or working on a fast day or a Sunday was liable to a fine. Similar punishments were imposed on anyone caught buying, selling, bargaining, carting, ferrying, or trading. The state church did, however, make apparently hypocritical exceptions for traders engaged in any import or export business which benefited the city–republic's economy. On holy days hunting and fishing were banned whether as a form of work or as a sport. In Château-d'Oex divine services were held not only on Sunday, but also on market day when farmers from the outlying homesteads and hamlets came into the village. Loitering during the hour of market-day worship was an offence, particularly when men were suspected of furtively frequenting the taverns and women of indulging their taste for the exotic fruits or sweet gingerbreads available from street hawkers.

In 1649 failure to respect the ascetic restrictions on the use of Sunday leisure erupted in a confrontation between the citizens and the authorities. The lord-bailiff of the highland travelled to Château-d'Oex from his castle to preside in person over a court hearing. No less than 22 men from many of the leading Château-d'Oex families were

arraigned before him on charges of scandalous behaviour not conso-
nant with the dignity of the sabbath. The men had apparently been
drinking on Sunday morning rather than attending divine worship and
had shown no proper respect either for the church or for their Bern
overlords. The affair was deemed to have involved a serious challenge
to authority and the case dragged on for 15 months. In the end most
of the accused agreed to pay a fine of ten florins. Three of them, however, Jehan Roch, Claude Henchoz and Noé Ramel refused to pay. They
pleaded poverty, probably genuinely, but may also have been stubborn,
standing-up for local freedoms. They were sent to prison for their
recalcitrance. A fourth defendant, Jehan Morier-Genoud the Elder, was
even more outspoken in his challenge to authority and was charged
not only with licentious behaviour but also with impudently holding
the court in contempt.

Failing to be seen and counted as a loyal subject at Sunday worship
was an offence. So too was a failure to send children, maid-servants
and farmboys to catechism classes. All children, whether legitimate or
illegitimate, were baptised within a fortnight of birth and given three
godparents. They subsequently needed a Protestant education before
their baptism could be confirmed. Lessons in religious discipline were
integrated with schooling during the winter, from the end of October
until the middle of March, but took place in church during the summer when the schools were closed. In theory all children and adolescents between the ages of six and 20 were required to attend classes in
religious doctrine. In practice, and despite threats of chastisement, parents were reluctant to release child labour from the fields during the
summer. To the youths themselves, however, catechism was a splendid
excuse to escape from farm drudgery and truants ran off to play at the
fair-ground regardless of the threatened fines. When they did attend
classes the reluctant catechumens were clearly a pain to their pastor.
They normally spoke to one another in the Romanic vernacular and
pretended not to understand the pastor's French. In one exercise book,
surviving in the Château-d'Oex archives, an exasperated pastor glossed
some passages with vernacular translations. He was particularly out-
raged when ribald farm children translated the concept of God's
'unique' son into words implying that he was his 'eunuch' son.
Eventually, however, all citizens were confirmed and thereafter were
required to take holy communion on four occasions in each year.

Failure to attend communion led to investigation of the cause of
absence. In the case of absentee women the investigation was conducted in private and the local church consistory appointed assessors

to visit the defaulter in her home. In the case of men, however, the enquiry into the cause of absence was conducted in public. A man who failed to take communion was suspected of immoral behaviour and was called upon to justify himself before the consistory court. A case arose in 1770 when the master clockmaker of Château-d'Oex failed to attend communion. The ensuing investigation established that he had 'kissed' Salomé Minod, treating her as though she were a whore. In exchange for the embrace he had rewarded her with a gift of shirt buttons. The Minod family, who were probably descendants of the first permanent pastor to be appointed to the Protestant church of Château-d'Oex, were willing to arrange a private reconciliation with the clockmaker. The Château-d'Oex chatelain who had presided over the court decided, however, that the case was too serious to be quietly resolved. In accordance with law number fifteen of the Bern church code he referred the matter to the lord-bailiff. Such exactitude in matters of male behaviour was especially stringently applied in the weeks immediately preceding the four communion services of Easter, Pentecost, Michaelmas and Christmas.

One of the great concerns of the church in a small farming community such as Château-d'Oex was the regulation of courting customs among young couples. The more draconian the regulations became, however, the less successful the consistory was in applying them. Boisterous young soldiers back from wars had become accustomed to swinging their camp-followers in a cascade of petticoats during rumbustious dances. The scandalised church elders tried to moderate their ardour by introducing barn dancing, men on one side of the hall and women on the other, but the sport lacked piquancy. The only authorised occasion on which couples might be permitted to dance as partners was at the celebration of a wedding. The consistory clearly had great difficulty in imposing its restrictions. One case arose when Pierre Morier-Genoud and Madeleine Isoz were charged with scandalously dancing together before the celebration of their marriage. The court clearly suspected that dancing had led to even more licentious forms of intimacy. Morier-Genoud swore his innocence but was nevertheless fined by a court conscious of recent Bern legislation designed to tighten the restrictions on dancing that had been set out in 1728:

> In the matter of Dancing several of our Citizens and Subjects, not content to benefit from such Divertissments on Nuptial Days, abuse of the licence and deliver themselves to dancing on all types of Occasion, doing so in hiding and in far-away places, as much in the

night-time as by day. We therefore desire and order that whomsoever should furnish a Place for such illicit Dancing, shall pay twenty *livres*, and each Dancer two *livres*, and each women dancer one *livre*, as a Punishment.

Weddings became such privileged occasions that guests came from miles around to enjoy the dancing. Catholic musicians provided music once Protestants had lost the art of playing musical instruments. At any good marriage feast the revelries lasted throughout the night and into the following dawn. Disapproving church elders, although conscious of the Biblical claim that it was better to marry than to burn, nevertheless tried to impose limitations. Sumptuary laws about the desirability of sober dress, and sermons about catering modestly and only for family guests, had little effect on the scale and magnificence of marriage celebrations. Weddings became occasions for burlesque ribaldry. Stag night processions wove their way through the village, singing provocative songs, waving forbidden torches and celebrating as loudly as had formerly been the custom during Catholic carnivals. The worst excesses were committed by young drinkers belonging to the 'charivari' associations. Their ritualised high spirits were partially tolerated to defuse generational conflict when the young and the powerless directed popular anger at the vice and hypocrisy of their elders. Charivari exuberance became boundless, however, when one of their number got married and the newly-wed couple found it expedient to pay the drinkers well to take their carousing elsewhere lest the bride's wedding chamber be invaded by chanting bands.

Finding an acceptable bride was particularly difficult in a farming society where neighbours were often closely related by blood and where the church was particularly severe in forbidding a range of potentially incestuous choices in the matter of marriage partners. Any romantically inclined bachelor tempted to revive ancient tradition and seek a young beauty from the lower valley of Gruyère, now faced stiff Bern prohibitions. The lower valley remained Catholic, under Fribourg ownership, and anyone marrying a Catholic wife was severely dealt with by Bern. Loss of citizenship and banishment in perpetuity from all of the Bern territories was the supreme penalty, but any citizen of Château-d'Oex who married a Catholic also had his possessions confiscated and was precluded from subsequently inheriting property in any Bern province. When it came to the risk of Catholic infiltration or subversion Bern was totally intransigent and there is little evidence of Catholic wives settling in Château-d'Oex after the Reformation.

In the absence of Catholic consorts a different pattern of exogamous marriage alliances developed in Château-d'Oex. Matchmaking took place within a common Protestant culture but across the linguistic boundary of the upper valley. Courting rituals that linked Château-d'Oex with Saanen survived into the twentieth century. On the first day of the New Year a young man of Château-d'Oex would decorate his horse-sleigh with green boughs and coloured ribbons and invite a young lady who was not betrothed to accompany him up the valley to the great field at Feutersoey where a New Year ball was held. It was there that the exchange of dancing partners enabled potential grooms and prospective brides to meet suitors who were not incestuously linked to their own family circle. Once introductions had been made familiarity was enhanced through the custom of bundling, revealingly known in Château-d'Oex by the Alemannic name of 'kiltgang'. Since young men were away in the mountains with the cattle during the summer and winter conditions were not conducive to a girl 'walking out' with her suitor, pre-nuptial socialising took place inside the home. The eligible lady, with the tacit approval of social convention, admitted her chosen suitor to her chamber through the window and permitted him to keep warm under her eiderdown while getting acquainted. In contrast to some neighbouring farming communities, where proof of fertility in a bride was welcomed, Château-d'Oex bundling customs were not expected to lead to pregnancy.

In the old customs of the Gruyère highland the binding prelude to matrimony was the commitment of betrothal. In the more rustic Alemannic hamlets betrothal was commonly formalised by a three day 'trial marriage'. In Château-d'Oex a betrothal was sealed by the drinking of toasts and by the giving and accepting of symbolic gifts. Betrothal gifts could be mundane household objects or more valuable presents of gold. The exchange of betrothal gifts was probably a prelude to cohabitation, especially when the expense of marriage feast could not immediately be contemplated, and the church went to great pain to limit breaches of promise. In one case, heard by the consistory court in 1637, Suzanne Chable strenuously denied that she had drunk a toast and received a gold coin, as a sign that she accepted a marriage proposal from Antoine Mange. In another case lighthearted badinage in a tavern at Rossinière led a would-be suitor to offer some walnuts to a young widow. The widow's sister urgently advised her to throw the nuts on the floor, but she declined to do so and by eating them found herself bound to a promise of marriage which she subsequently had to contest in the courts. Although betrothals were binding, the church insisted that marriage itself should be proclaimed in front of the congregation, not because it was a sacrament but in order to remove any public doubt concerning its validity.

Outside of marriage the laws of Bern, as applied in Château-d'Oex, provided draconian penalties for sexual offences. Anyone, man or woman, caught in adultery for the third time could be sent into permanent exile, a harsh punishment in the frightening Swiss world of warring states and jealously guarded citizenship. Persistent offenders could be sentenced to a public whipping by a professional executioner or might even be beheaded. Evidence of aggravated adultery does survive in the court records of Château-d'Oex. In 1699 Esther Pilet was held in the dungeon at Rougemont castle accused of committing adultery with David Lenoir, a carpenter at Les Moulins. Esther's mother testified that the carpenter had visited her daughter at night 'without lighting a candle' though she had been unable to overhear their 'conversation'. Esther herself strenuously protested that she did light a candle whenever a visitor called on her. The carpenter's wife supported the accusation of adultery and testified that her husband had subsequently lost any appetite for his conjugal rights. The case was deemed so serious that Esther spent a long time in prison while it was being investigated. Her legs became so swollen in their iron fetters that she was eventually unchained in order to receive medical treatment. She took the opportunity to abscond and gained refuge in the Catholic village of Montbovon. The case did not end there, however, and when Lord-Bailiff Tribollet, who had been determined to secure a penalty of death, retired after six irascible years as governor of the highland, Esther deemed it safe to return from exile. Her troubles, however, began again and her enemies accused her of trafficking in stolen ribbons, of attending a Catholic mass, of selling her favours to casual strangers, and of having been associated with Madeleine Byrde, a notorious Château-d'Oex bawd who was later beheaded for threatening public morals. The new lord-bailiff, Fischer, was unimpressed by Esther's protestations of innocence and resorted to thumb screws to obtain a confession. As her fingers were crushed Esther screamed but still denied the original charge of having committed adultery with Lenoir the carpenter.

The obsession of the Bern legislators with sexual behaviour involved not only the protection of men from predatory women, but also the control of women by their male custodians. A husband was permitted to mete out unlimited punishment to a wife caught *in delicto flagrante*. A virgin who was seduced was liable to be deemed guilty of bringing about her own downfall and therefore forfeited her *chapalet* or betrothal fee. This fee, paid upon the legitimate deflowering of a first-time bride, was a significant inducement to preserve proven virginity and one Rougemont bridegroom promised his bride-to-be 2000 florins for her maidenhood in addition to the ceremonial wedding gown and a silver girdle. But for all the prohibitions and inducements sexual conduct did not always obey church law and the punishments for deviation were clearly published as a warning to all who might stray from the path of morality. A 25 crown prostitute was put in the stocks and a high class courtesan had her earnings confiscated on behalf of the wronged wives and children of her clients 'should these be necessitous thereof'. The procurers who lived off the earnings of public women might be branded with a hot iron. Bern attempted to establish a puritanical culture very different from the raucous debauchery which had prevailed in the pre-Reformation towns of Savoy which men from Château-d'Oex had hitherto enjoyed visiting.

While Protestant morality provided one inspiration for legal custom, financial self-interest provided another. The Château-d'Oex borough fathers, like their contemporaries elsewhere, were particularly anxious to avoid having to finance the raising of an illegitimate child when no father had been convicted of paternity and declared liable for the necessary expenses. Borough officials went to great lengths to drive unsupported pregnant women off their territory. In February 1798, in the winter of the Swiss Revolution, the heavily pregnant Marie Madeleine, daughter of the late Abraham Chabloz, struggled home to Château-d'Oex. She claimed that the father of her expected child was a revolutionary French soldier whom she had married on the plain. Chatelain Louis-David Berthod demanded that she prove her claim with documentary evidence. When she failed to do so he heartlessly drove her out of the borough before the birth could become a community responsibility and the child could claim Château-d'Oex citizenship. Other cases of uncertain paternity were dealt with even more harshly. A woman who refused to name the father of her love-child was tortured by inquisitors, supervised by the pastor himself, during her pangs of labour. The reformed church in Château-d'Oex was not generous in its funding of social responsibility.

One of the traditions of the highland which the reformed church of Château-d'Oex, like most Protestant churches, found it particularly difficult to handle was the practice of witchcraft. Childbirth was one field where ancient rituals smacking of paganism were prevalent. In order to root out superstition the church insisted that any registered midwife be carefully instructed to avoid all use of charms, signs of the cross and mysterious murmurings. Magic nevertheless remained a normal part of everyday life. Spells were used to exorcise evil spirits, to make weapons of war invincible, to overcome human disease, to protect crops from plagues of caterpillars, to make cows more fertile and to deceive rivals in commercial bargains. Any woman convicted of consulting a sorcerer was liable to a fine, while a man convicted of the same crime paid a penalty twice as heavy. By and large the people of Château-d'Oex were afraid to denounce suspected sorcerers lest they themselves should become victims of evil spells. Bern tried to overcome local reticence by offering informers half of any fine imposed in a case of witchcraft. Convicted magicians, and persons covertly possessing books of magical practices, were stripped of their honours, incarcerated in prison, or even driven into exile. The church seized all denounced books on witchcraft.

Cases of witchcraft caused serious panic in the highland. In 1712 the village of Rougemont was in torment when witches threatened its peace and the burghers petitioned the church court to take action. The case revolved around the deposition of Madeleine Saugy, a child of 12 who had been sent to Vanel to buy some cloth from an Alemannic country weaver. On the lonely road she was accosted by a deformed crone and took fright. The deaf old woman with decaying teeth and a distorted speech tried to find out whose daughter the child was, but the more insistent she became the more she frightened the girl with her heavy breathing. The child finally escaped and ran distraught until she collapsed from heart palpitations. She eventually revived herself, ate some wild berries, and went home. She then told her agitated family stories of the strange woman who had sometimes appeared to behave like a fox, sometimes like a cat, sometimes like a raven or a dog. The village was immediately convinced that it was facing a case of witchcraft and demanded immediate action to exorcise the evil. The now bewildered child was brought before a terrifying tribunal of church elders which concluded from her testimony that she had been bewitched. To the shock of her father she asked him one day 'What does *ich glaub nicht in Gott* mean?' The German sentence 'I do not believe in God' seemed a sure sign that the child had been given to the devil by an Alemannic witch living across the cultural boundary. Moral panic became so acute that Lord-Bailiff Watteville decided that the matter was far too grave for him to handle. Poor Madeleine Saugy was sent to Bern accompanied by both her father and her grandfather. The supreme consistory was charged with hearing her case though its judgment has not yet come to light in the archives.

Another long-running case of witchcraft, this time unconnected with the fear of old women speaking Alemannic dialect in a dark forest, had broken out a few years earlier in Château-d'Oex. This case concerned the economic well-being of a dairy-farming community on the far side of the valley from the village. The pastures on the slopes of the Braye were north-facing ones and, as was to be expected, the cows yielded less milk than those pastured above the south-facing village. Not all farmers were satisfied with this elementary climatic explanation for their poor performance. They felt sure that their dairying activities were being hindered by witchcraft. In 1696 the matter came before the fiery Lord-Bailiff Tribollet, the governor who had held Esther Pilet in leg irons in his castle prison, and detailed depositions were taken from many witnesses, Moïse Berthod claimed that when his neighbour Pierre Rosat married the daughter of Antoine Marmier in 1680 the effect was a loss of milk yield, of cream production and of cheese quality on his farm. Abraham Lude supported the allegation and claimed that in the seven or eight years during which he had been a neighbour of Pierre Rosat his milk production had also suffered. David Turrian reported similar occurrences and claimed that as soon as he took his cows away from the Braye pastures near the Rosat farm their performance immediately improved. The court assumed that it was dealing with a case of witchcraft and of magical interference with the milk yields of cows. Both Rosat and his wife had previous convictions for witchcraft and had served long prison sentences. It was reported that while they had been in prison the cows of their neighbours had miraculously recovered. On their release from gaol, however, the milch-cows on the Braye again began to show symptoms of disturbance, became reluctant to drink water, or ceased to yield milk. Worse still the farmers themselves began to complain of aches and pains and said that their cheeses tasted bad and their butter would not set in the churn. The lord-bailiff took extensive notes which he sent to Bern to rid himself of a vexatious case of supernatural disturbance in his turbulent highland domain.

The puritanical laws that Bern introduced to the highland did not lead to conspicuously pious, chaste and deferential behaviour after the Reformation. One Château-d'Oex farmer, struggling to calculate the complex weighing of his cheeses and the value of his butter, was wont when daydreaming to write down the drinking songs that he learnt in the pub in his account book. Such songs had double meanings to which translation would not do justice but they would certainly have caused the pulse of a consistory judge to quicken. One of the less innocent songs that captured his bachelor fancy was a lullaby that highland mothers were said to sing to their children. It referred to the ribald exploits of husbands serving as musketeers in Paris and compared their prowess unfavourably with the strong, silent cowmen who stayed at home and satisfied their mistresses in more ways than one. Another surviving song lewdly but humorously compared the pleasures of the flesh with the pleasures of drinking. An excessive consumption of alcohol, both of wine from the plain and of locally distilled gentian gin from the highland, was a matter of constant concern to the church. So too was the Château-d'Oex addiction to gambling.

Protestant moral codes seem to have been, and remained, much more strongly opposed to gambling than were Catholic ones. Gaming with dice was particularly condemned, but all forms of gambling remained an abiding passion in the Château-d'Oex valley. Those who profaned the sabbath by playing at cards could be sentenced to a fine of ten *livres*, with additional fines for any publican who encouraged such indecent and frivolous pastimes. Penalties for betting did not stop people from gambling and a sweepstake was organised in the valley in which many, if not most, citizens covertly participated. The surviving, but undated, record of one lottery agent presents a much more cheerful picture of society than the records of the church tribunals. Lottery tickets, supplied by such eminent dignitaries as the chatelain of Rougemont and the borough clerk of Chateau-d'Oex, were touted round the villages and sold to clients using pseudonyms such as 'the first fruit of marriage', 'the Bernese girl', 'the good cheese tavern', 'my pipe is my delight', 'the pretty little bride', 'I love profit but hate work', and many scores of others. A small prize of forty florins was won by 'she who laughs while her husband weeps' but the jackpot, 250 florins, went to the holder of 'I hope, but you fear'. Not all punters used a disguise when buying their lottery tickets. The Pilet family of Rossinière bought seven tickets, one for Abraham the elder, one for Abraham who likes women, one for Aaron who likes cheese, one for stubborn David, one for good-boy John, one for pretty Marie and one for Samuel who aspires to become a lawyer.

Gambling in pubs caused the church courts more grief than the sweepstake in which public officials took a leading part. In 1771 an itinerant butcher from Burgundy came to the winter fair at Rougemont and bought some livestock with which he planned to walk home. At the fair he met Joseph Pilet, a schoolmaster, and they agreed to invite a few friends to a popular roadside tavern at Les Moulins. The publican supplied them with wine and discreetly settled them in an upstairs room where they began a long gambling session with playing cards. By the end of the session Pilet had won five or six fattened pigs which were surreptitiously delivered to his pig sty a few hundred yards up the hill. The Burgundian pig merchant disappeared down the valley with the rest of his purchases without complaining to anyone about his serious gambling losses. The matter nevertheless came to the attention of the church elders who took a grave view and investigated the activities of their schoolmaster. For days on end witnesses were called to testify before the church tribunal but none of the alleged gamblers would reveal who had been present, although rumours about their identity were rife throughout the village. The publican swore that his customers had played only to decide who should pay for each round of drinks. The players alleged that their stakes had only been pockets of chestnuts which the publican had roasted for them on his fire. The pigs, they all said, had been legitimately sold by the itinerant butcher and properly bought and paid for by the schoolmaster. Since gambling, even for food and drink, was illegal the church court imposed fines of five florins all round. The plaintiffs, declaring that they were peasants and not property-owners, protested that they could not afford such fines and appealed against their conviction to a higher court in Bern. Their ultimate fate is not recorded.

One way in which the Reformation changed the rôle of the church in Château-d'Oex was by attempting to limit the natural exuberance displayed in leisure pursuits by successful farmers who enjoyed drinking, singing and gambling. A quite different religious change concerned the church's perception of its social responsibility and its attitude to the deprived and marginal members of the community. The old Catholic church had been relatively well provided with property and income, but the new Protestant church was much less well endowed after the state had stripped many of its assets. The control of surviving church income was in the hands of the reformed dean and chapter of the now Protestant cathedral of Lausanne. The dean, however, was not given a free hand in managing the finances of his highland parishes. Traditionally church income had been used not only to pay the stipends of the priests but also to alleviate the sufferings of the poor. In reformed Château-d'Oex revenues from church properties were diverted from philanthropic causes to subsidise the salary of Bern's lord-bailiff of the highland. The parish constantly struggled to raise funds to heat the parsonage, feed the pastor, pay the deacon, and meet the needs of the sick, the maimed, the deranged, the elderly, the orphaned, and the outcasts. The tradition of charity remained an essential part of community life in Protestant Château-d'Oex but the resources available never satisfied the need. One important charitable foundation which did make the transition from the old order to the new was the bursary fund dedicated to the care of men and women suffering from leprosy.

Château-d'Oex took some care to avoid circumstances in which lepers became a burden on charity or public welfare. Much as people abhorred having lepers living in their midst, they deemed that preferable to having to sustain them at the community's expense. Wherever possible lepers remained with their families and spouses were not permitted to eject leprous partners from the household, or even to deny sufferers the right to share the conjugal bed. Lone lepers, however, confronted extreme social ostracism, more extreme it was alleged than plague victims, who were more infectious but who died more quickly and could be forgotten. Disabled and disfigured victims of the disease had traditionally been enrolled in a leprosarium using rituals resembling those performed by monks entering a monastery. On pre-ordained days lepers were allowed out to beg, but had to be muffled in hoods, cloaks, shoes and gloves. The response to charitable appeals for the maintenance of leper hospitals was commensurate with the horror which the disease caused. The hospital was also able to demand that prospective inmates who owned property should endow the leprosarium with their worldly wealth. The Château-d'Oex leper foundation came to hold important assets by the time leprosy burnt itself out in the western Alps in the seventeenth century. One late victim of leprosy was recorded in the lake-side port of Vevey in 1649. Although the leprosarium at Château-d'Oex was still in existence 22 years later, the building probably served as a general infirmary while still retaining its old name, the *maladière*, and its old charitable endowments.

Charity in Château-d'Oex was shown not only to outcasts but also to widows. In the case of widows the distinction between voluntary philanthropy and legal welfare obligations could be a fine one as illustrated in the account-book of Samuel Henchoz. Henchoz kept meticulous records of his regular 'gifts' to Widow Ramel who lived ten minutes walk from his home farm. In September 1758 he took her half a mature cheese weighing eleven pounds and worth six farthings a pound. In October he took her another five pounds of cheese and his wife delivered four penny-worth of lard, presumably after the fat pig had come down from the high alp and been slaughtered for the winter. In November Madame Henchoz delivered a whole cheese weighing 15 pounds and worth 27 pence. It then emerged that the 'charity' shown by the Henchoz ménage to Widow Ramel was being carefully monitored by the borough treasurer. The widow was entitled to 56½ pence per quarter year as a subsistence allowance from the community. Henchoz was expected to pay this but did so reluctantly and mainly in farm produce on which he put his own valuation. By Christmas 1758 Henchoz's payments were in arrears and he owed her one more cheese and eleven pence in coin. In the spring the widow had to send her granddaughter to plead for her cheeses during the hungry season. Eventually a licensed notary, acting as a trustee of the poor chest, obtained a cash settlement for Widow Ramel. As far as Samuel Henchoz was concerned giving to the deserving poor had become an institutionalised and disagreeable obligation.

Less parsimonious members of the highland community made a virtue of their welfare obligations. Josué Marmillod of Rossinière was the legal custodian of his aunt's financial affairs and went to great lengths to ensure her comfort. In July 1724, when she was in poor health, he arranged for her to be carried to the sulphur baths at Etivaz and spent twelve florins on lodging and bathing for a fortnight. He also bought her suitable blouses, stockings, bonnets, gloves and shoes, as well as a coarse shirt to be worn while taking the public waters. As luxuries he bought her some sugar and authorised expenditure on some lace, the kind of inessential vanity that would not have found a place in Samuel Henchoz' account book. During the autumn the Marmillod accounts covered the cost of the wine harvest and its atten- dant bacchanalia, of New Year presents including a load of firewood, of a straw mattress and two secondhand bed sheets bought at auction, and of quantities of dried peas and barley flour, Marmillod even recorded an expense of ten farthings incurred when his aunt's kitchen apron needed to be newly dyed. Taking care of an aunt's estate was a legal obligation rather than a philanthropic one, but concern for the wellbeing and dignity of an elderly relative could nonetheless be carried out with charitable good grace.

The Christian philanthropists of Château-d'Oex were not exclusively concerned with the essential alleviation of suffering. By the end of the Bern era they also put their money into public works and even into the open celebration of municipal pride. The most joyous and pervasive feature of the Château-d'Oex church was its carillon of bells. Whatever the early Protestant attitude to the silencing of bells may have been, the seventeenth-century bells were an important symbol of the congre- gation's loyal attachment to the church. Even in the remote hamlet of Etivaz the local farmers felt that when they built their tiny chapel it ought to be endowed with a suitable bell to call the faithful to Sunday worship, or to toll for the passing of a funeral. The church bell also announced the evening 'curfew' when fires were to be damped down and the embers covered over with a safety-plate of iron. David Henchoz, an Etivaz landowner, persuaded Château-d'Oex to contribute 900 florins towards the cost of the Etivaz church bell while he was serving as borough chatelain. His bell was cast of bronze in Bern on 26 September 1682 by Abraham Gerber. It was richly decorated with the coats-of-arms of Lord-Bailiff Béatus Fischer, Chief Magistrate Jean Isot, Pastor Samuel Favre, Deacon Jean Isoz and Chatelain Henchoz himself. The Henchoz coat-of-arms showed the family ink-well complete with a strikingly feathery quill pen cast in heavy bronze. On one side of the bell the lumbering bear of Bern climbed up the coat-of-arms.

While the chapel of Etivaz installed a single magnificent bell, the mother church of St Donat boasted a carillon of four great bells at Château-d'Oex. Unfortunately very little is known about their history since on the night of 28 July 1800 fire swept through the graveyard, set light to the church, and ignited the roof of the dungeon whose ten-foot-thick walls held the bells. When the embers had cooled 14 days later the bells were nothing but a twisted mass of half-melted bronze. 'Dean' Bridel, the energetic pastor, immediately set about replacing them with characteristic imagination. Finding the cost of new bells to be prohibitive he went to the military arsenal at Morges castle where the French artillery was casting some new bronze cannons. As raw material the coppersmiths had collected plundered or damaged church bells which they planned to melt down for military purposes. The arsenal agreed to sell Bridel two sound bells and to discount from the price the value of the molten remains lying in the Château-d'Oex dungeon. The bronze scrap proved insufficient, however, to pay for the large 29 hundredweight bell which the enthusiastic pastor had chosen and he had to settle for the smaller bell alone. He took his bell by lake barge to Vevey, then by cart up the steep vineyard tracks, and finally hauled it through the highland valley to reach Château-d'Oex before the November snows set in. The government agreed to meet the cost of fitting the bell to an oaken yoke and raising it in the refurbished belfry. The bell had been cast in 1538, 17 years before the Château-d'Oex Reformation. It was ironically christened 'the Catholic bell'.

4
The Milk of the Land

Over the course of nearly three centuries of Bern sovereignty the dairy industry came to dominate the economy of Château-d'Oex. Milk production came to eclipse other economic activity and most milk was turned into cheese. Fields that were formerly cultivated were turned into meadows growing hay to feed milch-cows. Farmhouse cheeses of several varieties became the staff of life for all members of the community and export cheeses became the highland's source of income. One of the earliest records of cheesemaking in Château-d'Oex is dated 1328. A cheese of that year was sent down to the plain as a feudal tribute to the sovereign prince in his castle at Gruyère village. At that time the making of cheese was a community occupation. Local folklore vividly preserved picturesque accounts of the old cheesemaking customs. The prime example was the song of the cowman, the *Ranz des Vaches*, which was later translated and written down in eighteenth-century French. The title referred to 'the procession of the cows' which wound its way up the steep hairpin paths to the highest Alpine pastures. The song went on to illustrate in dramatic detail the nature of summer dairying on the high commons. Historically the song was sung in the local Romanic vernacular of Gruyère and was spread across Europe by mercenaries in French army service. It was claimed, though without documented substantiation, that the song caused homesick soldiers such nostalgic memories of their highland homes that army officers tried to ban the singing lest it cause desertion or suicide. The tune was a catchy one and variations on it were played in polite salons at the court of Queen Anne in England. In Château-d'Oex the song was appreciated because it recalled the olden times before sixteenth-century land enclosure brought cattle pasture into private ownership, gradually driving the poorest peasants into foreign service and distant exile.

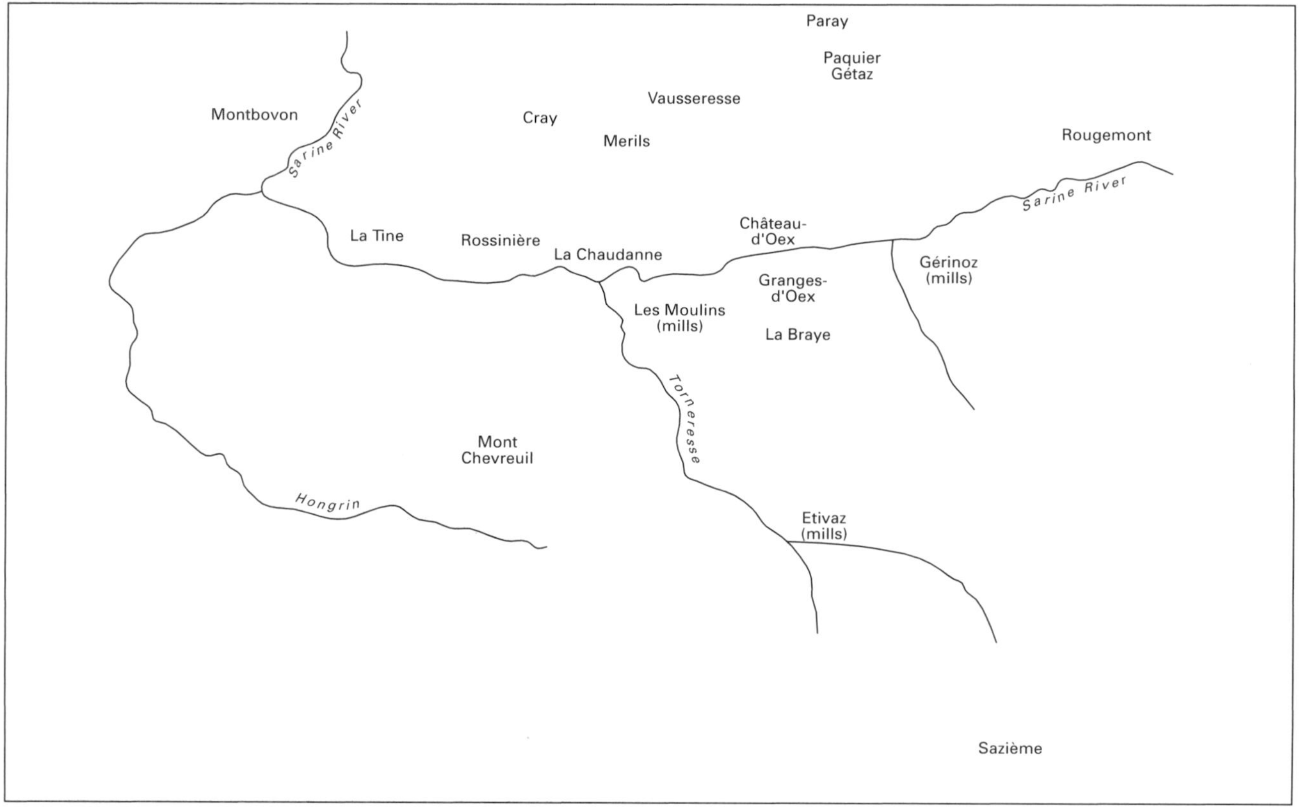

Montbovon

Sarine River

La Tine

Rossinière

Cray

Vausseresse

Merils

Paray

Paquier
Gétaz

Château-
d'Oex

Rougemont

Sarine River

Gérinoz
(mills)

La Chaudanne

Les Moulins
(mills)

Granges-
d'Oex

La Braye

Torneresse

Etivaz
(mills)

Mont
Chevreuil

Hongrin

Sazième

Sketch map 4.1 Streams and alps around Château-d'Oex

The old cowmen on the highland commons lived in very simple huts and did their milking out-of-doors. As the snow-line retreated and the grass sprouted they moved up the mountainside driving their cows and carrying their wooden milking pails and copper cheese cauldrons. The chorus of the cowman's song celebrated their way of life:

Cows, cows, come to be milked,	Liauba! Liauba! Por aria,
Come one, come all,	Vinidé toté,
White and black,	Billantz' et nairé,
Red and mottled,	Rodz' ct motailé,
Young and old,	Dzjouven' et otro,
Under the oak	Dézo on tschâno
I shall milk you,	Io vo z' ario,
Beside the alder	Dézo on treinbllo
I shall cut the cheese curds,	Io ï treintzo,
Cows, cows, come to be milked.	Liauba! Liauba! Por aria.

Open-air life wandering across the high commons was not always easy. The melting snows and the spring rains frequently caused the streams to rise dangerously and made access to the best pastures hazardous. It was just such a hazard that became the dramatic focus in the song of the cowman. Peter was a cheesemaster from Colombette, a Catholic village in the lower Gruyère valley, who had followed the communal herd into the highland. When he encountered a stream in full spate, which the cows could not cross, Peter sent his cowman down to the village to ask the priest to offer a rain prayer that would improve the weather and open the way up the hillside. The priest was quite willing to pray for better weather, but asked Peter to reward him with a good quality cheese. The priest emphasised that he did not want a lean curd-cheese but a rich one for ripening. Peter agreed to pay the cheese and invited the priest to send his housemaid to choose one. The priest, however, was unwilling to send a maid to collect a cheese from bachelor cowmen on a distant Alp. Peter was indignant and told the priest that his men would never steal kisses that belonged to the church. Eventually the deal was struck, an *Ave Maria* was sung, the rain stopped and Peter was able to take his cows across the torrent where he found lush highland grazing. So rich was the grass that Peter had filled his cauldron to the brim, and made his first highland cheese of the new season, before his cowmen had milked even half of the herd.

Medieval cheesemaking in the open air had many attendant risks. It was difficult to keep the equipment clean and the cheese free of undesirable bacteria that could cause it to swell up with bloat and deteriorate instead of maturing. Cheeses made in temporary shelters were smaller and less valuable than the ones that could be made in a well-constructed dairy. Good cheeses needed to be preserved at an even temperature, ideally in a stone-built cheese cellar. To improve the quality of cheeses, and to make them fit for export, permanent milking parlours began to be built on the high Alpine meadows. The first stone-built highland dairies, with shingle roofs and giant chimneys, were probably designed by the priory monks of Rougemont on the pastures which they owned high above their monastery. Over time permanent buildings were constructed at each level of altitude on the pastures. Whole chains of grazing plots, linked by steep footpaths, were established. Wherever cattle stopped to graze the Alpine slopes for a few weeks of the short summer season a dairy was built. Many of the working dairies in use in Château-d'Oex in the twentieth century were built in the eighteenth century, and some date back to the sixteenth century and to the earliest days of the highland enclosure policy.

It may not be pure coincidence that the first community of the highland to enclose its pastures was Rougemont, the community in which monks apparently pioneered the building of stone farmhouses. Once improved dairying facilities had been built successful farmers aspired to turn the commons into private farms. The move was an extension of the one which had enabled serfs to become landowners and so ensure that their property was protected and passed to their descendants. The borough of Rougemont made the decision to sell common land to private owners in 1527. This was nearly 30 years before the principality of Gruyère was dismembered and the medieval order was terminated by the flight of the prince into exile in the Netherlands. By the time the mercantile burghers of Bern assumed sovereignty over Rougemont, in 1555, much of the land was already privately owned. When in the same year the monastery was dissolved, as a result of Bern's imposition of the Reformation, further land became available to families of the local property-owning class. The Rougemont precedent, however, was not immediately followed by Château-d'Oex. There the decision to sell the commons was not taken until 1585, 30 years after the Bern purchase of the Gruyère highland. The policy on commons enclosure, and on the sale of land, was different again in the third borough of the highland, Rossinière. The citizens of this small village decided not to sell their joint heritage but to continue to exploit at least one third of their territory in common. The surviving commons of Rossinière included not only summer grazing but also tracts of forest. Over the following four centuries these commons provided an endowment for the whole village. The citizens of Rossinière, who had previously won the right to have their own ecclesiastical parish, their own civic borough, and their own legal code, also exercised their independence in the matter of sixteenth-century land enclosure. In the twentieth century envious neighbours sometimes referred disparagingly to Rossinière as the 'communist borough'.

The 'enclosure' of land as private property rather than as communal grazing was primarily a legal change. Not all of the newly privatised fields and meadows were fenced or hedged. They were, however, rigorously measured and marked with square-cut boundary stones. The ruling senate of Bern was concerned to establish field boundaries not merely to avoid conflict between neighbours but also to identify which lands were subject to which types of taxation. The state clearly approved of the privatisation of land ownership and even granted some tax incentives to the new owners of the enclosed commons. When Bern decided in the 1660s to up-date the Château-d'Oex land and tax register, the matter was one of great controversy and officers supervised by the lord-bailiff walked the boundary of every patch of grass, marsh, wood and garden. As they did so they recorded their observations in copper-plate writing entered in huge leather-bound ledgers. The location of every boundary stone, the current state of every stream bed, and the condition of each distinctive tree was noted. This survey was later up-dated in 1799, soon after Bonaparte had conquered Switzerland, and again in the nineteenth century when detailed coloured maps were drawn. The French invaders had demanded that every penny of taxable land should be identified though Château-d'Oex protested strenuously that much of the flat, and to an untutored eye apparently valuable, land in the borough was actually marsh that was virtually valueless, and only produced swamp reeds which were dried to make litter for cow byres and manure for hay fields.

Much more valuable to the landowners of Château-d'Oex than the flat marshes were the dark coniferous woods, known by their old Celtic name of 'jeur'. Tenant farmers were expected to cut and clear the undergrowth from even the smallest stand of trees in order to facilitate the growth of timber on any soils too poor or too steep for cattle pasture. The ownership of a coppice, once the commons had been divided up, was an important source of wealth for the new landowners. One of the heaviest tasks of the farm workers during the late summer was felling, barking, hauling, splitting and stacking firewood for the next season. The woodpiles had an elegant Swiss precision about their construction and were carefully protected against winter snow and ventilated to prevent wood rot. On dairy farms wood was especially needed to fuel the fire beneath each cheese cauldron. Most farms maintained a firewood plantation, carefully protected from wood poaching by neighbours, and located away from the likely course of any avalanche that could sweep fully grown trees into inaccessible gorges. Only very high dairies were located beyond the tree line but farms above 2000 metres in altitude had to carry their wood up the mountain for the cauldron fire. Around the village, farmhouses needed wood to make lattice palings to keep stray animals out of vegetable gardens and cultivated fields.

No detailed account of the communal joint use of land by dairy cattle is available from Château-d'Oex before the borough adopted a policy of land enclosure and privatisation. When the decision to sell its highland pastures and forests was made in 1585, however, one particularly steepsided valley that tumbled down the mountain above the village was excluded from the enclosure law. This valley, called the Vauseresse, was too rugged to be coveted by cheese farmers, so the burghers decided not to partition it into individually-owned plots but to retain a communal pattern of exploitation. The borough also decided, parsimoniously and sanctimoniously, that a part-share of the inaccessible and impoverished slope should be set aside as an endowment for the village rectory whose incumbent was entitled to a supply of winter fuel and summer grazing from his parishioners. The church's ministers were not overwhelmed with gratitude to be offered pasture and firewood in a dangerous gulley prone to avalanches. They also complained that the sheep which they sent up the Vauseresse mountain in summer were liable to be killed by wild bears. Successive pastors insisted that their firewood entitlement was supposed to consist of good quality beech logs from the valley and not of stunted fir trees that struggled to survive erosion on the borough's most sterile piece of land. Despite their complaints, the parish pastors remained institutional holders of rights on the last surviving common.

In the year 1776 the record of the men, women and public institutions which held grazing entitlements on the steep Vauseresse common was set out by Samuel Henchoz, the Château-d'Oex captain of militia, by Maître Gronicod, the public notary, and by Colonel Gabriel de Watteville, pompously described in the deed as 'the Noble, Magnificent, Generous and Very Honoured Lord-Bailiff'. Like all important political pronouncements the record was read from the pulpit after a Sunday service. The meticulous care taken in measuring the

372 units of sheep grazing was emphasized by the fact that some titles included fractions of a unit by which a sheep was allowed on the mountain for a half, or even a third, of the season. All claimants to common grazing had to produce authenticated legal titles. The lord-bailiff, who claimed the revenue from 36 units of common grazing, produced documents dated 12 May 1710 and 3 August 1712 to prove his title. The pastor's title to 24 units dated back to the original Château-d'Oex enclosure legislation of 1585. More recent titles were held by borough officers, thus reinforcing the belief of farmers that the law, rather than agriculture, was the profession which really earned money in the highland. Among ordinary folk old family rights were based on deeds and wills carefully treasured among inherited parchments. The complexity of the record, and the need for farmers to have literate advisers to protect their rights, was illustrated by the case of the ten grazing units held by

Jean, son of Daniel Morier of Le Mont, in his own name and that of the heirs of the late Honourable Moïse Byrde, according to an old title of land shared between the children of the late Pierre Byrde, dated 8 April 1624 and signed by Notary Jean Perronet who was better known as 'Besson'.

Since the Vauseresse could not be divided or fenced, and since trouble had arisen when individuals had made unauthorised hay or illicitly extracted firewood, it was decided in the eighteenth century to auction the whole common annually to a shepherd who would take responsibility for recruiting a flock of sheep to graze it. To avoid over-grazing the shepherd was forbidden to recruit more than 372 sheep, but he was permitted to keep a few milch-goats up the mountain to provide milk for his personal sustenance. The shepherd lived alone on the mountain over the summer, communicating with the village only in a true emergency by calling 'wolf' on his horn. In choosing sheep for his flock the shepherd was required to give preference to sheep from the village. When local sheep-owners had been accommodated he was permitted to seek sheep from outside the borough to make up the complement. To provide the shepherd with a shelter, the *chaumière* in which he would live throughout the season, an old cabin perched on a rock ledge was refurbished by an itinerant Italian stone mason at the joint expense of the commons-holders. The holders were reluctant, however, to incur further expense by improving the safety of access and widening the path that had been hewn along the cliff face to reach the entrance to the common. The joint fund available for maintenance purposes was managed by an elected commissioner who spent hours accounting for tiny sums of expense and revenue. In poor years the yield of the Vauseresse could be as little as three farthings for each unit of sheep-grazing. No citizen who was both literate and numerate was willing to accept election to the thankless task of commissioner. The lord-bailiff, who was *ex-officio* the chief beneficiary, threatened to punish all commons titleholders for insubordination before he could secure the nomination of an accountant. Anyone failing to attend the annual meeting of the Vauseresse association when summoned by the town crier was fined eight farthings, equivalent to a season's earnings on two sheep. The management of the sheep commons may have been democratic, but it was not lucrative compared to the profits made on private land by cheesemakers.

The greatest problem that arose in stocking the sheep commons concerned access to the mountain across the village's rich cow pastures. Litigation over access became particularly fraught in the case of Widow Chabloz, née Esther Chappalay. The widow, who incidentally held a small stake of three and a half sheep-units on the common, owned the farm of Grelateyre immediately below the mountain and exploitation of the common caused her endless problems. Lumberjacks who went up the mountain left logs lying on her fields and failed to clear the bark chippings that they had strewn on her meadow. Commoners illicitly made hay on the mountain and did great damage to her property when hauling it down to their barns. The most strident of her protests, however, concerned the damage done to her crops by the sheep and goats which passed through her farm in summer. In desperation she barricaded the shepherd's path in 1781 and the lawyers who held grazing rights took her to court. They proved that once the autumn feast of St Denis had passed, and cows no longer grazed out-of-doors, they were entitled to cross privatised land on traditional trails using both handcarts and horse sleighs. They also demonstrated that woodmen were permitted to haul timber across land that was covered with snow, though they conceded that bark chippings had to be cleared before they soured the soil. But above all the lawyers defeated Widow Chabloz by establishing that shepherds had the customary right to take their flocks to and from the commons provided they kept their animals 'as closely as possible' to the path. The old right-of-way ran up the east bank of the Vauseresse stream, through what had been common cow pasture before 1585, as one witness whose memory went back almost one hundred years attested. Bern had authorised the enclosure of the cow pasture on the express condition that the right-of-way for both sheep and goats should remain open on a daily basis. The widow finally lost her law suit in 1796 and was forced to pay 187 florins in legal costs. The sum spent on litigation dwarfed the revenue from Château-d'Oex's last common. The shepherd who won the bidding to stock the Vauseresse with sheep in 1796 was Rudolph Rittner. He won the whole season's grazing with an auction bid of only 80 florins.

Sheep and goat rearing had, by the eighteenth century, become marginal when compared to cattle raising. Goat herds shrank though the sixteenth-century enclosure laws preserved an important goat trail which climbed from the riverside sawmills of Gérignoz to the north-facing mountains south of the river. This trail, carefully marked with boundary stones, led through woods and pastures to rough scrubland that was unpalatable to cattle. Beyond this scrub the land was so inaccessible that it remained the domain of wild chamois. In 1779, when land pressure was at its peak, Lord-Bailiff Bonstetten watched the chamois grazing on the highest cliffs, and dreamed of finding herd-boys so daring that they could take goats up there and turn even the wildest corner of his Alpine bailliwick to economic profit. Goats, however, were more difficult to manage than sheep and had to be brought down to a hamlet each night to be milked. Their daily trespassing, and their insatiable appetites, caused great damage as can been seen from the nineteenth-century records when goat herds revived in the highland.

Nineteenth-century Rossinière maintained goats in the traditional manner. Each goat lived with its owner in the village where it was milked morning and evening. During the day all goats were taken by a communal herdsman, elected by the village, to browse coarse vegetation on the highest mountain ledges. The terrain, however, was dangerous and the goat-herder was personally responsible for the safety of his flock. In one nineteenth-century village drama a goat was carried over a cliff by a rolling boulder. The herdsman saw his annual earnings vanish in a single accident. The tragedy potentially threatened not only his own livelihood but that of his family as well: at the time paupers were being heartlessly shipped to the Americas by the borough. The shepherd was saved by a voluntary subscription organised among the citizens of Rossinière and supported by the first tentative holiday-makers arriving in the Alps.

The village of Rossinière, although it retained a traditional goat herd and continued to use communal cow pastures, was nevertheless able to benefit from the rise of the dairy industry. One set of records which happened to survive in the attic of a farmhouse illustrates how cheese farming was practised in the late eighteenth century. It was a highly organised operation which retained many of the features of the communal medieval industry. On 25 May 1776 the 21 cows that were to be sent for the summer to one of the high commons were listed in writing. The cows belonged to 21 different owners and each animal was described in detail, identified by the colour of its tail, muzzle, head or moustache. The youngest was three years old and the oldest one was nine. There was no standardisation of breed and the cows were red, grey, black and brown. Rossinière assembled several jointly-owned herds of dairy cows each season. Each herd consisted not only of milking cows but also of calves, yearlings, heifers, bullocks and of course the bull, who would guarantee a new generation of calves and a new season of milking. Some pasture was rented from private Rossinière owners but the community herds primarily grazed on common land. Each herd was regularly visited by a cattle inspector elected by the village. Between the ascent of the cattle on 25 May and their descent on 5 October the inspector chosen in 1776 climbed the mountain eleven times to ensure that animals were properly cared for by the cheesemaker and the cowmen and herd-boys.

The on-going custom of the dairy industry required owners of single cows to unite and form a herd big enough to produce sufficient milk to make one cheese each day. In order to succeed they needed to choose a reliable cheesemaker to take the assembled herd up the mountain for the season. The job of cheesemaker required experience and a sense of responsibility. Election to the post led to a critical appraisal of the professional and personal qualities of each candidate. Some dairyworkers were rejected because too many of their cheeses had turned rotten in the previous season. Some cowmen were alleged to be too fond of milk maids to concentrate on their task when posted alone to the mountain for three months. The survival of the whole community depended on choosing a reliable cheesemaker for each herd.

When the cheesemaker and his cowmen had been chosen they had to inspect their Alpine dairy, repair the wooden hurdles, check the briar hedges and make sure that cattle could not stray over precipices or wander onto neighbouring pasture. The pasture itself had to be preserved from the encroachment of the wilderness by the uprooting of harmful weeds and saplings. When the cattle arrived the cowmen were not only responsible for milking them but also had to tend the pigs which were fattened on the whey which was left in the dairy cauldrons when the last ounce of cheese curd had been extracted for human consumption. They had to protect the calves from attacks by wolves. They had to avoid the violent tantrums of the bull which roamed among the cows and heifers seeking out those that were in season. At the end of the summer cowmen had to manure the alp by breaking up and scattering dry cow pats to fertilise the new spring grass when the next season's snow melted. Manure which had been stacked up all summer beside the cowshed was also taken out to the fields in heavy wooden wheelbarrows. But above all the cowmen of the high alps spent seven or eight hours each day milking cows. A lax cowman who failed to maximise his profit by extracting the last drop of milk from each cow was liable to find his herd drying up before the end of the summer. Milking for the cheese industry required total dedication to a hard life.

The seasonal migration of cattle from the village to the alp and back was strongly marked by ancient tradition throughout the Gruyère valley. For the ascent the cows wore their largest bells and their most ornate collars. On arrival at the dairy these huge bells were removed and slung on poles across the front of the farmhouse and the cows were fitted with working bells. These bells were worn day and night throughout the season so that a cowman could keep an ear open for any change in the clanging rhythm of all-night grazing which might signal danger. The bull did not wear a bell. This too was a long-standing tradition as witnessed in many old pictures of cattle processions. Some of these rustic pictures, called 'poyas', were painted above barn doors. Others were finely cut from paper with scissors and showed silhouettes of pastoral scenes. For the autumn descent to the valley the cows were richly decked out with small spruce trees and wild flowers attached to their horns. The queen of the herd carried the single-legged milking stool, symbol of the whole Alpine dairy industry, fixed to her horns with garlands. The herd was escorted through the village by children proudly wearing their best velvet costumes, straw caps and linen pinafores. Onlookers showered them with sweets and toffees.

As the management of the dairy industry became more organised, and production grew in scale, the pattern of transhumance up and down the mountain took on a new routine. Instead of migrating slowly up the mountainside as far as the barren rockscapes during the summer and then migrating down again during the autumn, the cattle processions adopted complex patterns of grazing on well-defined steps in a chain of Alpine pastures. The complexity of this cattle movement was illustrated by the working schedule of Emile Raynaud, a twentieth-generation Château-d'Oex cheese farmer. Raynaud managed a herd of

75 cows and rented two large Alpine farms which had been given to the borough of Château-d'Oex in 1814. The milking season began in May when the procession of cattle was led from the home farm, lying at about 1000 metres above sea level, to the first of the rented seasonal dairies, the Paquier Gétaz, situated at 1600 metres. There the cows grazed 'the first flower' of the Alpine meadow, a diet which included many wild blue geraniums. A few weeks later, on 15 June, the whole herd, accompanied by the cauldron and all the paraphernalia of the dairy industry, moved up to the second dairy, Paray Charbon, on one of the highest of the Château-d'Oex alps at 2200 metres. The first visit to this high dairy lasted about two weeks during which time the first grass was fully grazed to encourage new growth. On 1 July the herd, the staff and the equipment, returned to the halfway dairy where the cows spent the next two weeks eating the second flowering on the Paquier Gétaz. On 15 July the whole caravan returned to the high alp for the main summer season which lasted six weeks. On 1 September the cows, now almost dry of milk, trundled back down to the middle dairy to enjoy the third and last grazing. They were kept there until October, producing little cheese but feeding out-of-doors until early snow storms forced them back down to the village and eventually into their winter stalls where they had to be fed on hay until the following May.

The making of hay was the most important ancillary activity of the dairy industry. The standard measurement of a valley field was determined by the amount that a skilled worker could mow in a morning. Land measurements used on the mountain, by contrast, were determined by the extent of pasture required to feed a standard milking cow for a 90-day summer season. The practice of haymaking fluctuated over the centuries as farmers experimented with different patterns of cropping. On balance the best advantage was gained by cutting hay twice over the course of the summer, though in the twentieth century hay was commonly cut three times a year. The work was very labour intensive but cutting the grass encouraged further growth. Haymaking success depended on having the right weather at the right time and enough people to bring the hay under cover as soon as it was dry and before it was spoiled by rain. While most men followed the herds into the mountains, women remained in the valley and harvested the hay. Scything was normally done by a man but turning, raking and hauling was often done by women and children. The finished hay was stored in small barns scattered throughout the valley. Once winter came it was transported to the cattle byres on sledges.

Winter was a bleak time in Château-d'Oex with little to rejoice about and sometimes little to eat. Men tried to supplement their farm income by working as foresters. In order to do a full week's work in the furthest sections of woodland a lumberjack had to leave home on Sunday afternoon carrying enough food to keep himself in his remote logging cabin until the following Saturday. Meanwhile women tried to earn a living in winter by knitting woollen stockings, straining their eyes by the light of a lone candle. Neither foresters nor knitters gained much from their hours of labour. Old folk went out foraging for winter fuel, sometimes losing their lives trying to haul firewood along short-cuts over the thin ice which covered streams and ponds. After a particularly bad harvest in 1780 famine threatened Château-d'Oex and the winter hunger was so severe that the normally parsimonious republic of Bern spent 900 000 *livres* buying in French corn for its Romanic-speaking subjects of the highland and the plain.

For many farmers the worst day of the winter was the quarter day when debts had to be settled. Those who could not pay were liable to have their land sold and their chattels seized. Insecurity always threatened on the edge of the Alpine wilderness, even in one of Switzerland's most successful dairy-farming highlands. In 1751 Daniel Massard of Rossinière was unable to satisfy his creditors but succeeded in negotiating a reasonable price for the sale of his farm. The buyer, however, was a stranger from outside the valley and the members of the borough council refused to authorise the sale. Instead they insisted that Massard sell his land to his relatives who offered him a much lower price and one which did not enable him to pay his debts. In despair Massard appealed to the lord-bailiff for legal help, claiming that his own feebleness of mind had enabled his family to cheat him out of 400 florins. The Rossinière justice of the peace endorsed Massard's appeal and shrewdly pointed out to the lord-bailiff that a better sale price would entitle the castle to higher stamp duty. Massard was partially reprieved, but famine and debt regularly drove other families out of the highland to fend for themselves in the harsh, competitive labour market of the plain. In Château-d'Oex many frail folk did not survive the hungry season at the end of winter.

In the highland the prospect of spring was greeted with urgent anticipation as the supply of salted pig meat ran low and the neatly piled stacks of logs for the kitchen range became exhausted. Dried vegetables in the cellars often ran out before the first wild dandelion leaves brought fresh salad to the table. The anticipated green shoots of spring had traditionally been associated with the celebration of carnival but the Reformation had brought an end to such pre-Lenten debauchery. A modified spring rite persisted in March when the children from the hamlet schoolrooms trooped down to the village at the end of the school year to receive their class prizes from the pastor. Older children prepared themselves for their baptismal confirmation and for the great family ritual of the first Easter communion. After Easter the snowfields began to melt, cowmen made reconnaissance visits to the mountain dairies to repair the ravages of the winter and scrub out the drinking troughs. Spring also presented farmers with an old ecological problem in deciding which of their trees needed to be preserved as protection against erosion and which needed to be cut to let in sunlight and warmth. In the early season tall trees cast such long shadows across the pasture that morning frosts did not melt and the growth of new grass was delayed. By June the feast of St John the Baptist heralded summer and high season could get under way as garlanded cows and grunting pigs reached the summer alps.

In the dairy industry the feast of St Madeleine on 22 July was celebrated even more elaborately than the ascent and descent of the cattle processions. The great festival broke the lonely drudgery of the cheesemaking season. Even puritanical pastors and grudging bailiffs recognized that unless some excitement was permitted in the lives of farmers the young of Château-d'Oex would drift away to the plain and the cities. Summer dancing on the alp therefore survived the Reformation. The ball of St Madeleine coincided with the most important economic event of the year, the annual weighing of the milk. The tradition of milk weighing, as once practised on the open commons, was still required since the herds remained mixed ones, made up of cows belonging to many owners, and it was necessary to have a formula to determine what share of the season's cheese production should go to each owner. The milk of each cow – the red one with the white tail, the black one with the white head, the dappled one belonging to the widow, the hairy one from the castle, the foreign one with the crumpled horn brought up from Fribourg – was ceremonially and individually weighed on St Madeleine's day. Everyone came to the weighing and everyone checked the records. Each peasant's livelihood next winter depended almost entirely on how much milk his or her cow gave on St Madeleine's day. Any error in the cheesemaker's measurements would affect the equitable sharing out of the cheeses in the autumn.

When the milk-weighing was completed the feasting could begin. One alp on which the feast was particularly popular was Sazième. This remote farm, at the furthest end of the Etivaz valley, was the highest one on the territory of Château-d'Oex. The festival dated back to medieval times and on one occasion Prince Anthony of Gruyère was among the revellers. The romantically-inclined Dean Bridel imaginatively described the fifteenth-century tournament three centuries after the event. He claimed that the dancing had lasted for two days and two nights and that the cowmen and milkmaids of Château-d'Oex had been joined by those of Gruyère in the lower valley, by those of Ormont on the Rhône side of the mountain, and by those of Saanen in the Alemannic Oberland. The feasting had involved the roasting of ten whole chamois and the eating of untold quantities of fresh cheeses. Before the celebrations were over, however, a summer thunderstorm descended on the mountain. The prince's marquee was torn down in the gale. The dancers were lucky to escape drowning as they fled across the Torneresse, the now-raging torrent which normally turned the saw mills. Despite this cataclysm the alp of Sazième, famed for its high quality grass and its rich cheese, never lost its popularity as a place for festivals. The haunting sound of the long alphorn echoed round the mountains inviting all to join the feast. The village girls eagerly climbed the mountain at dawn. By the eighteenth century they carried coffee and sugar loaves to brew in the great cauldron, as soon as the day's cheese had been made, and served thick, sweet coffee with gallons of rich cream. Men who had remained in the valley to scythe hay also climbed the mountain carrying shoulder-vats of wine to enliven the dancing on the close-cropped turf. Music and frivolity made the ball a high-point of the Château-d'Oex milking season.

Normal daily life on a cheese farm began early. The cows had to be called in from the fields where they normally grazed all night, untroubled by heat and day-time flies. Each cow had to be milked before breakfast, a skilled cowman milking twenty cows in three-and-a-half hours. To make a full-size Gruyère cheese 150 litres of warm, frothy, morning milk were poured into the cauldron. An equal quantity of cooled, skimmed milk from the evening milking was then added. This milk had been kept in shallow wooden bowls which were stored over night in a well-ventilated stone-walled dairy and then skimmed with a wooden scoop to reduce the fat content of the final cheese to a level that would produce the distinctive Gruyère texture and flavour. The surplus cream was later churned with a paddle in a small barrel to make butter.

When full the copper cauldron, hanging by an enormous iron handle from a giant swivel post made of a solid tree trunk, was swung over the log fire. The open hearth was under a wide wooden chimney with a large hinged lid that could be closed to keep out rain and snow. The fire was carefully stoked with split logs of spruce or fir and the milk was slowly warmed. Exactly the right temperature had to be reached, but the dairyman could afford to use only a minimum of scarce fuel. The cheesemaker's thermometer was calibrated on the Réaumur scale, with freezing at zero and boiling point at 80 degrees. When the cauldron reached 25 degrees Réaumur exactly, it was swivelled away from the fire. A carefully measured and tested quantity of rennet, taken from the dried stomach of a calf and mixed with some of the previous day's whey, was then poured into the cauldron causing the warm milk to set as cheese curds. When the curdled milk had set the curds were sliced with a many-stranded wire cutter on a wooden frame. The cheesemaker went on slicing through the cauldron until the curd crumbs were as fine as barley seeds, quite unlike the large curd cubes used to make cheeses such as English Cheddar. When ready the cauldron was brought back over a low fire and stirred steadily for an hour or more with a wicker paddle. To break up the eddies in the swirling curds a moulded wooden plank was fixed to the inside wall of the cauldron. An iron screen was also placed in front of the fire to channel the flow of hot air evenly round the outside of the cauldron. When the temperature in the cauldron reached 44 Réaumur degrees the cheesemaker tested a handful of the bland, saltless, curds for their texture and flavour. When satisfied that it was time to separate the curds from the whey the door was shut to keep out cooling drafts and the dairyman prepared to scoop out the cheese. A sterile cheese cloth was wetted in hot whey and fixed to a flexible rod that could be bent to the shape of the inside of the cauldron. The maker and assistant then ran their arms under cold water so as not to be burned when they plunged them into the simmering cauldron. The heavy, 60-pound bundle of hot curds was swiftly scooped out and put into a round wooden mould on a heavy draining slab. The cheese was then placed under a pressure of 1200 pounds applied by an ingenious system of boulders, pulleys and levers assembled in the dairy roof.

After the new cheese had been pressed and drained of excess whey it was marked with the cheesemaker's personal symbol so that it could be distinguished at the annual cheese sale. When a cheese had dried for a day or two it was lifted on to a flat cheese yoke and head-loaded down to the valley. There it was placed in a salt bath in an underground, stone-lined, cheese cellar. A large cheese was kept in the brine bath at a salinity level of 22 per cent for three days. It was then taken out of the bath and stored flat on cellar shelves from which it was moved every day to be turned and rubbed with fresh salt. The cellarkeeper had to check the cheeses for any signs of cracking or swelling, thus indicating some defect in the process which could be traced back to a fault in the herd, or a problem in the dairy. At the end of the season, when the cheesemakers came down from the mountain, the cheeses were weighed and put into store for the winter to become fully mature and ready for sale the following summer. A few selected cheeses were coated in preserving oil and kept in dry airing barns for another three years. These hard cheeses had to be sliced with a carpenter's plane but the flavour of the elegantly curled shavings was greatly esteemed. Some vintage cheeses were put aside on the occasion of a child's christening and kept to celebrate his or her wedding 20 or more years later. In 1779 Lord-Bailiff Bonstetten claimed to have received a cheese that had been laid down in 1646; one might be permitted to wonder if after 133 years it had passed its prime.

The daily life of a cheese farmer was marked by long hours, repetitive work and monotonous food. After three or four hours of morning milking the dairyworkers treated themselves to some of the evening's thick cream for breakfast. The meal traditionally began with morning prayers followed by a rather more pagan ceremony. Each person tapped the edge of the great wooden cream-bowl at the centre of the kitchen table with a wooden spoon in order to to salute the '*diédze*', the spirit of the mountain. The cowmen then dipped their ornately carved oval cream spoons into the communal dish. The rest of the meal was cheese, occasionally eaten with bread when it was available. The cheese was washed down with tea made over the cheese fire, by boiling a pan of water and then throwing into it a handful of tea-leaf, some sawn up lumps of sugar-loaf and a stick of cinnamon. Later in the day, when the new cheese had been made, lunch began with bowls of hot whey scooped out of the cauldron. Food on the alp offered little variety and even when cultivated fruit and vegetables were available in the village they rarely reached the mountain dairies. The cowmen sometimes suffered from agonising constipation as a result of their ill-balanced diet and lack of wild berries. Apart from cheese the staple of the midday meal was a hard biscuit called *gatelet*. Traditionally these circular biscuits, one foot in diameter, were prepared from a mixture of milled barley and pounded broad beans. In the eighteenth century, however, the normally conservative farmers discovered that if they grew potatoes instead of barley they could avoid paying tithes on the crop. They therefore began to mix potato flour into their biscuit mixture and reduced the proportion of barley. The hard-tack biscuits were baked about four times a year in the parish oven and then tied in bundles and hung in chimneys to preserve them from vermin and mildew. Curing them in the smoke gave the biscuits a wood-like texture and they were eaten with new cheese after being soaked in hot whey to soften them.

The making of soft whey cheeses was the second stage of the cheese-making process. When the great Gruyère cheese had been scooped out of the cauldron and pressed into its mould, the fire was stoked again and the cauldron of whey was swung back over the hearth. Vigorous heating caused a thick froth to rise to the surface. This froth was poured into perforated moulds, each about six inches in height and six inches in diameter, to form the small whey cheeses that were the common fare of working folk. A skilled cheesemaker could expect to get one pound of whey cheese, called *séré*, from his cauldron residue for every two pounds of full-fat Gruyère cheese produced. Some of the whey cheeses were smoked to preserve them for a short while and some were salted, but most were eaten fresh. The local market value of whey cheese in the eighteenth century was a little over half that of mature cheese, about seven farthings a pound compared to eleven farthings.

One private landlord who kept meticulous records of the eighteenth-century functioning of the Château-d'Oex dairy industry was Samuel Henchoz. His great ledger of daily income and expenditure survives for the period from 1745 to shortly before his death in 1787. In his youth Samuel Henchoz had made an advantageous marriage to Marie Desquartiers and thus furthered his career as a landowner as well as being a soldier, a public servant, a moneylender, a farmer and an all-round entrepreneur. As a prudent accountant he kept a record of every rood of grass he rented out, every horseshoe he replaced, every cheese he sold and every pint of Swiss wine that his wife and her friends drank on blistering hot days in the hay fields. His smaller properties were scattered throughout the rural borough. Close by his wife's elegant apartment, in a fine timber chalet overlooking the church, he owned two moderately level meadows which he rented out for hay cropping. Below the church he owned a large farm which was called La Glacière in the title deed of 1551 because it lay in a frost pocket. This farm he leased to his cousin Moses for 160 crowns a year. This and other transactions between the two cousins involved complex barter deals. In 1782, for instance, Moses took in Samuel's horse for 16 days in June and charged him twenty pence for the fodder which it ate. He also charged him fifteen crowns for taking a cow up to a high alp for the season and six crowns for fattening a pig on whey. Moses paid part of his rent in cheeses, one good fifty-pound cheese being valued at 13 farthings per pound. At the end of the farming year, however, all the barter deals left a balance which had to be paid in cash and on 14 November Moses paid Samuel fifteen new gold sovereigns bearing the effigy of King Louis of France. The final settlement was made on 20 February 1783 when Moses paid a further 118 crowns, seven pence, and two farthings in coin.

The properties owned by Samuel Henchoz and his wife included not only hay fields in the bottom of the valley but also Alpine pastures in the mountains. One dairy farm was on the Braye, the cold side of the valley where previous farmers had suspected witches of interfering with the mysteries of cheesemaking. The tenant there was Samuel's nephew, Joshua, and the barter deals between the two men reflected the complexity of agricultural economics in Château-d'Oex. A Flemish sheep was valued at four crowns and a whey trough for fattening pigs at 25 crowns, though the cost of hauling it up the mountain was greater than the value of the trough. Joshua sold his uncle a cow worth 36 crowns at the end of the season and paid a first instalment on his rent with a hundredweight of fresh cheeses. Later payments were made in mature cheeses. Joshua also made butter in the rented dairy and sold it to his uncle in five-pound pats at 12 farthings a pound. As the tenant of an Alpine dairy Joshua was responsible for repairs to the buildings but could deduct the cost of materials and labour from his rent. He bought eight rounds of spliced spruce shingles to repair the dairy roof and charged his uncle four pence a day plus food for the labour involved in laying them. In addition to the dairy and its pasture the property included important forests and Joshua contracted to pay part of his rent by cutting and delivering firewood to Samuel at his home. Although Joshua felled the chosen trees and took them down to the riverbank he failed to deliver them to his uncle's door high up on the sunny side of the village.

The largest mountain farms in the borough of Château-d'Oex were in the valley of Etivaz, the frontier land on which a fierce battle had been fought in 1502 and on which the ball of St Madeleine was held. Samuel Henchoz owned two of these large farms. The lower one, free of marshes and screes, had 28 hectares of pasture, a firewood plantation appropriate to the needs of a cheese dairy, and a grazing capacity of 18 milking cows. Samuel's tenant was his brother-in-law, Moses Desquartiers, who paid his rent in both unsalted whey cheeses and heavy Gruyère cheeses. This farm also supplied Samuel with some of his meat, suet and leather. A side of beef was worth more, pound for pound, than soft cheese but less than prime cheese suitable for ripening. In 1782 this farm had a good year and yielded 13 gold sovereigns of rent, but the following year was less bountiful and it only yielded ten sovereigns. The remotest of Samuel Henchoz's estates was a huge Alpine pasture carved from the former commons at the far end of the Etivaz valley. The farmhouse was situated at 1500 metres and the pasture rose up to a range of rocks at 2000 metres. The estate was denuded of protective forest and the tenant had to build great stone walls to deflect avalanches. This farm had a short summer season and provided grazing for only 60 days a year.

Once the Château-d'Oex cattle lands had ceased to be commons there was scope for moneylenders and landlords such as Samuel Henchoz to rationalise their land holdings. The consolidation of estates was noted, and condemned, by a young contemporary of Samuel Henchoz who arrived in the highland in 1779. Charles-Victor von Bonstetten belonged to the highest nobility of Bern and had been educated in French by scholars of the Enlightenment. During his eight months in the highland as acting lord-bailiff at Rougemont castle he wrote the standard analysis of Swiss mountain society at the end of the *ancien régime*. His manuscript was subsequently lost by a publisher in Geneva, but an indifferent translation into German had been made in Basel and a retranslation into French survives. It is the work of an enthusiastic young man of 35 who on arrival in his domain climbed the nearest hill and was amazed at the way in which each new shoulder of the mountain opened up a new vista. He got to know his bailliwick intimately, and from the summits of his very own mountains he could admire the whole Swiss plain and beyond it he could see the Jura mountains stretching from the Catholic bishopric of Basel through the Prussian-owned principality of Neuchâtel to the Calvinist city–state of Geneva. Immediately beneath his feet he marvelled at the undulating meadows of Château-d'Oex filled with mixed flowers.

Bonstetten's shepherd kingdom, his 'Hirtenland' which became the classic Alpine model of latter-day social scientists, was viewed through rose-coloured spectacles. As he ascended from the fertile plain of Fribourg wheat and Vaud wine he imagined he could feel the falling away of the shackles by which manor-house lords oppressed the labouring poor. In his mountains men were free. They lived, he claimed, in great harmonious families of ancestors, aunts, brothers, children all residing under one roof and sharing one purse. He confessed, however, that his bachelor enthusiasm was not unconnected with the ravishing beauty of mountain peasant girls. He was, moreover, apparently unaware of the strains that communal life placed on families struggling to make a living in his springtime paradise. When looking across the frontier to his neighbours in the Ormont valley above the Rhône he did half-recognize the Alpine problems of poverty and over-population which were to attract Thomas Malthus to study the demography of that valley a few years later. Meanwhile, however, Bonstetten believed that in Château-d'Oex insulation from the corruptions of the outer world had bred its own rustic bliss. The more remote the hamlet, he said, the more enchanting its old customs, its betrothal ceremonies and its burial services. Bonstetten rejoiced in the first fall of snow when travel became easy, the laws of trespass were suspended, leisure time was available and country folk went to weddings. They travelled, he said, on long 'Lapland skates' and one may wonder whether by the eighteenth century the custom of nailing barrel staves to the soles of boots had already introduced rudimentary skis to Château-d'Oex. Bonstetten's lyrical accounts of the oceans of fog that lapped the feet of his mountains ring true, though his claim that hail storms were rare does not. Hailstones the size of pullet's eggs in fact did extensive damage in Château-d'Oex in 1991 and four years later a great landslip carried a ten-foot wall of mud to the edge of the village, reminding villagers of the power of the elements.

Bonstetten's concept of farming was sometimes as romantic as that of Queen Marie Antoinette. He believed that bringing hay down from the highest mountains on sledges was but a painless sport rather than an arduous and very dangerous means to economic survival. In summer he savoured the sweet smell of hay but had no concept of the muscle-aching hours of labour that went into making it. He claimed that his idealised cow herders had never had any concept of tilling the soil and was apparently unaware of the eight centuries of battle between man and nature that had gone into winning the land and holding back the wilderness. He joked about families who numbered the timbers of their farms so that they could rebuild them after an avalanche had demolished them. He had little concept of the labour involved when a barn had to be moved to a safer location away from the changing avalanche paths down the mountains. His aristocratic mind unjustly imagined that in their happy innocence the Château-d'Oex farmers knew nothing of drainage or irrigation. He never understood about the management of marshes, the protection of stream banks, the politics of water pipes, the maintenance of cattle troughs, all of them matters of vital daily importance to his subjects, including the now venerable Samuel Henchoz.

Gardening was something with which Bonstetten was a little more familiar. He noted that vines grew in the mildest section of the highland valley at Rossinière and that plums ripened as far up-stream as Rougemont. He complained that people put so much effort into their cheeses that they did not prune their apple and pear trees adequately, though in Saanen he obtained excellent cherry jam flavoured with cloves and cinnamon and cherry chutney spiced with wild mustard. The famous broad beans, which gave the people of Château-d'Oex their nickname of bean-eaters, were deemed the staple food. Bean leaves were fed to sheep and dried bean stalks were used for cattle litter. The young tax-collecting lord-bailiff noted that tithes had fallen by a half in the 40 years since potatoes had begun to replace corn in farm gardens. He acknowledged, however, that the potatoes which fed the large highland population had a good flavour and cooked to a fine flour-like consistency. Bonstetten did notice that Château-d'Oex peasants, his happy innocents, practised manuring and crop rotation. On newly broken and well fertilised soil they sowed barley or spelt, in preference to oats or rye, and thereafter grew a season of potatoes and one of flax or hemp, before returning the land for several seasons of grass and hay. The academic horticulturalist did not, however, notice that by growing beans the gardeners fixed nitrogen in the soil, nor was he aware that cereal crops were needed to supply straw as well as grain.

Bonstetten was opposed to the rising domination of the dairy industry since the growing of grass and hay had reduced other crops to a marginal role. He would have preferred a mixed farming economy to a monoculture and advocated the development of rural craft industries which generated export revenues and new taxes. He was impressed by the Château-d'Oex hemp gardens which yielded 16 sovereigns a year in tithes to the treasury. One eighth of a hogshead of raw fibre could produce 15 pounds of homespun thread. Some of the fibre was sundried to produce a red textile and some was dried in the shade to produce white material. Bonstetten aspired to expand the cloth industry and eradicate idleness and begging among the poor who had been marginalised by the all-conquering cheese industry. Bonstetten's enthusiasm for innovation showed his aristocratic ignorance of the fine economic judgments that peasants constantly had to make in deciding how to use their time, their family labour, and their land to ward off penury and keep themselves out of the Château-d'Oex workhouse. Although Bonstetten knew full well that stretches of England, the world's most advanced agricultural country, were still covered in heathland he nevertheless wanted his own mountain kingdom to be productive to the last inch of tamed wilderness, with inaccessible deserts turned into meadows and fearsome forests into gardens.

Political economy was Bonstetten's forte. Adam Smith's *The Wealth of Nations* had been published three years before he analysed the herding economy of Château-d'Oex. Bonstetten's cost-benefit analysis of the revolution in dairy farming concentrated on demographic change and maximising the use of underemployed labour. The big eighteenth-century landowners had been reducing their production costs by minimising their labour input and maximising the economies of scale in cheese production. In particular they had switched from grazing their meadows once and mowing them for hay twice to grazing them twice and cutting them only once. The policy favoured richer farmers who had more land than labour. It harmed poor farmers with large families but few fields. Rich farmers reduced the labour costs involved in mowing, drying and carting quantities of hay. The victims of the policy were landless workers or small farmers who rented out family labour. The victims became indebted, fell prey to moneylenders, lost their land and were forced to leave the highland. It was the labour of such marginalised people, the victims of land consolidation, that Bonstetten wished to recoup and employ in diversified local production. As a member of the Bern parliament he explained the advantages of reversing the trend towards bigger cheese farms. His case was that bigger farms adversely affected Bern's international balance of payments.

When capitalist farmers in Château-d'Oex economised on labour and only mowed hay once a year they did not produce enough winter fodder to keep their dairy herds in the highland all year round. In order to make their large cheeses they therefore hired transhumant summer cattle from plains dwellers in the republic of Fribourg. Although they saved on mowing wages, they had to pay rent for each cow of between 40 and 60 *livres*. Bonstetten was convinced that this economy of transhumance benefited the cattle owners of Fribourg, but robbed Château-d'Oex and the republic of Bern, of its highland wealth. The city–republic of Fribourg profited so much from the cattle migrations that in 1758 its senate passed legislation favouring haymaking in order to ensure that adequate winter fodder was available for the great herds which were sent up to Château-d'Oex each summer. Bonstetten pointed at the cost in foreign exchange of the cow rentals. The Château-d'Oex landowners, by contrast, told a different story. They said that growing competition among plainsmen to send their cattle to the highland increased the value of Château-d'Oex's grazing. Either way, however, labour became redundant and the poor were forced to emigrate, to Bonstetten's dismay. Worse still, he felt, the highland rich became gentlemen, puffed up with pride and a restless vanity that obscured their ancestral peasant virtues. In Rossinière, he said, ladies now wore fashionable hats while gentlemen felt it demeaning to tend their own cows.

The rich highland citizens whom Bonstetten lampooned were some of the greatest cheesemongers in the Alps. They dispatched cheeses to the markets of the Swiss plain and negotiated sales in fairs across most of Europe. A prime cheese, almost the size of a small cartwheel, weighed one hundred pounds and was worth two gold sovereigns. Such cheeses played a key political role in the highland and were customarily offered each New Year to the lord-bailiff in his castle. Cheeses were also given as tribute to the church. The best cheeses, however, were dispatched to such distant but wealthy customers as the sugar planters of the French West Indies and the tea merchants of British India.

5
Fairs and Markets

The Gruyère cheese produced in the highland dairies of Château-d'Oex became one of Europe's most famous cheeses. A small and apparently isolated village in the Alpine highlands became the hub of a network of mountain trade paths. The cheesemongers of the *ancien régime* sold their cheeses not only to their neighbours but also to overseas customers. Château-d'Oex's prosperity depended increasingly on its commercial relations with foreigners who bought cheese and supplied in return the commodities that were not available in the local highland and sometimes not even in the surrounding Alpine communities of Switzerland. Many of the essential tools and raw materials which Château-d'Oex required for its dairy industry came from outside the Gruyère valley and had to be bought from European suppliers who visited the fairs of the Swiss plain. Copper was needed for the cheese cauldrons and iron for the hay scythes. Even more costly was the need to ensure a regular supply of the salt required for the curing of cheese. Château-d'Oex thus sold its cheeses not only to satisfy consumer demand for imported necessities and luxuries but also to obtain the coin and the credit it needed to pay for its salt imports.

The focal point of business in Château-d'Oex was the Thursday market which provided an opportunity to buy and sell local produce and retail foreign wares. The market was the social hub of village life and of community relations throughout the valley where other village markets were held on other days of the week. Most farmers, men and women, walked down to the village on market-day, conducted their business on the square or under the arches, and had a drink in the Town Hall inn or the Bear public house. Rural schools were closed on market day so that children were free to carry baskets of produce fitted with heavy leather shoulder straps. A church service was held on market day for the benefit of parishioners on remote farms who could not make two journeys into the village each week. Once the service was over blacksmiths could resume their hammering, and bakers could sell their sweet pastries to out-of-village clients.

More important for serious trading than the Thursday market was the annual cycle of the Château-d'Oex fairs. In 1721 five fairs were scheduled for Château-d'Oex. The winter fair was to be held on 6 February, the spring one on 21 May, and the three autumn ones on 17 September, 20 October and 27 November. The autumn fairs were particularly brisk. The cowmen were down from the high alps with their annual wages in their pockets. The farmers had brought their fat-stock to market at the end of the season. The cheesemongers had sold last year's mature cheeses to make space in the dairy cellars for the fresh cheeses that were to be ripened over the winter. People had money to spend as they crowded round the hundreds of stalls built along the Château-d'Oex highway, curiously known as the 'royal' road. Château-d'Oex continued to call its fairs by the names of saints though the official record, the Bern state almanac, used calendar dates. In deference to the archaic traditions of farmers, however, the almanac listed the dates of the fairs in the old style of the Julian calendar regardless of the fact that this calendar had officially been superceded in 1700 by the new Gregorian calendar used in Catholic Switzerland.

The farmers and cheesemongers of Château-d'Oex were avid readers of almanacs. They used them not only to plan their trading journeys but also to plan their seasonal routine. A much more lively almanac than the official one issued by Bern was the almanac of Vevey, Château-d'Oex's nearest market town. This was called the *Messager Boiteux*, the voice of the peglegged courier. The courier was a war veteran on crutches who walked through the highland from village to village disseminating news and selling pamphlets. His almanac was full of miraculous weather predictions, advice from old wives, and traditional folklore. Although it was much appreciated by farmers, the church took offence at the superstitions which the popular almanac peddled along with necessary information about markets and fairs. When Dean Bridel was rector of Château-d'Oex in the 1790s he published a 'morally improving' almanac to wean any farmer who could read French off the old pagan superstitions and provide him or her with 'curious and useful' information. The fourth issue of the Château-d'Oex almanac, approved by the censorship office in Bern, portentously became the *Etrennes Helvetiennes et Patriotiques*, a nationalistic tract to counter subversive ideas from France with uplifting anecdotes from the 'glorious'

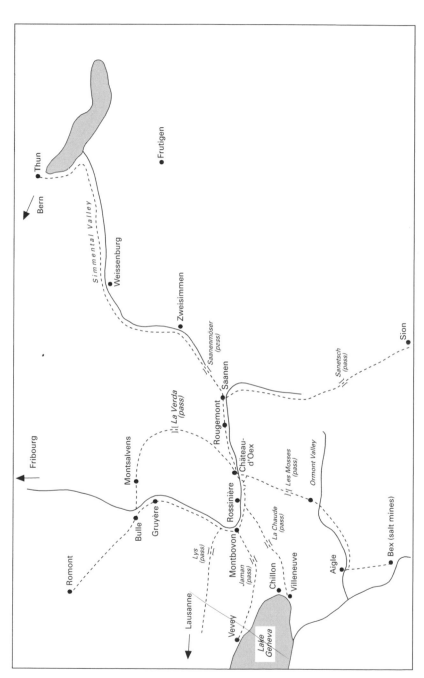

Sketch map 5.1   Trade paths out of Château-d'Oex

history of Switzerland itself. The farmers, however, continued to rely on the peglegged courier for gossip, news and advice. His almanac was their window on a world in which they sold their cheeses to customers in Burgundy and Lombardy, Savoy and Lorraine, Germany and France.

Château-d'Oex's own greatest fair was the autumn fair of St Gall. All household necessities were on sale. Life may have been spartan in the highland, but some homesteads accumulated a wide range of some-times ornate material property. One household inventory which gives an indication of the goods that would have been displayed to cus-tomers at the fair was drawn up on 28 October 1772 for Widow Martin, née Favre, of Rossinière. To begin with the Martin household listed the cauldrons of various sizes which it possessed. Smaller items made of copper included a bucket, a bedwarmer, a jug, a stove and two cheese-curd sieves. Less valuable than the copper artefacts were the imple-ments made of iron including three saucepans, a biscuit iron, a frying-pan, one large three-legged cooking pot and one small one, two pairs of pruning secateurs, two picks, three axes, two tree-felling cross-saws, three hand-saws, four scythes, two shingle-splicers, a small plane, a carpenter's wedge and sundry tools for repairing horse harnesses. Other assorted items, some of which might have been bought at the fair rather than locally manufactured with imported materials, included a brass oil lamp, six knives and forks, several cushions and pillows, six towels, two pairs of shoes, an old Bible, 20 ells of woven cloth, two walnut coffers, two muskets complete with bayonets and cartridge boxes, two sabres and a brand new laundry tub of spruce wood. The current assets which Widow Martin possessed, and which her heirs could have sold on the weekly market, constituted the work-ing capital of her farm. They included three cows, two goats, one pig, 20 pounds of clarified butter, 12 jars of walnut oil, 20 quarters of wheat, four quarters of beans, 16 small cheeses, ten pounds of spun flax, 15 pounds of raw flax, four cartloads of firewood, and a large pile of handsawn wooden planks. In addition to having a working family farm and a well-equipped household Widow Martin probably engaged in commerce on her own account. Two items suggested that she under-took retail trade and piecework. One was a consignment of ten kegs of wine from her brother-in-law's vineyard on the plain and the other was a stock of 43 new men's shirts.

One of the permanent problems of Château-d'Oex, and indeed of all the surrounding highlands of the western Alps, was that it had no local supply of iron, copper, or any other metal. All metal objects, from iron hoes to golden earrings, depended on imported or recycled raw material. Local craftsmen became extremely skilled at mending, adapting and re-forging metal artefacts with great economy. Essential furnishings such as metal door-locks, buckles for harnesses and shoes for horses, were all obtained either by visiting a market on the plain, usually at Vevey, or by patronising the travelling salesmen at the five annual fairs. However skilled and self-sufficient a dairy farmer might be in making bowls of wood, hats of straw, or homespun cheese cloths, he still needed copper for his cauldron. When refurbishing one of the farmhouses which he rented out Samuel Henchoz had to buy new iron bars for the fire grate and eight metal catches for the windows, spending in all three carefully hoarded florins. The local nailmaker was able, however, to repair for him an old lock and chain which he used to secure a valuable cow bell. Samuel Henchoz, as the custodian of the town hall, was particularly familiar with the functioning of the Château-d'Oex fair and rented out store rooms to travelling merchants. The tinkers who came regularly from the Austrian Tyrol paid him 25 pence for the hire of a store and tipped him each year with a small present from their stock, cobblers' tools, a hanging lamp of pewter, a striking-plate for his gunflint, a single spur which had lost its partner, a soup ladle and a pair of scissors.

Next to tools and utensils the most important section of the Château-d'Oex fair was devoted to textiles and clothing. People often arranged for their clothes to be cut locally but the cloth, buttons and other haberdashery had to be carried up to the highland and sold at the fair. Salomé Minod, the seamstress who had fallen foul of the church by selling a kiss, had done so in exchange for a supply of shirt buttons, presumably attractive foreign ones from the fair rather than local buttons carved from cow horn. The clothing used in the highland ranged from coarse to fairly luxurious. The working habit of a male farmer, at least until the mid-twentieth century, was a loose knee-length shift that covered and protected other clothes. Traditionally this smock was of homespun wool and had been sent to Saanen to be dyed blue. By the eighteenth century, as the profits from cheese escalated, women could afford more varied costumes than their old woollen ones. They began to adopt fancy pinafores, skirts, bloomers, petticoats, dresses and even nightgowns. The travelling drapers at the fairs tempted them with cotton materials from the cities and occasionally with Italian silk. Men's styles changed too as they adopted large-rimmed felt hats which could not be made locally as traditional straw and velvet skullcaps had been. Women also treated themselves to elaborate head wear, though their fine bonnets of black lace were made locally during the long dark winters. Both men and women prided themselves on their ceremonial costumes notwithstanding the disapproval of the Church of Bern. Ballgowns and velvet jackets were trimmed with embroidered Zürich ribbon. In contrast to ceremonial costume people of substance also owned mourning suits. Death from accident and disease was the constant companion of daily life, and the bereaved took great care to wear their dark clothes when going down to the village to attend the market. In sharp contrast to the sombre formal clothing of civilians, military men wore brilliant uniforms. Whole books of regulations about military costume were published and tested the ingenuity of the most skilled tailors who scoured the fair for the necessary materials.

Dairy farmers were great patrons of the Château-d'Oex fairs but it was not at these fairs that they sold the majority of their great cheeses or their more limited supply of butter. These they preferred to carry down to the plain. By taking their cheeses to market on the plain the cheesemongers could improve their profit margin by providing their own transport. They took great care of each cheese by selecting strong and experienced porters. Carrying a 60-pound cheese, wrapped in cloth and tied to a flat wooden head yoke supported on shoulder struts, required stamina and a stout pair of shoes. Women usually specialised in the butter trade and carried heavy baskets of butter over the mountain to Vevey on Monday, sold them on Tuesday and climbed back up the mountain on Wednesday. In spring they sometimes waded through snow drifts in long skirts and in autumn they battled against gale-force winds and driving rain. It was not only the elements, however, that made the long trip to market hazardous. The footpath over the Jaman pass crossed a section of potentially hostile foreign territory belonging to the Catholic republic of Fribourg. Customs officers and tollgate keepers were an endless source of chicanery to the cheesemongers and buttermaids who struggled through in all kinds of weather. Once they had reached the summit, the footpath down to the lake 1000 metres below, was steep and ill-repaired. A small rustic borough was supposed to maintain a plank bridge across a ravine which tumbled into the lake at Montreux, but the local citizens often failed to make the necessary repairs and forced the dairy porters to take a long detour. Avalanches which occasionally swept men and women into the abyss above Montreux were described with terrified awe by the Renaissance geographer Mercator, a Netherlander working at the Habsburg imperial court in Brussels.

Vevey was not only a cheese and butter market town but a lakeside harbour from which cheeses were exported further afield. The cheeses that arrived there were carefully inspected, graded and sealed into barrels. The coopers of Vevey, whose main business was making barrels for wine, had an important side line in making cheese barrels. Each barrel was built around ten cheeses, the smallest cheeses at the top and the bottom and the largest ones at the waist of the barrel. Barrels as a means of transport had the advantage that they could be rolled when they weighed several hundredweight and were much too heavy to carry. Barrels also helped to preserve the cheese, if necessary for years, by keeping out moisture. The cheese coopers' business rose and fell with the rise and fall of cheese exports from Château-d'Oex and from neighbouring farm provinces which used Vevey as their port. Cheese prices had risen spectacularly during the Thirty Years War when large armies had to be sustained but conscripted farmers across Europe were no longer producing food. When the war ended in 1648 cheese prices fell by as much as half and whole herds of Swiss cattle emigrated to Burgundy. Some farmers switched their meadows to horse raising, but in time the cheese industry recovered. In the late seventeenth century cheeses were successfully exported to Piedmont in exchange for Italian rice and sugar. This market dwindled when the Italian Alps developed their own cheese industry, but in the early eighteenth century prices were buoyant during the War of Spanish Succession. In the 1740s trade was again booming and 30 000 cheeses passed through Vevey each year of which about 3000 probably came down from the Château-d'Oex highland each season. One large order was placed by the French navy which wanted 400 barrels of Gruyère cheese to supply naval vessels out on long patrols in the Atlantic. France had always been an important customer but the country's exchequer had constantly worried about its loss of foreign exchange. It had even tried to ban payments for cheese being made in gold coin, and one Gruyère cheesemonger was caught at the frontier with 730 gold sovereigns secreted about his person. To improve trade relations with the French the Château-d'Oex cheese-mongers appointed a member of the Raynaud family to be their own agent in Marseille.

Vevey's importance to Château-d'Oex extended beyond its market and its harbour. The town was also the local metropolis and the focus of city entertainment for those who could get away from the austere highland. Vevey was also a place of coffee shops and supplied Château-d'Oex with coffee, a drink which Bonstetten decried as an unnecessary luxury for peasants. Bonstetten apparently failed to recognize that coffee did not lead to the alcoholism which so affected some isolated mountain farmers. It was in Vevey that the hapless Esther Pilet was accused of selling stolen haberdashery to supplement her income from part-time prostitution. The last count of Gruyère had a castle of his own, the Tour-de-Peilz, on the mild lake shore at Vevey. It is perhaps symbolic of Prince Michael's profligate life style that his castle later became a museum of games and gambling. At Clarens, near Vevey, the lord-bailiff of the highland had an official lowland estate which supplied his castle at Rougemont. It had a good vineyard and a vegetable garden which grew crops that were not available in the colder climate of the mountains. Vevey was also an important industrial centre for the highlanders. Its metal industries were important and when Château-d'Oex was burnt down in July 1800 the borough sent the scrap metal it was able to recuperate from twisted locks and melted hinges to the iron merchants of Vevey. It was also in Vevey that Dean Bridel initially tried to commission a new set of bronze bells for his burnt-out church, but the prices asked by the foundry were far beyond the means of even the richest of cheese farmers. Vevey was accustomed to a much wealthier wine-making clientele, one of which had built some of the finest churches in the Alps.

For many visitors the chief attraction of Vevey was its taverns. When Château-d'Oex sent borough officers to the city on official business they received a drinking allowance. The steep, south-facing terraces of vines produced Switzerland's best wine, quantities of which were drunk in the highland inns. Each year many vats of wine were carried over the mountain by returning cheese-porters to be drunk at the festivals of the agricultural year. Vevey white wine was the main alcoholic complement to the bitter local gin which was distilled from the root of the yellow gentian. Dean Bridel claimed that 20 middle-class Château-d'Oex families, including his own, kept private cellars in which Vevey wine was laid down to mature. During the October wine harvest, young men from Château-d'Oex came over the mountain for the season to work in the vineyards and carry the great shoulder vats of grapes down the steep terraces to the huge wine presses. The wine harvest supplemented the annual farm income after the cheesemaking season was over. The work was long and hard but unlike the lone bachelor days on the alp the company was congenially mixed. The highland porters could demand a kiss from any girl who missed a bunch of grapes on the row she was harvesting. The owners approved of the practice which made the girls more attentive to their work and encouraged the porters to supervise each girl's performance very closely.

Companionship and festive drinking also led to late night romance and Pierre Dubuis was jailed for ten days in Blonay castle for having put Margarite, a local girl, in the family way during the grape harvest of 1780. He was later required to make good her loss of earnings by paying her three crowns for her 'trouble' in suckling his illegitimate child.

The wine makers of Vevey organized themselves as a secular guild under the patronage of St Urban. The guild trained each new cohort of apprentice vintners to improve the quality of vine growing and wine making. About once in each generation, six times during the prosperous eighteenth century and four during the poorer nineteenth, they held a wine festival. A huge Bacchus of painted plaster was carried in a procession through the streets. The rôle of the attendant goddess Ceres was acted out by a butcher's boy in the 1747 festival, but by 1791 Vevey daringly used a woman as an actress in its pageant. The festival became such a success that the throngs could not crowd into the streets and raked stands were built for paying spectators. The farmers from Château-d'Oex came down in their hundreds, the halt and the lame struggling over the mountain to witness the great festival. By the twentieth century the Vevey celebrations of 1955 spanned a fortnight, with 11 three-hour processions, and in 1977 the Michelin Guide, with incautious hyperbole, described the Vevey feast of the vintners as the greatest festival in Europe.

Once Château-d'Oex's cheeses had been safely packed in barrels by the coopers of Vevey the valuable cargo was shipped in twin-sailed barges to Geneva, a larger and far more cosmopolitan city than Vevey. By the early fifteenth century Geneva was claiming that its independent fair was the most vibrant one in all Europe. The fair, which lasted for ten days and was held every three months, was located at the continental crossroads of the Alpine routes joining France and Italy and of the plains routes linking Germany to the Mediterranean. The ruling mercantile burghers of Geneva rented out warehouses and stalls, provided hostelries and theatres and supplied police protection to merchants carrying large sums of bullion. Caravans brought woollens from England, metal wares from Nuremberg, fruit and wine from France, salt from the Mediterranean and cheeses from the Alps. The city's dozen banks included the most profitable branch of the Medici Bank of Florence. In the mid-fifteenth century, before the sea gold of Guinea and Mexico had begun to reach Europe, coin was so scarce that Geneva expanded trade by using credit notes with floating exchange rates, which avoided contravening the laws on usury. In 1480 Geneva expelled its traditional Jewish financiers and replaced them with Italian bankers from Lombardy and Piedmont. A change of bankers, however, did not solve Geneva's economic crisis, a crisis which deeply affected the cheese trade.

A confrontation between Geneva and France broke out in 1462 when Louis XI, dismayed at his loss of foreign exchange, closed his frontier with Geneva. He then established a rival fair at Lyon, two days down the Rhône, which he planned to hold on the same dates each year as the Geneva fair. Bern decided that it must safeguard its French outlet for cheeses by switching at least some of its business to the new Lyon fair. Mobs of Geneva highwaymen retaliated vigorously against traders going to Lyon and relieved one passing merchant of his consignment of silver bullion. The loss was so severe that Bern called upon its neighbour, the count of Gruyère, to restore order and retrieve the robbed silver but a tribunal meeting at Saanen was unable to establish the facts of the case. Meanwhile the Medici bank moved its branch to Lyon as Geneva's trade declined. The lakeside city tried to recover its losses by trading with Burgundy during the war of 1476, but Burgundy was destroyed and Geneva was fined an indemnity of 26 000 gold crowns by Bern and branded as a war criminal. After further confrontations between Geneva and the Swiss republics trade relations were restored but much of Château-d'Oex's cheese continued to be sold on the Lyon market in order to guarantee imported supplies of high quality French salt.

The scale of the Château-d'Oex salt purchases was large. The salt content of mature Gruyère was almost two per cent of gross weight. Further quantities of salt were needed to fortify the cattle diet and salt licks were fixed to modern milking stalls. In earlier times cowmen had carried leather satchels of powdered salt and before milking each cow had put a pinch of salt on its tongue. In the eighteenth century, as in the twentieth, the number of cows needing salt licks to keep them healthy was probably about 2000. Since eighteenth-century milk yields were probably only about one-fifth of late-twentieth century ones the amount of salt needed for brine baths and cheese curing was considerably less than the five tonnes used in 1995. The logistics of getting even one tonne of salt over the mountains each season were nevertheless formidable and the cost of salt in Château-d'Oex was high.

Salt was one of the most politically sensitive of commodities in early modern Europe, as in any other continent and at any other period before the railway era. Romans had paid 'salaries' to employees in salt, Venice had taxed salt at 200 per cent in the twelfth century and Louis XIV had raised one-quarter of France's state revenue through his salt monopoly. In 1653 Swiss salt prices caused a peasant war of such ferocity that 35 ringleaders were executed in Bern and Lucerne. The salt came from Genoa, Venice, Austria, Germany, Alsace, France and Burgundy. Italian salt, wrapped in oil-cloth, was carried over the Alps by mule trains and was used not only for making cheese and butter but for tanning leather and preserving fish, meat and vegetables. French salt was packed in barrels on the Mediterranean salt pans of Aigues Mortes and brought by barge up the Rhône. By the time it reached Geneva the salt had been subjected to duty payments at 46 tollgates and was worth 16 times more than when it left the coast.

Salt was so expensive in the Alps that it was the dream of every highland cheese farmer to get rich by finding his own salt mine. In 1725 a Château-d'Oex lieutenant of militia, a member of the Desquartiers clan into which Samuel Henchoz later married, thought that he had discovered a salt spring high in the mountains. News of his discovery could not be suppressed, such was its potential value, and someone disloyally reported the find to the castle. Lord-Bailiff Effinger took energetic steps to find the salt on behalf of Bern as well as in his own interest. He sent an expedition, accompanied by his son, to investigate the quality of the alleged brine. Château-d'Oex appointed pastor Perissod, magistrate Perronet and surgeon Cokisberg to secure the interests of the borough in the affair, but the great expedition failed to find the salty eldorado. Before he reached his mountain Desquartiers was taken ill and brought to the rectory for questioning. It then emerged that the man was under intolerable strain. He had been subjected to threats of every kind since the village realised that he had revealed the salt location to officials from Bern. He had been insulted by an unidentified woman and attacked with pistol shots fired into his barn. Pastor Perissod investigated the bullet marks and was shown a burn hole in one of Desquartiers' shirts. Sceptical city officials gave the lieutenant a severe reprimand but the pastor was convinced that malicious persons with evil intent and genuinely threatened his life. He judged Desquartiers to be an honest man and warned the castle that if he were put under further pressure he would become deranged.

Threats by strange women, violence by unidentified gunmen, the psychiatric collapse of an officer of the militia and a high level investigation by the castle itself were all indications of the importance attached to discovering salt. The idea that local salt might be found in Château-d'Oex was not entirely fanciful since genuine salt had been found in a mountain spring only 30 kms away. That discovery, so legend claimed, had been made by a wandering goat-boy above the village of Bex on the Rhône. Sixty years later, in the 1530s, the Bern senate farmed out Bex salt-mining rights to Nicholas von Graffenried, an influential city aristocrat. Since the brine from the springs only had a salinity level of three per cent the venture struggled to make any profit. Enormous quantities of expensive wood were needed to boil the brine dry and the contractors searched the mountains as far as Château-d'Oex for fuel supplies. Carrying logs down the mountain was arduous but in 1695 engineers solved the transport problem with the newest technology. They built the first of the modern Alpine dams on a mountain stream. The pioneering dam had two bow-fronted rock faces, a water-tight clay core and was 30 metres long by eight metres high. At its base an ingenious sluice gate enabled the water to be let out in a sudden jet. Fuel logs for the fires under the brine pans were cut into metre lengths and piled high in front of the closed sluice gate while the lake filled up. When the sluice was opened the rush of water carried the log pile down to the Rhône 1000 metres below. The dramatic mechanism remained in use until late in the nineteenth century but was eventually demolished in 1945. Carrying timber to the bottom of the mountain had become easy but bringing the salt back up to the cheese farms remained laborious.

Château-d'Oex supplied the Rhône mines not only with fuel but also with pipes to carry brine from the springs to the vats in which it was boiled. The pipes were made of larch wood which did not corrode in salt as more expensive metal pipes would have done. Teams of specialist carpenters extended and repaired the wooden pipelines by boring tree trunks with giant handtwisted gouges. The best larch trees had to be selected and harvested in January. Popular custom required that they be felled under a waning moon and thousands of them were taken to the mines. Pipe drillers, experienced in making conduits to bring drinking water to the mountain cattle troughs, were recruited by the mines until farmers complained of a scarcity of drinking troughs for the dairy industry. The craftsmen hoped to use the demand for their skills to improve their wages in a competitive market but Bern threatened to import foreign labour to undercut costs and increase the supply of pipes. Similar competition occurred in the iron industry when farmers complained that highland blacksmiths were being taken to the mines to forge giant boiling vats for the salt. Sour relations between the salt industry and its cheesemaking customers were further embittered by the low quality of Swiss salt compared to the imported salt from southern France or Spanish Burgundy.

In 1668 the international politics of Château-d'Oex's preferred salt supply were dramatically altered. Young Louis XIV of France invaded

Spanish Burgundy and gained control of both the major sources of salt which supplied western Switzerland. The king was then able to increase the already high salt prices and demand that Bern supply his armies with more mercenaries from the highlands by way of payment for salt. To overcome the crisis Bern intensified its efforts to produce salt from its home territories. Rock miners, using gunpowder and supplied with air pumped underground by huge bellows, cut a 700 metre gallery into the Rhône mountainside at Bex. They found new sources of salt-bearing rock that could be broken up, dissolved and pumped out of the mine to be dried in the vats. The huge caverns and deep shafts quarried in the mountain inspired awe in the French novelist Alexandre Dumas when he visited them. Halfway down the 49 flights of ladders he stopped to muse that a fall from that point would still be longer than falling from the spire of Strasbourg cathedral. The impressive engineering, however, was not matched by economic performance and the yield of 2000 tonnes of low grade salt a year remained disappointing.

Salt reached the Château-d'Oex cheese dairies in small consignments, as revealed in the accounts of Samuel Henchoz whose farm tenants were significant consumers of salt. In 1753 he received seven deliveries of salt totalling 115 pounds in weight between March and October. The salt was supplied by a cousin at about a penny per pound until in February 1756 he received a larger consignment of 245 pounds worth two gold sovereigns. No further purchases were recorded until 1762 when Cousin Henchoz, now Chatelain Henchoz, made ten deliveries totalling 200 pounds weight during the course of the year. This salt was paid for by bartering the cost of pasturing seven sheep and six lambs during the summer and by the supply of a new Louis XV sovereign worth 160 pence. In the following year another 300 pounds of salt were delivered. The consignments came in 20 pound barrels and the purchaser had to pay the cost of the barrel staves. Buying salt was a constant drain on the finances of a working farm but in 1765 Samuel Henchoz had a stroke of luck. He and nine of his friends, including the borough treasurer and the pastor, bought a lucky ticket for the Lausanne sweepstake and Samuel was able to put his winnings of 45 pence towards that year's salt bill of 140 pence.

One of the problems that Château-d'Oex faced as an international centre of salt buying and cheese selling was the absence of any standardised system of currency matched by a single system of accounting. In the mid-eighteenth century Samuel Henchoz kept his cheese accounts in a German system of values based on the florin. The florin was divided into four *Batzen* and each *Batz* was quartered into four *Kreutzer*. Bern issued copper coins for the two smaller denominations, the large *Batz* coin being roughly similar to an English 'cartwheel' penny and the small *Kreutzer* to an English farthing. But Samuel Henchoz did not use florins to measure his property deals, his land rentals or his borrowing and lending of capital. These he calculated in the French system of pounds, shillings and pence, or *livres*, *sols* and *deniers*. The French *denier* was worth one twelfth of a French *sol* but was too small, by the eighteenth century, to be of much account. The French *livre*, on the other hand, was widely used as a measure of value, and was equivalent to two and a half German florins. Neither the *livre* nor the florin, however, existed as coins in circulation.

The gold and silver coins in eighteenth-century Château-d'Oex came from all over Europe. Traders needed a fine pair of scales and a reliable set of weights to be able to assess the value of the coins that they were offered on the market or in the fair. The biggest gold coins, double sovereigns, came from Portugal bearing the effigy of John V and were made of gold from the Brazilian mines that had been developed early in the eighteenth century. These Portuguese coins circulated widely in England, as they did in Switzerland. An older and much appreciated gold coin was the French sovereign, issued by Louis XI in the fifteenth century when he was the ally of Bern against Charles the Bold of Burgundy. A smaller gold coin in regular use was the 'new' sovereign issued by Louis XV. The silver coinage which Samuel Henchoz and the Château-d'Oex cheesemongers used for daily transactions was the crown or *écu*. Like the gold sovereign the silver crown varied in size. The most commonly cited crown was the small crown worth about one eighth of a small sovereign. In Samuel Henchoz's great ledger the small crown was equivalent to five German florins or to two French *livres*. The *livre*, renamed the franc and divided into a hundred decimal cents, eventually became the basis of nineteenth-century Swiss accounts, somewhat to the dismay of the Alemannic Swiss who would have preferred to retain florins as their currency. The *sol* or *sou*, one-twentieth of a franc, continued to be used in popular Château-d'Oex parlance during the twentieth century.

Coinage was not the only complex hinderance to trade in Château-d'Oex. Commercial activity also suffered from a problem of diverse weights and measures. Even in 1848 when the rival Swiss nations agreed to a common market they did not rapidly harmonise the units according to which items were bought and sold. The pound weight traditionally used in Château-d'Oex was the one used in Gruyère and was divided into eighteen ounces. The liquid measure used in the highland, however, was one with twice the volume of that used on the lake shore at Vevey. In Château-d'Oex a 'fathom' of closely-stacked firewood measured three metres but in Rougemont it only measured two. Textiles were measured in ells but the Château-d'Oex ell was one inch longer than the 'royal' ell recognized in France. Land measurements, made in feet, were particularly difficult to reconcile since Château-d'Oex used both the Bern standard and the French standard. Distances were measured in leagues, Vevey being seven leagues away on the footpath over the Jaman pass but twelve leagues by the cart track down the valley and through the plain.

One of the surprising aspects of cheese and salt transport in Château-d'Oex was the very limited use of carts or pack animals. Indeed the highland kept few auxiliary animals at all. The hunting dogs and guard dogs of the medieval period are rarely mentioned in the eighteenth century and even the shepherds and goat-herds who took small livestock to remote corners of the mountains apparently did not have dogs to help them. The dairy farms did have cats to keep down vermin, the mousehunter travelling up and down the mountain on top of the backpacked luggage with each seasonal move. Cultivation which survived the dairy revolution and the change from tilled fields to hay meadows was done with spades and hoes rather than with ploughs and oxen. Pack animals were scarcely used to bring salt up to the mountain or carry cheese back down and Château-d'Oex depended largely on human labour for transport.

Transport practices contrasted sharply with those used in the Italian Alps where donkeys, and more especially mules, were extensively used as pack animals both by cheesemongers and by the local militias. On the plain, where Château-d'Oex bought its corn, oxen and ox carts were the common feature of heavy transport but few reached the highland, though bulls were occasionally used for exceptionally heavy work such as dragging roof timbers up to the village from the river. In Château-d'Oex horses were the only working animal and these were used sparingly and mostly for forestry. No farmer wished to devote grazing land or winter fodder to feeding a horse when his supply could be used to feed a milch-cow instead. The political economists in the Bern treasury were equally adamant that horses had to be kept out of the highland to maximise the profit from their dairy land. Where horses were used they doubled as cavalry horses for military officers such as Samuel Henchoz, the drill master of the Château-d'Oex militia. He rode his horse when summoned to military tattoos on the Oberland training ground at Erlangen. These prestige horses were expensive to buy and to maintain and in 1753 Samuel Henchoz laid out five sovereigns, two hundred florins, to buy a horse. The horse fair patronised by Château-d'Oex was at Romont, a former Savoy principality out on the plain beyond Gruyère castle. On one occasion Samuel Henchoz sent his wife's brother, Desquartiers, to attend the horse fair on his behalf. He left Château-d'Oex on a Sunday taking one horse and one mare to market. His first night was spent in the market town of Bulle where an innkeeper charged him eight pence for his own lodging and 14 pence for the stabling of his two animals. He also had to buy each horse three pennyworth of hay for each day of the journey. The success of his transactions is not recorded but on his return he treated himself to half a jar of wine at Montbovon and bought three boxes of the much prized cherries which he may have distilled as cherry brandy.

The greatest change in transport policy in Château-d'Oex, at least until the digging of the Jaman tunnel in 1904, was the eighteenth-century construction of a cart track from the plain to the highland. This track was built on a wave of prosperity which led both Bern and Fribourg to build roads across the Swiss plain. The two states even dug a small, rather unsuccessful, canal for barges to carry wine barrels from the Rhône to the Rhine. The dairy industry was also thriving at the time but the impact of the cart track was surprisingly limited. After seven centuries of reliance on footpaths the cheesemongers continued to carry most of their cheeses on their heads to Vevey. The track was used to import bulky goods and wheat and barley may have become cheaper, though their importance was receding with the spread of the potato. The cart track may have been used to bring in the small barrels of salt that Samuel Henchoz bought at one penny a pound.

The lack of success of the cart track was partly due to difficulties encountered in its use. Where it entered the highland through the narrow gorge at La Tine, below Rossinière, rock falls frequently interrupted traffic. Elsewhere soft soils made the poorly surfaced roadway impassably muddy in wet weather. Worse still the customs post erected by Fribourg and Bern when they partitioned Gruyère in 1555 continued to impede traffic. So exorbitant were the Fribourg tolls that in the eighteenth century an alternative route to the plain was opened by the great Château-d'Oex landowners. The new route, across the high Hongrin valley, was designed to run entirely through Bern's economic space and so avoid foreign customs duties. It crossed the mountain a few miles east of the Jaman footpath and reached the lake at Villeneuve, six miles from Vevey. The track could not take wheeled vehicles but, unlike the Jaman path, it could be negotiated by pack horses. For a few years some cheesemongers tied their cheeses to pack saddles and led strings of surefooted mountain horses over the trail before it was closed each autumn by snow. Although it avoided a troublesome customs post the pack trail was not an economic success and the route fell into abeyance. The cart track, on the other hand, survived and was gradually upgraded over the years.

Among those who gained what advantage they could from the development of a cart track the most prominent were the Rossinière members of the great Henchoz congerie of clans which had spread through all three boroughs of the highlands since the Middle Ages. The Henchoz family of Rossinière, although not immediately related to Samuel Henchoz of Château-d'Oex, practised similar pursuits, consolidating land-ownership, lending money, entering public service and above all trading in cheeses. In the late-fifteenth century 'Honestum Henricum Henchod' of Etivaz, a freeman but not a nobleman, had been appointed chatelain of Château-d'Oex by the count of Gruyère, thereby initiating a tradition of public service that was to live on in the family for five centuries. The Henchoz coat-of-arms was adorned with the quill and inkwell of a scribe. In the sixteenth century one of the Henchoz farmers from Etivaz bought some good, almost level, land on the eastern outskirts of Rossinière, a few hundred paces from the densely packed wooden village. The site was close to the medieval stone bridge which linked Rossinière to the left bank of the Sarine and the cart track. This was convenient for winter trade with Château-d'Oex when heavy sledges were permitted to cross snow covered land on their trading journeys up and down the valley. In the seventeenth century old Abraham Henchoz was elected by the village to serve as its schoolmaster during the winter months when children were available to attend classes. His son Gabriel, born in 1675, was sufficiently educated to become a public notary, a barrister-at-law, a justice of the peace and Rossinière's town clerk. He also maintained the family farm and diversified its activities into beekeeping to produce candle wax and honey. As land consolidation gained pace in the highland, driving small farming families into exile on the plain, Gabriel Henchoz successfully made auction bids for the properties of bankrupted peasants. Although Rossinière had retained one-third of its land in common ownership, there was still scope for speculating and profiteering on the other two-thirds. Gabriel increased the number of his holdings, enlarged the size of his fields, and sold off fragmented marginal plots. As an agricultural moderniser and innovator he built terraces against erosion, barriers against avalanches, and walls between his fields. As crops continued to retreat before the advancing dairy revolution his wheat and flax gardens were turned into cattle pasture.

Gabriel Henchoz, like Samuel Henchoz, was a wily entrepreneur who made a very advantageous marriage. His wife brought with her a dowry of 5000 imperial florins and a life interest in several barns and pastures. By the age of 32 Gabriel was elected 'governor' of Rossinière, a post equivalent to that of chatelain in Château-d'Oex. He served in office for a record five terms. His home built for his father in 1686 by carpenters of the Geneyne family, was so well-appointed that he was able to receive the lord-bailiff as his guest. In return Gabriel was invited to the castle. Each New Year he delivered the cermonial cheeses of the citizens of Rossinière to the lord-bailiff. He also oiled the wheels of administration and diplomacy by giving presents of tobacco to his excellency and of sweetmeats to the castle ladies. By the time he died in 1752 the estate of Gabriel Henchoz was worth 92 413 florins. He had become one of the richest cheesemongers of the highland.

In 1725 Old Gabriel sent his sons away to school, first to Vevey and later to the academy city of Lausanne on its fortress hill high above Lake Geneva. In Lausanne the boys paid Madame Panchaud 120 florins a year for their lodgings. For their board they brought with them 24 pounds of mature Gruyère cheese, 18 pounds of dried salt meat, and five pounds of clarified butter together with the necessary money for other items of food. For their tuition they paid the rector of the academy one silver crown each per month plus two florins for elocution classes to improve their French. The investment in education proved justified. When Jean-David Henchoz graduated as a lawyer, at the age of 22, he was granted an audience with the lord-bailiff in Rougemont castle. For the occasion he commissioned his brother, who had gone into trade in the city of Bern, to purchase him a symbolic silver sword as a sign that the son of a chessemonger could aspire to honourable status. His excellency read the boy's credentials, tested his knowledge and appointed him clerk of the Rossinière magistrates. Four years later Jean-David married into the family which owned the great house on the main square in Rossinière. His wife's dowry enabled him to buy two mountain farms.

Jean-David Henchoz's new wife epitomised the part that women of drive and experience were able to play in the enterprise culture of the highland. Madame Henchoz was a highly successful businesswoman who traded in cereals, cultivated flax, preserved winter vegetables, spun and wove woollen and linen cloth, and cut gentlemen's suits to order. She played political hostess to the valley and to any travelling business people who passed through. She also helped her husband with his extensive moneylending activities and with the accounts of his brothers who served as the pastor of Rossinière and as the judge of Château-d'Oex. A fourth brother, the one who had gone into business in the city of Bern, had died prematurely thus warning Jean-David to keep his account books up to date so that if disease should strike him down his wife could instantly take over his affairs. In 1752 Jean-David Henchoz began to prepare for himself a lasting memorial. He planned to build a chalet that would be even larger than his father-in-law's great house on the village square. The project, however, was not entirely founded on vainglorious pride. His economic rationale was to build a house with cellars big enough to serve the highland cheese industry on a huge scale. Gruyère cheeses, as has been noted, required careful curing in large salt baths and had to be matured in cellars maintained at an even temperature. By attempting to monopolise the year-long storage of Rossinière cheeses Jean-David Henchoz sought to generate for himself a comfortable income both from private cheese farmers and from the peasants who jointly exploited the communal pastures. He also calculated that since most cheese farmers were in debt to him, and sometimes tardy in paying their interest, he would be able to hold their cheeses in caution against their debts. He would also be able to insist that any farmer wanting a loan would have to bring his cheeses to the giant new Henchoz cellar and pay the appropriate fees for having them ripened. Like other big moneylenders, sometimes politely known as bankers, Jean-David Henchoz engaged in finance as a supplementary activity to farming and trading.

The design of the 'Great Chalet' of Rossinière, the biggest chalet ever built in the Swiss Alps, was a bold one. To get a large number of cheese cellars under one roof, while still building a house that was elegantly proportioned in the traditional style, required daring experiments in architecture and engineering. To obtain the necessary skills and materials Henchoz used his extensive network of trading contacts not only in the valley but also down on the plain. The house was built in two halves on each side of a huge 'Burgundian' chimney of stone. Each half provided autonomous accommodation for a household on two habitation floors with very generous storage space under the roof. Jean-David was his own architect and master-of-works. He began selecting and felling timbers in 1752, the year in which his father died, and hired a team of eight lumberjacks at three pence per man per day to lower logs from barely accessible mountains and haul them over the snow to the building site. Over two years he assembled beams, planks, laths and shingles for the project. When his master-carpenter walked off the site Jean-David took over supervising the jobbing carpenters and day-labourers himself for the next three years. The master-plasterer came on site at two each morning to light up his lime kiln. The stone door-way for the great cheese-cellar was bought secondhand from an aban-doned castle near Fribourg, the price being a mere 15 florins plus the ceremonial wine required to authenticate the contract. When it came to making the 113 metal windows the Rossinière blacksmiths had diffi-culty meeting the precise specifications needed for windows designed to hold panes of clear glass. When the problem of the new style win-dow frames had been solved glaziers were brought up from the plain to install the glass. New methods were also needed to hold down the enormous roof. Instead of laying laths and heavy stones over the top of the shingles Jean-David adopted the new fashion for nailing shingles on laths fixed beneath the roof's surface. A roofing contractor from Montbovon, three miles away across the frontier, commissioned black-smiths throughout the valley to fashion quantities of handmade roof-ing nails. In preference to fitting standard doors of solid wood, joiners from the city were brought on site to make elegant panel doors for each room.

Once the construction was finished the Grand Chalet was carefully decorated. Family and friends followed tradition by giving the new owner engraved window panels. Pious texts were carved on the outer beams or painted on the sheltered timbers under the eves. The letter-ings for the 2800 characters were designed by Marie Perronet. Her hus-band, Jean Raynaud, spent 43 days on a scaffold meticulously painting praises to the Almighty on both the front and the back of the building. Although this artwork was effaced by the weather over the nineteenth century another sample of the artists' work does survive. In Château-d'Oex Marie Desquartiers, the wife of Samuel Henchoz, commissioned Marie Perronet and Jean Raynaud to paint the ceiling of her bedcham-ber. This painted bedroom ceiling was later sold and incorporated into another house before being moved yet again and displayed in the highland museum as a fine sample of eighteenth-century mural art. Meanwhile in Rossinière Jean-David Henchoz, the greatest cheesemon-ger of the Château-d'Oex highland, did not live long enough to enjoy his architectural and artistic achievements. It was his son, Young Gabriel, who became the patriarch of Rossinière. After his father's death he lived in the village for four score years and, as Dean Henchoz, became one of the great patriots of the Swiss Revolution.

6
The Green Flag of Liberty

The French Revolution and its new concepts of liberty, equality and fraternity had repercussions throughout Europe. The ensuing Napoleonic wars disrupted the lives of peoples across the whole continent. In the highland of Château-d'Oex wealthy members of the élite worried that their business activities would be disrupted by the political turbulence in France. Madeleine Isoz, née Rosat, feared that unreliable mail from England would deprive her of news of her overseas relatives. Worse still her lawyer, in Lausanne, was deprived of news of the 1100 sterling shares which she held in London. She agonised over whether her letters of instruction would be more reliably delivered via the city mail to Bern or via the local postman who walked over the mountain to Vevey. Meanwhile down on the plain revolutionary ideas caused much excitement and even talk of an uprising against the authority of Bern. In the autumn of 1797 the young general Bonaparte made a semi-clandestine visit to Vaud, the westernmost province of the Swiss plain which had by now been under Bern occupation for 261 years. The daughters of revolutionary-minded citizens welcomed him with white flowers as a symbol of freedom. The dictator's coach ride through the Swiss night was not at all appreciated by Bern, even if one officer tried to ingratiate himself by recalling how he remembered meeting Bonaparte in Corsica. Bonaparte dismissed such flattery; he harboured no sympathy for the haughty Bern captains who had dominated the French army when he was a mere lieutenant. He was much more receptive to the Vaud dreams of liberty and years later, after Switzerland had been through its own difficult revolution, he was able to help the people of Vaud to win their freedom. In 1803 they adopted the green and white flag of liberty. The Romanic-speaking villages of the highland behind Vevey, including Château-d'Oex, were attached to the revolutionary new republic.

In the Château-d'Oex highland attitudes to the revolutionary ideas spreading from France were divided. The most eloquent voice to be heard was that of 'Dean' Bridel, the newly appointed pastor who had arrived from Basel in 1796. In Basel he had served as pastor to a traumatised community of French refugees who had escaped the guillotine. Bridel became an articulate opponent of French revolutionary ideas and the romantic defender *par excellence* of archaic Swiss values. Château-d'Oex's Bern overlords represented the epitome of resistance to revolution and so Bridel mobilised support for Bern tradition and for the old order. Opposition to France and its revolutionary régime did, however, cause confusion and ambivalence in Switzerland. France had been the defender of Bern's independence for three centuries but now represented a world turned upside down. By contrast Austria, the other European superpower, had been the traditional enemy of Bern and of its Swiss allies but now seemed to be the great protector of the old order.

While Dean Bridel campaigned against the revolution in Château-d'Oex, his friend and neighbour, Dean Henchoz of Rossinière, publicly welcomed the new social and political order advocated by France. The pastor's kinsman, Judge Henchoz, received awed reports from his children at school in Lausanne. Their master had told them that France had abolished the aristocracy and no longer recognized either barons or counts. The excitement was enhanced when the village welcomed home as its local hero one of the boys of the Pilet family who had served in the élite royal guard at the Tuileries palace in Paris; he had survived the great massacre in which most of the Swiss guard who protected the king of France had been killed on 10 August 1792. Rossinière's revolutionary fervour apparently did not decline even when, in the following year, the French king was executed and many erstwhile sympathisers felt a revulsion against the excesses of the Paris regicides. In Château-d'Oex attitudes were more nuanced as citizens who supported radical change discreetly worked against the public lobbying of Bridel and his supporters of Bern.

One way in which the élite of Château-d'Oex responded to the challenges of the 1790s was to petition Bern for the right to set up a local military society. The old sporting 'abbey' of highland arquebusiers had been defunct for some years and the petitioners sought permission to set up a select company of marksmen to protect the customary liberties of their mountain village. The senate of Bern, although keen to defend the integrity of the republic including all its highland possessions, was reluctant to concede any military autonomy to the borough of Château-d'Oex. It did nevertheless want to revive the waning sport of target practice. In Rougemont, whose bourgeoisie lived in close symbiosis with the lord-bailiff in his castle, Bern had encouraged a revival of the martial arts through a voluntary association even before the fall of the Bastille in 1789. Five years later, as the French Revolution unleashed turbulence all around, Château-d'Oex was apparently seeking to establish a similar shooting club of its own, but Bern mistrusted the motives of some of its highland subjects.

The prospective founders of the new military sports association of Château-d'Oex were long-established citizens of landowning families. Their leader, David Lenoir, was actually a cavalry officer in the Dragoons rather than a marksman, but he advocated infantry target practice as a sport. After the revolutionary wars he became a wealthy and influential member of the community and served as its chief executive for 22 years. In 1794, when he proposed the founding of a new military society, he was still only 36 years old. His ten associates included three musketeers, four grenadiers, Bombardier Descoulayes who was then aged 22, Lieutenant Marmillod from Rossinière, and a civilian lawyer, Justice Byrde, who acted as the association's secretary. On the face of it none of the associates was a revolutionary and they planned to model their sport on established military practice. Entry to the club, however, was to be restricted to men of modest wealth whom the founders deemed 'honourable'. Admission would be exclusively controlled by a ruling council of 21. This council would manage all the assets of the club and would make all the decisions about the award of prizes. Members would have a free choice of weapon in any competition. The club's mission was to instil excellence in the martial arts, to enhance the glory of the Almighty and to defend the village in times of war.

Bern, perhaps surprisingly, rejected the club specifications proposed by Lenoir and his associates. The city oligarchs refused to accept either the restricted terms of club membership or the merely parochial defence objectives. They also balked at offering competitors a free choice of weapons instead of insisting that standard Bern militia guns be used. It took two years of negotiation to achieve a compromise and the first shooting festival did not take place until 1796. Lenoir agreed to allow his society a broader, perhaps less conspiratorial, membership in place of his one hundred handpicked followers. Thereafter membership was to pass automatically from grandfather to grandson and would be supplemented by open competition among applicants. The society was reluctantly granted permission to tax any capital wealth inherited by its members, but only at one-half of one per cent. The society income was to be used exclusively for the purchase of competition prizes and could not, as Lenoir had intended, be diverted to other club activities. Still more restrictively the ultimate authority over the club was not to be vested in an autonomous council but in the lord-bailiff appointed by Bern who was to receive two days' advance notice of any proposed shooting practice. On the matter of weapons Bern did concede a free choice to members provided that the club's motto should be the defence of the nation rather than merely the protection of the local highland. Ironically, however, neither the local nor the national defence objectives of the club were achieved and within two years of its foundation Château-d'Oex had been visited by troops from revolutionary France.

The Swiss Revolution broke out in 1798. It was both a spontaneous uprising by peoples oppressed by the oligarchies of Switzerland's six rural republics and seven city states, and also a response to a French invasion directed by Bonaparte. The French armies poured over the borders, but many Swiss were not happy to find themselves 'liberated' by Jacobins. In Château-d'Oex it would probably be wrong to cast David Lenoir, the self-styled 'abbot' of the military club, as a supporter of the French regicides even if his sympathies were tinged with revolutionary ardour. Once his society had been approved its founders had quietly set about designing the standard behind which they would parade at festivals. To the surprise of many they had chosen for their flag red, white and blue, the revolutionary colours of France, rather than black, red and gold, the national colours of Bern. The records shed little light on this apparently subversive decision, and the club treasurer, who had spent 194 florins on the controversial flag, had great difficulty in obtaining a reimbursement of his expenses. Not everyone appreciated the revolutionary colours of the club's standard but the military society's desire to defend the highland against outsiders was quite genuine and Château-d'Oex set about resisting the French as plunderers rather than embracing them as liberators.

Many Château-d'Oex militiamen remained proud of being citizens of Bern. Some had married into Alemannic families in Saanen, as David Lenoir himself was later to do. When, amidst the collapse of the *ancien régime*, the last lord-bailiff fled back to Bern city from his castle at Rougemont many citizens of Château-d'Oex did not cheer his departure. When Dean Bridel preached against the revolution he found a positive response to his advocacy of old Swiss traditions and had little difficulty in persuading many of his parishioners of the dangers inherent in a French occupation of the highland. As war approached, and Château-d'Oex mobilised all men aged over 16, the conscripts listened to the cultured and humane, but fundamentally conservative, voice of their pastor as Bridel proclaimed loyalty to

> our legitimate sovereign against whom we have neither plaint nor grievance and we bless the Almighty for our fortune in living under the paternal government of Bern and hope that our children will have the same good fortune.

Bern sent troops to Château-d'Oex to defend the loyal highland and to attack rebels and invaders on the plain. Captain von Graffenried, one of whose forbears had so courageously taken possession of Château-d'Oex on behalf of Bern in 1556, built defensive fortifications at the gorge of La Tine and on the mountain pass of Jaman. Colonel Tscharner arrived from the Simmental with 1500 men and six portable artillery pieces. His instructions were to attack the market harbour of Vevey which had 'treasonably' welcomed the French. In retaliation against the Bern threat from the highland a French-led division commanded by General Brune, which included two rebellious Vaud battalions, was ordered to capture Château-d'Oex and advance on Bern along the mountain trail through the Simmental. In the event the highland war lasted only five days and all the fighting took place in the Ormont district, on the far side of the mountain from Château-d'Oex.

For their highland campaign the French had requisitioned horses from peasants on the plain but left their Vaud allies to pay the war debts later. France also incurred considerable expense in buying brandy for the troops. The cost of transport for the cannons was burdensome, and quantities of cartridges and flints had to be imported for the muskets. The resistance, meanwhile, remained chronically short of ammunition and even wooden pikes were in short supply, though some were issued to women to defend the villages. The Bern army managed to halt one French bayonet assault and even won a victory of sorts by killing a French colonel. Von Graffenried was soon forced to withdraw to Château-d'Oex but decided that the stone arch over the river was so inadequately defended by two small cannons and one mortar that he pulled his men back to Saanen. It was there that he learnt, on 5 March 1798, that a rapid French advance across the plain had captured Bern city itself. Further resistance in the highland was futile.

The Château-d'Oex militia, led by the young Bombardier Descoulayes, returned home two days after the fall of Bern. By noon on 7 March the borough had decided to acknowledge French victory. Its address to the new republic of Helvetia, which Bonaparte established, reminded the puppet rulers that the men of Château-d'Oex always kept faith with their sovereign. Alpine men, the borough fathers claimed, were incapable of cowardice or perfidy and would be loyal to the new régime as they had been to the old one. It was suspected that Dean Bridel not only knew how to craft diplomatic phrases but also, when he deemed it prudent, how to turn his coat. For all their fine words, however, the Château-d'Oex highlanders were among the most stubborn of citizens in the 'united and indivisible' republic by means of which Paris ruled the Swiss. Their disaffection with the puppet administration was fuelled by the constant demand for taxes and conscripts to fight France's European wars. Even the Vaud plainsdwellers, who had so loudly welcomed the Revolution, were soon disillusioned and 17 000 petitioners protested at the continued French occupation. On 28 June 1801 Château-d'Oex appealed to the government of Helvetia for permission to secede from the newly-formed province of Vaud and rejoin the old province of Bern. The words were probably those of Bridel:

> Do not be surprised if we wish to be Bernese and not Vaudois. Part of the political well-being of ourselves and of our children requires us to avoid doing violence to the affections of our hearts. We should regard as a misfortune any forced separation from Bern which linked us with a 'canton' whose political, geographical and moral conventions are not ours.
>
> [Archive Cantonale Vaudoise, file Hc 59, p. 25, 23 Oct. 1802]

This appeal to secede from Vaud immediately caused a protest from the anti-Bridel tendency in Château-d'Oex. Former Justice Byrde and former Chatelain Lenoir, the secretary and president of the military society, strongly opposed the return to Bern sovereignty:

> Our municipal government has not thought of the insurmountable inconvenience presented by differences of language and the inordinate cost of translating laws, decrees, civil suits and criminal appeals. [...] A throng of incidents would arise out of contested

translations and the eternal litigation would infallibly bring ruin to our citizens.

The energetic vice-governor of the highland who represented the Vaud government in Château-d'Oex wrote to his superiors at Lausanne on 21 February 1802 seeking urgent financial inducements to help him find 'enlightened spirits' who could dissuade the borough from re-joining Bern. He pointed to the benefits that would accrue to Vaud if it could retain control over the highland and over its export of cheeses which, he said, were earning Vaud 96000 silver francs per annum in foreign exchange. Château-d'Oex, however, was not minded to accept integration into Vaud and followed its romantic pastor in favouring Bern. Of the three highland boroughs only Rossinière favoured the Vaud connection and Dean Henchoz drafted a humble petition to Lausanne saying that the citizens were happy to be part of the Vaud 'Canton of Léman' and did not want to be restored to Bern. This petition was immediately forwarded to Paris while in Château-d'Oex local opinion was disregarded. Favre, the vice-governor who combined revolutionary correctness with patriotic loyalty by heading his notepaper with a William Tell crossbow, reported that Château-d'Oex was heartily disillusioned by the French intervention and as subversion and treason became rife he was ordered to find out who had sent a delegation to Bern seeking a restoration of the old sovereignty.

The matter of highland sovereignty was eventually decided on 22 Frimaire (12 December) 1802 by a Swiss commission meeting in Paris. Three Bern parliamentarians, Wattewil, Gruber and Mullinen, argued that Château-d'Oex was linked to the Oberland and to 'Old Switzerland' by moral practice, by traditional usage, by ancient custom and by patterns of work. Moreover, they claimed, the borough had been constitutionally attached to Bern not since 1555, the date of the partition of Gruyère, but since 26 June 1403 when the status of the men of Château-d'Oex as co-citizens of Bern was confirmed 'in perpetuity'. In reply to this bid for a restoration of the old order the founding fathers of Vaud, Muret, Monod and Secretan, brought forth counter-arguments of comparable historical weight. Château-d'Oex, they asserted, had been part of the principality of Gruyère which had become a medieval fief of the Savoy estates of Vaud. As for cultural links it was obvious, they declared, that the men of Château-d'Oex had never been German-speakers and should therefore be incorporated into a French-speaking Swiss republic. In Paris Vaud won the argument regarding the future sovereign affiliation of Château-d'Oex. Bern thereupon tried a more radical stratagem and proposed that the whole of Vaud should be restored to Bern tutelage. Bonaparte is said to have remarked that it was more likely that the sun should change its course in the heavens than that Bern should recover its territorial possessions.

France had invaded Swiss territory with two objectives in mind. The first was to seize the city treasure of Bern, the largest and possibly wealthiest of the Swiss republics. Part of this treasure had originally been plundered from Lausanne cathedral in 1536, but when recaptured by France it was not restored to the Lausanne city patriots who had cheered their French liberators but was loaded on long-distance wagons and hauled to Toulon to finance Bonaparte's attempted conquest of Egypt. The second objective of the French invaders was to recruit 18000 Swiss volunteers to fight against Austria but this was much more difficult to achieve. The province of Vaud was assessed for a contribution of 600 fighting men but not a single one volunteered from Château-d'Oex. The government's highland representative pointed out to the city politicians that it was traditional for recruiting sergeants to provide music and to offer wine if they wished to entice youths to follow them. The Château-d'Oex reluctance to enlist was hightened by the hope that Austria would soon be victorious and would drive the French off Swiss soil. The puppet politicians threatened to punish anyone who refused to 'defend' Switzerland against Austria although the illusion of Swiss independence was very thin. On 7 June 1800 the Vaud administration wrote to Rougemont on behalf of First Consul Bonaparte expressing extreme displeasure at the failure of the municipality to send five able-bodied men with their full military equipment to join the ranks. If within seven days the men were not received an armed column would be sent into the highland to press-gang them. Worse still the punitive expedition would remain in the district until it had seized enough money to reimburse itself for its costs. Bridel worked hard as a conciliator on behalf of the neighbouring village but the best he could achieve was a three day extension of the deadline. The grieving men of Rougemont were forced to draw lots to decide who should leave home to join the murderous wars of the revolution and face the risk of being maimed or killed.

During the revolutionary years daily life in Château-d'Oex was always tense. Three foolish young men were prosecuted for displaying a Bern flag but were acquitted with costs. Dean Bridel's sermons were checked for seditious content and although found to be within the law his continued popularity caused the government constant anxiety. The borough treasurer was asked to acknowledge receipt of the French

1 Market Square (Château-d'Oex Museum collection).

2 Castle motte (Museum, old postcard).

3 Rossinière old chalet (drawing by E. Gladbach in E. Henchoz, *Revue Historique Vaudoise*, March 1964).

4 Wooden interior (Museum collection)

5 Pack-mule (M. Henchoz and G. Morier-Genoud, *Château-d'Oex*, 1990).

6 Cheese porter (G. Fleury, Villars-sur-Glâne).

La Partie de cartes au chalet

7 Cowmen at play (Museum, old postcard).

8 Seventeenth-century cow bells (DBB).

9 Cheese dairy (Siegfried Eigstler, Thun).

10 Lumberjacks on the river (in André Jacot, *Chroniques*, n.d. [1996]).

Château-d'Œx — Un bon filard.

11 Hay-carrying (Museum, old postcard).

En Cray. — Armaillis du Pays d'Enhaut

5. Photogr. Borloz. Château d'Œx

12 Alpine dairymen (Museum, old postcard).

13 Winter sports (Museum, old postcard).

14 Luxury rail travel (M. O. B. railway company).

15 Paper cutout art (Château-d'Oex Museum exhibit by J. J. Hauswirth).

16 Barn decoration (G. Fleury, Villars-sur-Glâne, from Bulle Museum exhibit by Silvestre Pidoux).

military pension of Pierre-David Lenoir, six pounds and eighteen shillings in the currency of Tours, worth four pounds and twelve shillings in the Swiss equivalent. The war department refused, however, to pay David Rossier of Rougemont arrears to which he was entitled and admitted that a number of Château-d'Oex soldiers had never been paid at all for their mercenary services. In order to rescue military paupers an unauthorised loan was taken out of the coffers of the Château-d'Oex salt depot. On 30 December 1802 the borough was advised that it should expect to feed and lodge the third company of the Second Dragoons. The billeting clerk drew attention to the fact that the Dragoons had themselves received no pay, but since they were being sent to Château-d'Oex to levy arrears of taxation his appeal for generous hospitality fell on deaf ears.

The French invasion of Switzerland had been accompanied by the planting of 'Liberty Trees' in front of town halls and on 7 March 1798 Château-d'Oex had reluctantly complied with an order to plant one. Reluctance to conform was followed by other types of bureaucratic prevarication. The tax collector made clear his resistance in a letter of 12 May 1798 in which he referred to traditional dues formerly delivered to the castle of the bailliwick but now payable, he disdainfully said, 'to the canton of "Léman" to which, I am led to believe, we are currently annexed'. In 1801 the receiver's stationery was still headed Léman, the then official name for Vaud, but in later headed notepaper the canton name was left blank to allow for any modification of nomenclature. By then 'liberty' was turning sour on the plain as well as in the highland. At dead of night people maliciously damaged the trees of liberty, sawing halfway through their trunks without their neighbours bearing witness against them. The government tried to apprehend the dissidents and some governors wrote agonised letters apologising for the misbehaviour of their subjects. From Château-d'Oex, however, the response was curt:

> Concerning your circular of the ninth instant relating to Liberty Trees the one in Château-d'Oex was burnt in the great fire that destroyed the village and those of Rougemont and Rossinière have fallen down. I thought it prudent to not re-establish them and therefore no such trees exist in my district.
>
> [Archive Cantonale Vaudoise, file H 145, 24 Dec. 1801]

The vice-governor's 'prudence' in not inciting riots by restoring the commemorative tree in honour of a now bitterly resented régime was well founded. By 1802 the Swiss cantons were in a state of civil war and in 1803 the republic of Helvetia collapsed. Bonaparte is said to have remarked that the Swiss were ungovernable. In the turmoil the patriots of Lausanne won independence for Vaud. Their green and white flag of liberty was inscribed with the words freedom and nationhood, *liberté et patrie*. The opening of the new republic's parliament was celebrated on 14 April 1803. Rossinière got its wish to become a small self-governing borough within the highland district of the new state. Château-d'Oex did not return to Bern but had to adapt to celebrating 14 April as a public holiday to commemorate its reluctant 'independence'. Château-d'Oex became the new highland district capital and the castle of the old lords-bailifff at Rougemont was sold. Bridel, despite his reactionary political views, retained his post as minister-in-charge of the Château-d'Oex parish eventually becoming a dean of the new national Church of Vaud. David Lenoir, the discreetly revolutionary founder of the military society, became the mayor of the Château-d'Oex municipality.

Outside the highland the European war carried on for another 12 years, indirectly affecting economic and public life in Château-d'Oex. As the fortunes of war swung away from France and toward Austria the great powers continued to ignore Swiss neutrality. In 1813 Austrian troops and their Russian allies entered Switzerland as brazenly as the French had done 15 years before, though Austrians never reached Château-d'Oex. Peace eventually came in two stages, in 1814 and in 1815, separated by Napoleon's hundred-day return to imperial power. The second peace was in many ways a more uncompromising restoration of the old order, intended by Austria to restore the *status quo* which had preceded the French Revolution. As far as Château-d'Oex was concerned, however, no restoration of the *ancien régime* took place. Vaud not only saw its independence of 1803 confirmed by the great powers but also retained its hold on the Romanic-speaking corner of the Bernese Oberland.

It had been Bonaparte who had been responsible for the separation of Château-d'Oex from Bern in 1803. It was Tsar Alexander I of the Russians who determined that the divorce would not be annulled by the restoration of 1815. The tsar's childhood tutor had been Frédéric-César de la Harpe, a scholar who became one of the intellectual mentors of the Vaud independence movement. When Austria tried to restore the domination of Bern over the Swiss plain at the treaty of Vienna, Alexander was lobbied by his old teacher and obtained from the great powers a recognition of Vaud's independence of 1803. As part of that recognition the city politicians of Lausanne were able to retain control of Château-d'Oex and its lucrative cheese revenue. The parish had by now lost its silver-tongued pastor and no effective voice was heard to argue the case for a return to an affiliation with Bern. Vienna decided Château-d'Oex's fate in 1815 as decisively as Paris had done in 1803. But the Vienna settlement did not make Switzerland any less 'ungovernable' than Bonaparte had claimed it to be. Conflict, exacerbated by poverty and post-war recession, remained endemic throughout the first-half of the nineteenth century. Religion was commonly, though not universally, the trigger that led to confrontation and frequently to civil war. Neither Vaud nor Château-d'Oex was immune from religious strife and the revolutionary era did not end in 1815.

During the half-century of Vaud independence religion was one of the most controversial aspects of its politics and Château-d'Oex played a significant rôle in church affairs. The totalitarian enforcement of religious conformity maintained by Bern had been temporarily discontinued by the French invasion, and during the revolutionary years religious tolerations had been permitted on condition that no disorder be caused. The constitution imposed by Paris had decreed that:

> ... as Christians you shall retain your priests and pastors and shall live together as brothers, refraining from persecuting Quakers or Anabaptists, Jews or Muslims, and permitting them to celebrate their own forms of worship ...
>
> [J. Cart, *Histoire de la liberté des cultes dans le Canton de Vaud 1798–1889*, Lausanne, 1890, p.8]

No sooner had Vaud won its independence in 1803 and raised the green flag of liberty, than it returned to the Bern style of enforced religious conformity. All toleration was ended and any form of proselytising was outlawed. In 1814 the National Church was confirmed as the sole church of the Vaud republic except in the district of Echallens, outside Lausanne, where even Bern had been obliged to accept a Catholic tradition of worship. Once peace had returned, however, church uniformity was rapidly challenged by proponents of the evangelical revival which had spread to Switzerland under English influence. The Dean of Lausanne, threatened by the zeal of keen young ministers who had been inspired by Methodism, persuaded the Vaud parliament to condemn Sunday evening assemblies organised by evangelical parishioners. The rise of piety and the persecution of evangelicals led to rioting in 1822. Evangelical ministers were dismissed and religious assemblies were driven underground as outlawed sects. The pastor of Vevey, Charles Rochat, was condemned to three years exile in 1824 but in his absence his congregation founded an illegal dissenting church. A leaflet campaign in favour of toleration was repressed by the censors. Neither the oligarchic bourgeoisie of restoration Lausanne, nor the conservative peasantry in the farming districts, was sympathetic to the evangelicals. One lone voice of a politician, Henri Druey, pleading for toleration was scarcely heard until in late 1830, six months after the July Revolution in Paris, revolution broke out in Vaud.

On 18 December 1830 the parliament of Vaud, epitomised by the social conservatism of the restoration, was driven out of its chamber by the Lausanne mob. The victorious Liberals drew up a new Vaud constitution but they failed to make religious toleration acceptable to the electorate or to inscribe it into their constitution. Intolerance continued to grow and at the Vevey wine festival of 1833 Charles Rochat, returned from his evangelical exile, was thrown into the river by the mob. This scandal did persuade voters to concede some religious freedoms on the condition that non-conformist proselytising should not trouble the political serenity of life. The establishment had, however, become concerned by the moral turpitude arising from the inability of evangelicals to contract valid marriages and in 1835 civil marriages for dissenters were instituted. Any wider toleration was firmly rejected, however, and by 1844 Vaud was heading for an ecclesiastical revolution and Switzerland for a religious civil war.

In Château-d'Oex intolerance, evangelicalism and religious diversity probably developed as they had done in Vevey but the parish records have temporarily disappeared. In the later years of the century the Salvation Army gained a foothold in the highland after it had been sternly persecuted on the plain where one lowland magistrate had caused an international outcry by sentencing a young Scottish Sunday-school teacher to a hundred days incarceration in Chillon castle. This symbolic gesture of intolerance embarrassed even the Vaud government and the young prisoner was offered the chamber of the Duchess of Savoy as a cell and her meals were sent across the drawbridge from a local hotel. Another Anglo-Saxon movement which created a millenarian following was the church of the Seventh Day Adventists which established a congregation in Château-d'Oex. More influential than either, however, were the Plymouth Brethren. Their leading missionary in Switzerland was John Nelson Darby, an Irish curate who led believers away from the established church not only in Ireland and

England but also in Vaud. Darby's model congregations appointed their own elders, held autonomous meetings for church discipline, ran adult schools and each Sunday celebrated the 'Lord's Supper' at which members broke their own bread. The concept of self-reliant congregations without hierarchical order of ordained ministers spread quickly from its roots in Devon. The acrimonious conflict between the evangelicals and the Church of Vaud provided Darby with fertile ground. He had made a preliminary visit to Switzerland in about 1837 and by 1840 a regular meeting of Brethren broke bread together in Vevey. Darby became involved in theological disputes among the Lausanne Wesleyans and two years of virulent pamphlet warfare encouraged the founding of many small congregations including ones in Rossinière and Rougemont which Darby may have visited personally. In 1842 one of Darby's followers, from the Rougemont family of Saugy, wrote out some of Darby's sermons on the concept of apocalypse and later published them in 1847. Darby returned to England where his followers became known as the Exclusive Brethren while the highland Brethren became known as Darbyites.

The Darbyites probably had a more powerful impact on agricultural society in Château-d'Oex than any other religious sect. They retired from public life to devote themselves to their farming, their families and their evangelical assemblies run by self-taught elders. The austere modesty of their life style enabled them to survive the cyclical crises of cattle farming and hard, lonely work in remote Alpine dairies. Their numbers grew particularly in the Etivaz valley where some lived in isolated homesteads throughout the year. For a time they maintained a closed tradition and even sharing a meal with an outsider, let alone marrying a bride from beyond the worshipping circle, was proscribed. The congregation was occasionally revitalised by a visit from a travelling preacher and families could be rejuvenated by inter-marriage with Darbyite congregations on the lake shore beyond Lausanne and in the Jura hills beyond the plain. Self-sufficiency, moral fortitude and social responsibility were the strengths of a Darbyite community and they helped to preserve the social fabric and Alpine traditions of Château-d'Oex farming. Autonomous religious communities gradually gained acceptance and in 1922 a formal Darbyite place of worship was opened in Château-d'Oex. In the mean time, however, the much larger congregation of the National Church of Vaud had fallen prey to a spectacular schism which divided the parish for 120 years. This schism was linked to yet another revolution which broke out on the plain and had repercussions in the highland.

In 1845, three years before the pan-European revolutions of 1848, the government of Vaud was again caught up in turmoil and eventually overthrown once more by the Lausanne mob. The root cause of revolution might have been the potato blight that was threatening to spread famine across Europe. One of the driving forces of the demonstrators, however, continued to be religious intolerance. The *sans-culottes* whipped up hysterical accusations against evangelicals and the Lausanne crowd thronged the streets chanting abuse. Most ministers of the established church were caught in a dilemma since they broadly supported the Liberal government of 1830 but were also sympathetic to demonstrators who campaigned against the evangelicals. Some pastors may have helped to draft the petitions which poured in to Lausanne demanding an end to religious toleration and the renewed suppression of the evangelical assemblies. When the crowds turned revolutionary and began to burn down evangelical oratories the clergy felt qualms of conscience. Worse was to follow when the Radicals replaced the Liberals as the party in power and the clergy began to fear for its monopoly of ecclesiastical authority. Vaud Radicalism was seen by the conservative church as but a step away from revolutionary disorder. The ministers of the National Church were horrified when asked to repay the state's loyalty in repressing the evangelicals by endorsing the new Radical government and its policies of broad-based democracy and social transformation. The clergy rebelled and forty pastors refused to read from the pulpit an appeal in favour of a new Radical constitution for Vaud. Many pastors saw the ideals of the Radicals as 'communist' and refused to disseminate such propaganda despite the fact that it had always been common practice under the Church of Bern for pastors to read government statements from the pulpit. In this crisis of insubordination half the ordained ministers in Vaud left the church. They hoped that their congregations would follow them to create an independent and conservative Free Church opposed both to the Radical government and to the 'Methodist' evangelicals.

In Château-d'Oex the two Church of Vaud pastors both refused to take orders from a Radical government and so resigned their livings. To their dismay the great majority of their highland congregation did not support them. The impoverished farm labourers of Château-d'Oex, like the paupers of Lausanne, were optimistic about the policies of a Radical government. The only members of the village who supported the pastors were the professional élite. A handful of upper middle-class secessionists nevertheless tried to set up an independent Free Church, much as defecting dissidents had set up a Free Church in Scotland two years earlier. They met, however, with virulent persecution. The Radical politicians in Lausanne persuaded a new Vaud parliament to give them plenary powers to govern by emergency decree for the duration of the religious crisis. The police were empowered to break-up unauthorised religious assemblies. Pastors who had resigned their livings and were left without independent means of support were deported as paupers to their villages of origin. In Château-d'Oex Free Church meetings for worship were held secretly. The conspirators, including some of the wealthiest families in Château-d'Oex, planned their survival strategically.

The first service of the Free Church of Château-d'Oex was held on 2 April 1846 in a wood at the Pâquier des Vernes, beyond the gorge leading to the Etivaz valley. The clandestine congregation appointed as its elders Pastor Morel, Pastor Leresine, Notary Favrod-Coune, Notary Isoz, Louis Zulauf, Colin Gétaz and the former mayor Gronicod, who had been dismissed in the Revolution. On 16 August these men shrewdly tried to gain recognition by offering tithes to the new municipal government, but the authorities refused to acknowledge even their money. Next the Free Church 'brothers' discreetly tried to arrange a village service on a market day, as the National Church did, and Madame Rosat offered a private room for the purpose. They surreptitiously publicised communion services to be held at 9 a.m. and 2 p.m. By Easter the congregation had bought a communion chalice for 37 francs. The congregation remained small and autonomous but on 12 March 1847 it sent a delegate to a synod of 33 Free Church chapels meeting in Vevey. Although the government had banned independent congregations from owning property, the élite of Château-d'Oex was wealthy enough, and sufficiently knowledgeable about the law, to buy a house in the name of an individual church member and so open the first chapel in Vaud.

On 19 September 1847 members of the Château-d'Oex chapel honoured the Federal Fast Day, a day of abstinence which had been instituted in several Swiss states after the revolutions of 1830 in the hope of lowering the temperature of religious conflicts which had threatened to bring civil war to many of Switzerland's divided republics. The hope of religious peace proved vain, however, and in November chapel services were again banned and a catechism class was broken-up by municipal officers. Worship was once more organised in secret cells. An atmosphere of recrimination created conflicts within the Free Church and some members were debarred by their fellows from taking communion. By May 1848 proscription had eased and the Château-d'Oex chapel planned a revivalist meeting in the open air with a guest preacher. On the plain tension continued, and in 1849 pastor Scholl was driven out of Lausanne and took refuge in the highland where he gave new heart to the still unauthorised congregation of Château-d'Oex. Pastor Scholl, a relative by marriage of the Henchoz merchants of Rossinière, received shelter and sustenance from his mountain cousins, but less fortunate pastors faced severe poverty or were forced to emigrate to the Americas, to the dismay of their congregations.

The Vaud religious crisis dragged on for five years but by 1851 normality had returned, persecutions had ceased and chapels were tolerated. A Free Church association, sustained by most of the state's theologians, set up both a faculty of theology and a foreign missionary society, but relations between the Free Church and the National Church remained hostile. Even when ministers of the two Château-d'Oex congregations collaborated with some ecumenical harmony their parishioners only met, it was wryly remarked, at funerals. The national congregation lacked trained personnel and the free one lacked state funding. The schism, based on class, party politics and family tradition, was only healed in 1968, and even then some chapel members preferred to join former Darbyites in a new Evangelical Assembly rather than accept integration with the National Church. To make survival of the Free Church difficult the state refused to sell the old chapel to the new Evangelical Assembly and insisted that it be converted for private residential use.

The Vaud revolution of 1845, and the subsequent schism of the Church of Vaud, helped to trigger the civil war of 1847 which pitted most of the 25 Swiss republics against each other. Instability and religious conflict dominated Swiss politics throughout the restoration of 1815 to 1848. Although Château-d'Oex suffered from crises of economic recession and religious persecution it had been saved from the full-scale ravages of religious war which disrupted so many other Swiss boroughs in the post-Napoleonic years. By contrast the old forest republic of Schwytz, which gave Helvetia its popular name of Switzerland, was torn apart in 1832 by a civil war whose secular and ecclesiastical origins were rooted in disputes that had rumbled since the thirteenth century. No sooner had a compromise been achieved and Schwytz re-united, than Basel experienced a similar violent schism. This one proved irreconcilable and Basel city broke away from the republic of Basel to form a 'half-canton' which subsequently joined the Swiss confederation of 1848 with one senator instead of two. Closer to Château-d'Oex, war on the Rhône pitted the Romanic and

Alemannic mini-states of the Valais against each other. The inter-state Diet of the Swiss republics was convened at Zürich to consider peace proposals, but Zürich itself exploded with religious rage and two thousand armed farmers lynched a distinguished theologian of whose preaching they did not approve. Confrontations also broke out in Catholic territories over the status of the 59 Swiss monasteries whose ancient franchises had been restored under the Treaty of Vienna. In Aargau a Liberal government dissolved the ultra-conservative monasteries, accusing the monks of resisting modern social change or even of plotting rebellion. The Habsburgs of Austria, whose family roots were in Aargau and who had sponsored the monastic tradition there, protested vigorously and a finely balanced compromise was found at a meeting of the Swiss Diet, sitting at Bern, though it did not bring lasting peace to Switzerland. The Basel historian Zschokke witnessed rebellion in the Bernese Oberland, anarchy in St Gallen and mob rule in Solothurn. Time, he said, had increased hatred rather than weakened it so that the Swiss pact of 1815 no longer existed in practice but had become a collection of states 'linked by concordats and divided by reprisals'. Tension escalated until conflict engulfed all but two of Switzerland's republics and brought war to the Montbovon frontier within five miles of Château-d'Oex.

The virulence of Protestant Radicalism in the Vaud Revolution of 1845 had seriously disturbed the political confidence of the Catholic states of Switzerland, notably the republic of Fribourg, which hotheaded students at Lausanne threatened to invade while brandishing their swords. The immediate trigger which unleashed the Swiss 'civil war' was not Protestant extremism but Catholic extremism. When the austerely conventional old town of Lucerne faced a rising tide of social change in the cities of the Swiss plain it decided to restore traditional conservatism by inviting the Jesuits to return to the lakeside forest of ancient Switzerland and take charge of education. Nothing could have been more calculated to create alarm. The Jesuit order had been persecuted, repressed and eventually disbanded all over Europe, yet the Swiss ancestral republics proposed to bring back the militant arm of the Catholic Church and entrust to it the education of the élite. All but seven members of the Swiss Diet felt so threatened by such retrogression that they voted to resist by force. Technically the war of 1847 was not a civil war since each of the Swiss states was sovereign and had control over its own army, but in Château-d'Oex the war felt very immediate with Catholic states supporting Lucerne to the east and to the west of the village, and Protestant states supporting the Diet of

Switzerland to the north and to the south, none of them much more than an afternoon's march away.

Although the prelude to the civil war had been long, the fighting was mercifully brief. Vaud invaded Fribourg and symbolically captured the bishop of Lausanne who had been in exile there for three centuries. Zürich defeated Lucerne which lost its status as one of the rotating capitals in which the Swiss Diet has traditionally met. Geneva supplied a Protestant general, Dufour, to lead the anti-Catholic coalition. Bern hosted the victors who, in defiance of the great powers, agreed to alter the terms of the Vienna settlement and create a stronger alliance among the Swiss states. This alliance even establishment a constitution which gave Switzerland a minimal central government for the first time. In the aftermath of the war of 1847 Château-d'Oex became one of the three thousand boroughs which made up the new Confederation of Helvetia.

7
Butchers, Bakers and Candlestick-Makers

In Château-d'Oex the eighteenth century had been the century of the dairy industry *par excellence*. In the nineteenth century the highland cheese industry went into partial decline and had difficulty facing competition from factory cheeses manufactured in proximity to railway stations. Although industrial cheeses did not have the full flavour of cheeses made from the milk of cows that ate Alpine flowers, the lowland cheeses competed very favourably in price with the cheeses of highland artisans. As a consequence the raising of livestock for meat became an increasingly important part of the pastoral economy of the highland. Meat had always been a by-product of dairying, with livestock being sold on the Château-d'Oex cattle market and walked to the abattoirs of the plain. In the depressed years after the Napoleonic wars the meat industry partially eclipsed the dairy industry. Impoverished farmers exported everything they could produce and kept little for themselves. Prime beef was sold to the butchers of Lausanne and in Château-d'Oex even the relatively comfortable professional class was forced to eat meat that was both poor in quality and dear in price according to the complaints of Dean Bridel. Pig meat, rather than beef, was the staple food and local meat consumption consisted of smoked lard or sausage which could be preserved for the hungry season. During the winter, buyers from the neighbouring villages of Ormont, Saanen and Albeuve bought cattle from the Thursday market. At the great Château-d'Oex cattle fairs butchers regularly came from 20 leagues around. The city slaughterhouses on the plain bought young calves, fattened bullocks and exhausted milch-cows. An even wider market was maintained by the tradition of itinerant herdsmen. Before the French Revolution Château-d'Oex had sold cattle to buyers from as far afield as the grasslands of the Vendée on the Atlantic coast of France. Cattle merchants and their cowboys bought as many as 200 spring calves at a time during the May fair and then fattened them on the heathlands and roadsides of France as they herded them home, covering 300 miles during the course of the summer. Meat contractors also came to Château-d'Oex from Italy and walked home to Piedmont with their animals once the spring snows had melted on the St Bernard pass.

One of the great problems of the itinerant cattle trade was that it spread epidemic diseases along the trails. Until the middle of the nineteenth century Château-d'Oex had neither a doctor nor a vet to handle outbreaks of infection either among people or among animals. Experienced farmers had a wide range of herbal and traditional remedies capable of dealing with cattle complaints. They washed incisions with vinegar after performing minor operations. They blew infusions of garlic up the nostrils of cows that were indisposed. They even tried curing stomach bloat, caused through eating frosted grass, by making animals swallow cannon powder, or so Dean Bridel had his readers believe. Local lore in the meat industry also dealt with the complications arising from castrating sheep and bleeding goats. One important conventional cure for sick cows was alcohol distilled from gentian root. The disadvantage of this cure was that all attempts to ban the distilling of gentian gin in the highland and so curb the incidence of alcoholism among mountain farmers, was resisted with the argument that gin was an essential cure for ailing livestock.

Far more difficult to deal with than local and seasonal illnesses were the highly contagious and ultimately fatal outbreaks of foot and mouth disease. Old wives' remedies were quite insufficient to cure even individual cases let alone to prevent contamination from spreading. The government established after the Napoleonic wars by the Republic of Vaud therefore stepped in and took strong measure to protect its cattle wealth and its meat industry. The butchers' trails were closed in times of epidemics and policemen were posted on the Vaud frontiers to enforce the ban on all cattle movements. Cattle quarantine created acute dilemmas for the Château-d'Oex stock farmers. On one side they wanted to protect their herds from imported alien diseases, but on the other hand they needed to sell stock to the export markets in order to survive. Conflicts over the enforcement of quarantine, and over breaches of trade prohibition, were fierce and frequent. The crises affected not only the butchers but also the dairy farmers. Surviving cheesemakers continued to hire dairy cattle from the plain during the summer season. The government closure of the trails to beef cattle also

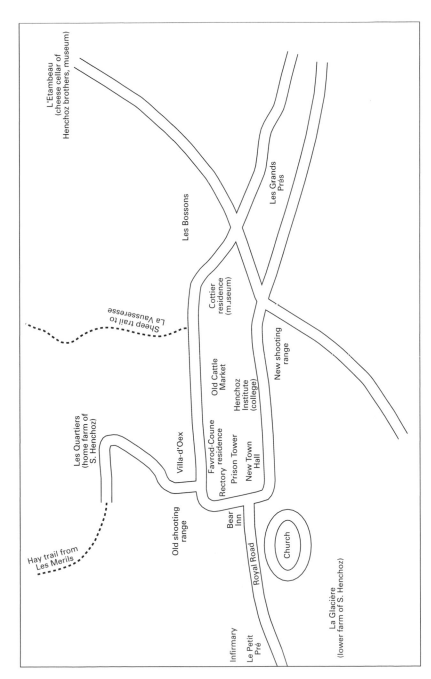

Sketch map 7.1 Château-d'Oex cart tracks before the railway

meant restrictions on the movement of dairy cows which were just as liable to carry infection.

In Château-d'Oex the meat trade was traditionally associated with a small ancillary industry of leather and skins. When domestic animals were butchered in Château-d'Oex, rather than exported on the hoof, their hides were tanned for local needs. The evidence can be found in the accounts of Samuel Henchoz who bargained carefully over the value of the leather on any side of beef which he bought to be dried for his own winter use. Trading in leather was yet another of his many-sided earning activities. In January 1756 he bought nine pounds of leather at seven-and-a-half pence a pound from David Morier, the tanner who worked at the lower end of the village. He also bought two rather expensive calf skins with which to make boots and six penny-worth of calf's hair for an undisclosed purpose. As usual Samuel was tardy in settling his account with the tanner but a year later he finally paid him with a Portuguese sovereign worth 205 pence and received as change a French sovereign worth 160 pence.

Farm work in the highlands required good footwear, summer and winter, and tanned leather had to be available for both local and itinerant bootmakers. David Massard, the eighteenth-century cobbler at the Villa d'Oex, made house visits to his customers and visited Samuel Henchoz at home to undertake his shoe repairs. On one occasion, rather than wait endlessly for a cash settlement, the cobbler accepted as a form of barter payment an old pair of boots which Samuel was sure he would be able to refurbish and sell. New boots represented a considerable outlay, one recorded pair requiring seven-and-a-half pounds of the best leather valued at 62½ pence. Making the boots required two days' labour, only a little more than the time taken in the twentieth century by an Italian cobbler in the village who charged 14 hours of labour for a pair of handmade boots. Old cobbler Massard charged Samuel Henchoz six pence for his time and craftsmanship plus an extra penny for the resin needed to glue on the wooden heels that helped keep his feet above the all pervasive farmyard mud. Once again he had to accept partial payment in kind, this time some worn leather uppers that he hoped to re-use to make secondhand boots. Nothing was ever wasted on a peasant holding or in a cobbler's workshop.

Toward the end of the nineteenth century state intervention brought about a new policy of improving and standardising Château-d'Oex's previously very mixed livestock. Up until then mixed herds had been maintained which indiscriminately produced cheese, butter, beef or leather depending on how the markets rose or fell. In the 1880s a decision was taken by the state of Vaud to concentrate on rearing only red-and-white Simmental cattle. The Simmental became internationally prized as a beef animal and the change of policy on breeds may have reflected the growth in relative importance of beef rearing as compared to highland dairying. In Vaud Simmentals became all-purpose animals used for haulage on the plain and for dairy production in the highland as well as for the meat trade. The Vaud department of agriculture licensed Château-d'Oex to pasture 853 Simmental cows, 776 heifers, 428 calves and 29 bulls, each bull being entitled to a double ration of grazing. The limits were very precisely calculated to prevent over-grazing, land deterioration and soil erosion. In addition to the licensed number of Simmentals, the borough was permitted to maintain 44 horses for cartage, 297 sheep to graze grass that was too steep for cows, 212 goats to browse shrubs too coarse for sheep and 195 pigs to live off scraps, whey and waste. Over a 20-year period state intervention so improved the quality of Château-d'Oex cattle that in 1906 the borough won no less than 100 prizes at the great autumn cattle fair held in Lausanne. The prize monies were worth 5889 francs to the farmers and the prize certificates were proudly nailed to the front of each barn. For the state of Vaud the reputation of its highland Simmentals became of international economic importance. A Château-d'Oex bull called Diamond won the supreme championship in Milan and a Château-d'Oex cow called Marquise was sold to the Ottoman sultan and shipped to Constantinople.

Despite the success of the Simmental breeding programme the Swiss Society for Alpine Economy expressed its anxiety over Château-d'Oex's animal husbandry in a report written in 1908. The society recognized that good farming practice had developed during the centuries of Bern domination, but complained that scientific methods had subsequently been neglected by backward highland pastoralists. The society's scientists had a rather weak perception of the economic factors which governed peasant choice over the use of land and labour in the highland, but their report provided interesting insights into nineteenth-century practices. Farming remained ecologically precarious and land saved from erosion for beef ranching still needed constant protection from noxious plants such as the inedible matt grass, known locally as dog's hair, which drove out edible sweet grasses. Other plants that persistently invaded the pasture were small spruce trees, Alpine rhododendrons, juniper bushes, bell heather, bilberries, yellow gentians and thistles. Once these inedible plants had been dug out the edible grasses needed to be encouraged by spreading slurry. With adequate investment this liquid manure could be taken to the fields in barrels on wheels, drawn by horses, but many farmers simply allowed their slurry to flow out of the farm buildings causing a stench around the house and quagmires by the water troughs. Spilt slurry and the over-manuring of fields below the cattle sheds encouraged nettles and docks rather than edible meadow grass.

In the nineteenth century farm improvements required capital investments which were not available in times of persistent economic depression. Farmers continued to switch from dairying to the simpler and cheaper practice of beef rearing. Despite the eighteenth-century land consolidations at the height of the dairy boom, many Château-d'Oex farms remained very small. In 1906 the high farms in the parish of Etivaz were large, but in the parish of Château-d'Oex proper, the average holding consisted of seventeen hectares of pasture, two hectares of woodland and one hectare of fenced land set aside for crops, orchards and vegetable gardens. Château-d'Oex had 145 working farms some with as few as ten head of cattle. The value of an average farm was 12 000 francs and the rent which an owner could expect to earn from a tenant was 400 francs, a return on capital of three per cent. To prevent any tenant from trying to squeeze a few additional francs from the holding, livestock controls were stringently maintained. In a bad season inspectors could compulsorily bring cattle down from a vulnerable alp regardless of any loss to the farmer or the tenant.

The economic result of the partial shift from cheesemaking to beef rearing enriched the butchers but had adverse social consequences for farm labourers in Château-d'Oex. Fewer farm staff were required than hitherto, since herding bullocks was less labour intensive than milking. The beef industry also required less skill than dairying and bullocks could be cared for by young herd-boys. The Château-d'Oex cheesemakers had to look elsewhere for employment. Since a Château-d'Oex apprenticeship in cheesemaking was deemed to be one of the best in Vaud, if not in Switzerland, selling dairying skills by seasonal migration became an option for some redundant farm workers. Each spring about one hundred Château-d'Oex dairymen, both married men and bachelors, set out to find seasonal employment in the new dairy farms of the Jura mountains on the far side of the Vaud plain. On the Jura farms they expected to receive free, if spartan, food and dry lodging in a hay barn. Those who did well could expect to return home in the autumn with savings of five gold sovereigns. Such a sum, although only about one-tenth of what Samuel Henchoz, the landowner, or Dean Bridel, the pastor, expected to earn in a year, was good money. The alternative to migrant farm work could have been domestic service in the city but Dean Bridel, in his inimitable way, pointed out that servants were expected to be so deferential and obsequious that free highlanders would have found the oppression unbearable. At least farm labourers ate at the same table as their employers. A labourer began working life in the stables at the age of ten and was paid in cheese rather than in coin. When tall enough to wield a scythe a labourer was able to earn piece-rate money in ratio to the amount of hay mown each day. This enabled him to start saving up to buy his first cow. A good mowing man could earn fifteen pence plus his food in a day. The problem with piece work, however, was that the available number of days of work was variable. For many, therefore, leaving home for a one-hundred-day season in the Jura was a more reliable source of income than remaining in Château-d'Oex and living off thin soup of potato, turnip or cabbage.

A decline in the dairy industry did not alter the harsh realities of Château-d'Oex's seasonal climate and beef cattle still needed a winter supply of hay. This hay continued to be harvested on even the steepest slopes. One of these was the Meril valley, next to the Vauseresse, under the high ridge which protected Château-d'Oex from the north wind. The track through a steep wood to the hay fields was maintained by an ancient fraternity. This voluntary association kept order among the haymakers and imposed on each a *corvée* of labour service. Some of the fields were so inaccessible that they could only be reached by ladders which scaled the rock. Such was the poverty of nineteenth-century cattlemen that they found it necessary to harvest hay in these inaccessible and dangerous places with the hope of sustaining one more animal over the winter and so improving their meagre earnings when the butchers came to the fair.

The high slopes of the Merils had two haymaking seasons. The summer crop was cut in July when hay harvesting had been completed in the valley. The autumn crop from the mountain was cut in September when the cows were expected down from the alp to eat the last grass around the village. The mountain haymakers set off early on Monday morning carrying a week's supply of food in large shoulder baskets together with scythes, hay-rakes, pitchforks, whet stones, ropes, and a pair of boots with steel spikes to hold their soles firm on slippery grass slopes. In the early years of the twentieth century the 25 owners of the 60-odd hay plots slept in ten shelters scattered across the mountain. Each shelter was built so low, almost underground, that a winter avalanche could pass over the top of it without doing serious damage. Each shed was equipped with a three-legged cast iron stove, a folding table and a sleeping shelf covered with hay on which the workers slept, fully-clothed, like sardines. Cutting began at dawn, providing that the dew was not too heavy on the grass. After an early lunch, tossing, turning and raking went on all afternoon often in torrid heat. In the evening dry hay was stacked into round ricks anchored to a central pole. If the work was completed in good time the cutting could begin again before nightfall. Children were sent up the mountain with fresh provisions and some stayed to help fathers and uncles rake and stack the hay. It was taken to the ricks in huge rope nets. Men bent double carried loads of nearly 100 kg. Twenty loads made a standard hay rick. In 1947, when the hay crop was particularly poor down in the valley, the mountain owners were able to harvest 100 ricks of hay off their Meril slopes. Some years later the quality of the hand-cut hay was so exceptional that farmers paid for the cost of bringing their nets of hay off the mountain by helicopter rather than waiting for winter to haul them down on hand sledges.

The valley of Meril, full of wild spring narcissi, was familiar territory to the people of Château-d'Oex. Each of its slopes retained its medieval Romanic name: Trontzet, or Planai, or Létchiaux, or Poutelanche, or Botsar. Since the Gruyère partition of 1555 the hay fields represented a foreign border running along the crest of the mountain, the 'frontier of sovereignty' as it was described on the maps. On the far side were Roman Catholic neighbours in the state of Fribourg whose herds of goats browsed the north-facing slope of the mountain. Sometimes their herdboys crept over the summit and allowed their beasts to eat their fill from the waiting Château-d'Oex hay ricks. On 9 September 1856 Louis David Chabloz, the special constable on duty that day, received complaints about illicit grazing and hay stealing on land belonging to the sisters Suzanne and Margarite Desquartiers. He climbed the steep track in haste and found three nanny-goats, three young kids, two billy-goats and one sheep eating from a hay rick. As he led them away he met a shepherd boy from Fribourg who gave his name as Joseph Pittan. The boy begged the constable not to impound the animals or charge him before the Château-d'Oex magistrates. He said he would be in mortal trouble with his adult employers, the goats' owners, if they knew he had been caught. The child agreed to pay a fine for trespassing and appropriate damages to the sisters Desquartiers, if only he could be permitted to take the goats back across the mountain to the village of Lessoc.

Trespassing and crop damage by herds of animals being led from one pasture to another, and from the farm to the slaughterhouse, were common. A few weeks after the Meril incident a cattle merchant at Saanen sent his son, Antoine Hauswirth, to deliver a flock of 60 sheep to Vevey market. He expected them to feed as they went, grazing the grass verges of the track that led through Château-d'Oex. When passing the village lime kilns the sheep broke into the land of David Moïse Rosat, illegally grazing his field, whereupon the shepherd was brought before the justice of the peace. The problems caused by errant animals on their way to market were compounded by the problems caused by dissolute shepherds on their way home from market. In December 1856 Abraham Lenoir, returning from Bulle market at eleven o'clock at night with his herd boy, stopped at the tavern in Les Moulins. He spent some of his market earnings by illegally ordering a late night brandy from a publican known for generously bending the licensing laws and permitting weary travellers some latitude in their drinking time. Like the shepherd from Saanen, Lenoir was caught by the police and taken before the justices.

Butchers walking their live animals to market had a relatively easy task in comparison with the transport problems of highland bakers. Bread of changing quality, consistency and content was a traditional staple food in Château-d'Oex. The bakers' bread ovens had traditionally been communal ones which were carefully regulated, in an attempt to minimise fire hazards, and taxed, to provide successive sovereign régimes with a regular income. In 1800 Château-d'Oex had four communal bread ovens which were listed among the buildings destroyed by the village fire. The village dependence on bakers meant that bakers were vulnerable to village anger when bread was scarce and expensive. The expense of bread was governed by the price and availability of corn. Historically the most important corn crop in Château-d'Oex had been barley which was mixed with wheat and bean flour to make bread. In the eighteenth century, as has been noted, potato flour was widely mixed with barley meal to make hard biscuits that served in place of bread. In the nineteenth century Château-d'Oex, like much of Europe, developed a growing taste for wheaten bread. Increasing quantities of wheat had to be imported from the plain along the unsatisfactory cart track. Once in the highland the loose grain was entrusted to millers to be ground into flour. Bakers, like all other consumers of flour, were dependent on the expensive and often restricted services of the millers. Some millers became bakers themselves, thereby competing with their wholesale customers and restricting the choice of supplier available to consumers.

Millers were among the most unpopular people in the whole of the Sarine valley. Everyone who took corn to the miller expected to be cheated. Every miller was accused of attempting to enhance his or her profits by 'losing' some of the raw grain, by 'stealing' some of the bran residue, or by falsifying the accounts and deliberately adding moisture to the finished flour to make it heavier. A set of regulations concerning the milling of flour is pinned in a watermill museum near Le Locle in the Jura:

> The miller is required to mill any grains that are brought to him. His wife and children are also required to work carefully in the mill. All grain is to be accurately weighed on delivery. The mill shall be open from 6 am in summer, 7 am in spring and autumn, and 8 am in winter with a lunch break from 11 till 2. Once ground the flour is again to be carefully weighed together with the bran that comes out of the grain and the loss of weight shall not exceed 6 per cent. The miller shall take particular care, especially in damp weather, that no moisture shall get into the flour and so increase its weight. He shall keep by him a smooth steel rod which tapers at one end. This rod shall be inserted into each sack and if any flour clings to it which cannot be shaken off by a gentle tap then he shall be deemed to have moistened the flour.

Château-d'Oex had four clusters of great waterwheels which provided power not only to grind corn but also to pound cloth, crush bones, saw planks and tan leather. The main corn mills were those situated along the banks of a leat which ran through the hamlet of Les Moulins, the 'village of the mills'. This leat came off the fast flowing stream that came down from Etivaz. The mills were conveniently close to the old stone bridge across the river and to the mile-long metalled road up which horses could haul carts to the village. In order to become a miller an aspiring entrepreneur required a license. Although the business had great potential for profit, it was also one with considerable financial risk. The most unpredictable risk was the weather. The torrents of Château-d'Oex were capable of such sudden fluxes that mills were frequently damaged by rolling boulders or clogged by floods of mud. The mills were also subjected to the more human risk of heavy demands from tax collectors. Since the days of the counts of Gruyère the mills had been licensed and millers had paid for their semi-monopolistic rights. Tax collecting from millers and bakers had once been farmed out to monks, but under the rule of Bern it was the state which controlled the licensing and taxing of mills.

In the late seventeenth century the licensee of one mill at Les Moulins had been a widowed immigrant. Her father had lived in the Ormont district on the south side of the mountain and her late husband had been Zachary Massard, a local citizen. Her financial 'tutor', François Turrian, obtained the mill license for her at an annual fee of six Lausanne pence plus 'six full-weight Château-d'Oex measures of local wheat carefully milled'. She also paid a turnover tax in silver at the feast of St Martin and a corn-harvest tax due at the feast of the Three Kings in January. In addition to a grindstone, the widow's water-wheel was equipped with a stamp mill for hemp. The fee for the stamp mill had to be paid either with six hogsheads of raw hemp or with the equivalent in hanks of finished hemp ready to be fitted to a spindle for spinning. The mill was also capable of fulling cloth for which a tax of twelve 'authentic' Lausanne pennies was charged each year. The mill was to be exempt from tax if it fell into ruin, but as an incentive to keep the mill working the miller was freed from feudal dues so long as she lived and worked on the premises. The concessions had been granted to her father-in-law, George Massard, on 26 August 1649 by the honourable senator John-Jacob Bucher of Bern then serving as lord-bailiff of the highland.

Disputes over water rights on the several mill races of Château-d'Oex kept the mill owners in a frequent state of conflict. In 1733 one such conflict broke out at Gérignoz, on a stream two miles up-river from Château-d'Oex. The lower mill had fallen into disrepair and the license was taken over by David 'the German' who wanted to bring the mill back into commission. He applied for the right to add a stamp mill for tanning hides to the installation. He also wanted to extend the capacity of the mill from one wheel to two. The licensee of the upper mill, Jacques-Louis Henchoz, officially objected, saying that the planning application went beyond the 'customary usage' for which rights had historically been granted. He produced parchment permits dated 1702, 1712 and 1716 showing that he had the right to operate a stamp mill and that his corn mill traditionally paid to the castle six measures of barley per annum. He further claimed that the lower mill had never had a tanning capacity, that it had only ever paid three measures of barley in tax and that it had never been licensed for two waterwheels. To emphasize his case Henchoz also protested that his new neighbour had only told him of his plans in Alemannic dialect and that he could not understand this 'German' speech.

The case of the Gérignoz mills was deemed sufficiently important to be heard by the 'avoyer' who presided over the Bern senate. Processing the complaint took four years and it did not reach the high court until

1737. The certified documentation relating to the rights and obligations of the lower mill had been mislaid, but the new licensee was able to produce a deed of sale dated 21 March 1583 which included reference to a fulling mill for cloth. Since the mill itself had been burnt down the tribunal could not inspect the machinery but was obliged to work from oral testimony in order to establish its traditional mode of functioning. One witness, an 80-year-old blacksmith called Jean Morier-Genoud, described how 62 years earlier he had met a former owner of the mill in Bern while he himself had been apprenticed to a blacksmith in the city. He recalled that the old mill owner had gained permission to rebuild the mill according to 'customary usage' but had failed to raise the necessary capital to bring it back into commission. When Morier-Genoud had finished his apprenticeship and qualified as a smith he returned to Château-d'Oex and helped the mill owner to restore the mill by forging for him the necessary iron pieces for the mechanism. The mill had been restarted, he testified, according to the terms of a valid license and despite the protests of rival mill owners. Such was the acrimony stretching across generations, it affected not only the competing saw mills, corn mills and stamp mills of Gérignoz, but also those at Etivaz where the river was called the Tourneresse, the stream which turns the saw mills.

In addition to the butchers, and all the trades associated with meat, and the bakers, together with the related millers, hauliers and corn merchants, Château-d'Oex boasted a tradition of artisans that might be epitomised by candlestick-makers. Some households probably had their own candle moulds, though none has been noted in wills or inventories, but other users probably bought ready-made candles. By the nineteenth century candles were extensively used though in earlier days domestic lighting had sometimes been supplied by small oil-lamps of pottery with floating wicks. Since little or no vegetable oil was available in Château-d'Oex the traditional fuel had been butter. Melted butter burning through a wick probably gave off unpleasant smoke for a limited amount of light. By the twentieth century paraffin made from mineral oil had become the main lamp fuel but it was imported and expensive. Candles, by contrast, could be made from local ingredients, the preferred raw material being beeswax. Bonstetten had been particularly interested in the potential of the highland for wax production and described the beekeeping practices of his Rougemont neighbours in some detail. At the other end of the valley the Henchoz family of Rossinière initially built up some of the capital that made them into wealthy cheesemongers by trading in wax. In the nineteenth century the wax industry grew in scale as beekeepers increased the quantities of honey they produced in association with candle wax.

The use of candles in a village built exclusively of timber was rigorously controlled by the police. Fire had always been, and long remained, one of the great causes of popular fear and insecurity in Switzerland. Several times a year one or another village of the highland, or small town of the plain, was seriously ravaged by fire. Any negligence by one burgher dropping a candle on a straw-strewn floor, or by one chambermaid taking a naked light up to a bedroom, put all members of the community at risk. A house fire could devastate neighbouring dwellings or even spread to a whole village. A cowman entering a stall with a lighted pipe in his mouth was punishable by fine. So too was any dairyman caught doing his early milking by the flame of an unprotected candle. Local by-laws insisted that candles must be encased in lanterns. Traditional lanterns were made of thin panels of translucent cow horn. These were later replaced by more efficient imported lanterns comprising metal holders with glass panels. Candles were used not only in cow sheds but also in the workrooms of women. In order to make lace after dark the light of a single candle on a workbench was magnified by surrounding it with glass decanters containing clear water. In spite of the strict regulations governing the use of candles accidents regularly occurred. To try to prevent disasters the Château-d'Oex voluntary fire brigade was regularly drilled and its fire-carts and fire-hoses were frequently inspected and repaired. Despite all precautions, however, the whole village was destroyed by fire on three occasions.

In 1798 Château-d'Oex had been lucky to escape the damage that the French invasion had inflicted on some Alpine villages which soldiers put to the torch while seeking food and hunting down escapees. Before the revolution was over, however, Château-d'Oex had nevertheless passed through the cataclysm of fire. Rumours that the fire had been the work of arsonists abounded, but in reality the disaster seems to have been due to an accident. The fire was not a particularly large one, in national terms, but it was spectacular and it attracted much sympathy from villages in other Swiss states. Château-d'Oex had been reasonably generous to other boroughs when they had appealed for help in rebuilding properties destroyed by the revolutionary armies of 1798. Château-d'Oex was, moreover, quite well known in cultural and literary circles through the patriotic writings and sentimental poems of its energetic pastor, Dean Bridel. Nearer to hand the people of Romanic Switzerland had seen the night sky light up behind the mountains and knew, even as far away as the Jura principality of

Neuchâtel, that another village had gone up in flames. The loss of life in the Château-d'Oex fire was limited to one old man who was visiting his relatives and died trying to rescue his possessions. The loss of property, on the other hand, was comprehensive.

The great fire, however frightful, did not come as a complete surprise. Château-d'Oex was a village notoriously at risk having already burnt down twice before, once in 1664 and again in 1741. In July 1800 the village was suffering from a scorching heat-wave and all the inhabitants had been asked to keep full pails of water on their door steps as a precautionary measure should any candle be dropped or should sparks escape from any kitchen or smithy during the drought. The fire broke out at half-past-one in the morning and spread across the thin roofs of wooden shingles around the square and down the street. Although the village fountain had a copious supply of water, and five good fire-pumps were available, there was no stopping the blaze. It spread up the church motte, through the bushes, and into the trees from which it reached the church bell tower. The tower roof fell in with a shower of sparks, thereby threatening isolated houses which had to be protected with wet blankets. Wooden palisades and dry bramble hedges also carried the fire like fuses of tinder and had to be hastily ripped up or cut down lest bush fires should creep as far as the dry galleries of forest that had seen no rain for a month. The final toll was 42 houses, 4 granaries, 18 barns and cow sheds, and 27 shops full of merchandise, all burnt down. Clay pots were vitrified by the heat and gold coin turned to tiny droplets under the debris. The Rossinière fire-pumps arrived to help but only three houses could be saved. The old rectory was sufficiently far up-wind to be unaffected, but the new rectory above the square was surrounded by burning buildings. Its timbers, holding a tiled roof above stone walls, were constantly sprayed with water by courageous firemen wrapped in wet clothing. They managed to save all of Dean Bridel's property and papers.

The new rectory was a fine eighteenth-century dwelling that had been built over the cellars of a large family house which had previously been destroyed in an isolated fire in 1716. The building and its cellars immediately became the repository for food aid as cheese, butter, milk and salt were brought in from the country farms. Four bakeries had been burnt down, together with their stocks of corn and flour, and Rougemont therefore baked large quantities of extra bread to feed the 52 Château-d'Oex families who were destitute. Two days later Saanen sent five hundredweight of loaves as a gift. Gruyère, Bulle, Lausanne and Vevey all sent carts loaded with clothing and bedding up the highland track. Teams of women sorted the gifts in the rectory store rooms, distributed the relief supplies to the victims and wrote touching letters of gratitude to the donors. On Sunday a service of worship was held in the burnt-out village square with the stone mounting-block serving as a pulpit. The congregation was crowded with parishioners in mourning and with strangers come to view the smouldering ashes. Bridel reported that no less than 36 of the village's great family Bibles had been lost and he appealed for help in replacing them. Although book dealers from Moudon and Lausanne were able to supply the congregation with a selection of religious pamphlets, only four bound Bibles were offered to the village.

The farming families who lived on the motte below the church lost their homes and their movable possessions, but managed to rescue any livestock that had not gone up to the alp and thereby saved their essential means of livelihood. The shopkeepers and the artisans, by contrast, depended for their subsistence on the tools of their trade and on their stocks of materials. It was they who lost virtually everything they possessed in the fire. Half of the victims were merchants who owned no land and therefore had no basic resource from which to rebuild family businesses. One preliminary estimate of the damage was 205 490 Helvetian francs. A wide-ranging appeal was needed to begin to raise such a sum and the village approached its pastor for help. Before agreeing to launch an appeal Bridel presented his stern conditions to the village. He would only try to assemble a building fund for Château-d'Oex on the strict condition that the village should be rebuilt in stone and mortar and that the houses should in future be roofed with baked tiles rather than wooden shingles. The terms were onerous since rebuilding in timber would have been quicker and cheaper than building in new materials unfamiliar to local craftsmen. But since the wooden village, built after the fire of 1741, had been burnt down again in less than 60 years the logic of Bridel's argument was persuasive. A general assembly in the village agreed to rebuild in stone. Permission was then obtained from the revolutionary provisional government to open public subscriptions in no less than three of the 'provinces' of the new Helvetia, in Léman otherwise known as Vaud, in Fribourg and in Oberland, the now autonomous highland of Bern. Bridel himself went further afield and undertook a lecture tour to Neuchâtel and Basel where he raised 5000 francs towards the appeal.

The largest public task that faced Château-d'Oex after the great fire was the building of a new town hall incorporating the public inn. A large plot of land was cleared on the eastern side of the square, where the arches of the old covered market had been, and children were hired at five pence a day to dig the new foundations. 'Citizen Director' Turrian sold boulders from his land to 'Borough Treasurer' Gétaz for the foundations. Since all architecture in Château-d'Oex had previously been based on carpentry no masons were locally available to lay stones and migrant masons from Italy had to be hired to build the walls. Cut stone to make the frames and lintels of the doors and windows was quarried on a farm called the *Chalet de Pierre* which the borough owned. On 27 June 1801, nearly a year after the fire, a payment of 160 florins was made in coin to the stonecutter while the carter who carried the stones was paid his wages in wine. To sift the large quantities of sand that Jean-David Favrod-Coune and David Marmie dug from the river bed on the farm of Chamaveau a large builder's sieve had to be bought in Vevey. To make enough lime for the building appropriate limestone was brought on sledges from the Etivaz quarry belonging to 'Borough President' Bornet. Aaron Rosat was paid three florins to stack the wood that was needed to fire the lime kiln. The great beams for the town hall roof were floated down the river from the saw mills at Gérignoz. When hauling the timbers up from the riverbank to the village square with a hired bull the rope broke. It had been borrowed from Béat Desquartiers and the borough had to buy a new one. The planks for the flooring were apparently cut over a saw pit on the site rather than in a saw mill. The sawyer, David Turrian, charged ten farthings for cutting short cross planks and seven pence for each long one.

To continue functioning normally the borough hired the services of a number of local specialists while the town hall was being re-built. Abraham Cottier charged 25 florins to restore the village sun dial and calculate the hour marks appropriate to the locality. The great press used to seal official documents had to be repaired and a new bench was bought on which to install it. Temporary office accommodation cost 40 florins in the house of David Gétaz, and David Pilet provided a temporary tavern for travellers. For eight months a strongroom had to be hired as the tax receiver's interim office. One of the mysteries of the fire concerned the archives which, according to records surviving from before the fire, had been housed in a secure, fire-proof, building. After the fire Albert Byrde was hired to repair the archive roof with materials supplied by Aaron Rosat, and Samuel Morier was commissioned to reorganise the surviving papers. The reorganisation may have been a little too radical, however, and although some early records of Château-d'Oex do survive in the borough archives, many others are no longer available. The loss of historic documents was compounded by the fact that when Château-d'Oex changed sovereignty two years before the fire some, but not all, of the village's national records were transferred from Bern to Lausanne.

By the autumn of 1801 the new town hall was ready to have the fire-proof tiles hung on its huge roof. A first delivery of 8550 tiles proved quite insufficient and another 4000 had to be ordered. They may have been fired locally in a kiln that had been set up on the stream at Les Bossons, a few hundred yards away, to supply the new stone buildings being erected along the high street. Nails to hang the tiles, 20 000 of them, had to be bought from Bulle market. The roof was topped with two zinc pommels costing 50 florins. The glass panes for the 24 casement windows cost 533 florins. The balcony of forged iron, from which ceremonial speeches were made on high days and holidays, was an expensive item costing 463 florins. The borough publican, Bertholet, bought two huge door locks in Vevey for the oak doors of the public bar on the ground floor. An Alemannic carpenter who came to build the doors lodged with Widow Zulauf for 16 days at the borough's expense. Heating the town hall adequately and safely required three stoves built of stone and decorated with glazed tiles which cost in all five gold sovereigns. To complete the work a master plasterer was brought from Albeuve, the village in the lower valley that had once belonged to the bishop of Lausanne. He painted the tribunal chamber in colour and whitewashed the cellar ceilings. The overall cost of the building had been considerable. The secretary to the commission for reconstruction received 30 433 florins, worth some 12 000 francs, in the first year of the appeal. This represented ten times the amount which the borough received in rent from its largest farm and 20 times the income generated by the town hall bar and hostelry. Much of the cost of construction was met from loans which Dean Bridel was able to negotiate at five per cent interest.

Large quantities of timber were required to rebuild the village even though walls were now built of stone. Timber was Château-d'Oex's most important economic asset after cheese and beef. Throughout the nineteenth century the logging industry continued to face great problems over transport. Medieval woodmen had been required to haul timber over the snow to their sovereign's castle, and early modern foresters had devised the ingenious sluice for flushing firewood off the mountain and down to the furnaces of the Bex salt works near the Rhône. Nineteenth-century solutions to the problem of how to improve the profits from forestry were equally diverse but the industry continued to sell raw wood rather than to increase its value by encouraging craft industries to make finished goods for export. The hauling of logs from the high forests to the local hamlets continued to be undertaken by horses until well past the middle of the twentieth century. There the great waterwheels were used to saw planks of spruce and fir which was stacked up high by the saw mills of Etivaz, Gérignoz and Les Moulins to be seasoned for the building industry. The entire supply of fuel for domestic heating and cooking was also hauled out of the forests. Beech was the favoured fuel but spruce was cheaper and much more commonly used both in the home and to heat the cauldrons in the dairy farms. Larch wood was the best quality coniferious timber and was used for making dairy equipment and kitchen utensils as well as water pipes and drinking troughs.

Logging was an arduous and controversial industry. The damage that the lumberjacks did by hauling logs and scattering bark chippings was notorious as has been seen in the legal case of the Widow Chabloz whose land adjoined the Vauseresse common forest. Clearing up the bark added to the labour and expense of timber extraction but provided little in the way of ancillary revenue. Unlike oak bark, which was a valuable resource in the tanning industry, spruce bark was of limited secondary use and not even appreciated as fuel. To survive, the logging industry depended on extremely cheap labour that would otherwise have been unemployed out of the hay mowing and cheese-making season. Lumberjacks, like the Meril haymakers, lived during the week in rudimentary mountain shacks and only came home to do their laundry and restock their food-baskets on Sundays. The greatest expense of logging was the maintenance of the teams of horses for whom scarce fodder, normally preserved for the dairy industry, had to be purchased. Whereas a dairy farmer could head-load a great cheese to Vevey or even bring a two hundredweight net of hay down from the mountain on his back, a logger required more than human strength. The lumberjacks who felled trees on the steep slopes above the farms therefore tied whole tree trunks together with chains for the horses to haul out over the snow. It was dangerous work and while hay-carriers often suffered from hernias, loggers commonly saw their careers blighted by broken limbs that had been poorly set by amateur physicians.

The nineteenth-century method of exporting timber was to float logs down the Sarine river. Timber floating was as difficult and dangerous as log rolling down the hillsides but in the absence of alternative economic opportunities the export of raw wood grew in scale. By the end of the century thousands of full-size tree trunks were being thrown into the river each season. With a little daring help from lumberjacks who jumped from trunk to trunk the logs shot the rapids at La Chaudanne and at La Tine and were carried down the lower valley. There they were purchased by the great saw mills of the state of Fribourg. River logging had many disadvantages quite apart from the danger to life and limb. The local Château-d'Oex saw mills, powered by water, lost part of their business to the much bigger mills of the plain. As the profits of these lowland mills grew they were able to switch their circular saws from direct water power to new and more versatile hydro-electric power. The big mills had the added advantage of being close to the new steam railways of the plain which could carry semi-processed timber to city building sites. Back in Château-d'Oex, meanwhile the floating of uncut logs did great damage to the farming industry. Fast flowing tree trunks constantly breached the dykes which protected the best watermeadows and damaged the bridges which the borough had to maintain at public expense. Objections to timber floating failed to stem the trade until the very end of the nineteenth century. Thereafter it was modernisation that stopped the river traffic when hydro-electric dams were built on the Sarine. The timber trade was then rescued from oblivion by the construction of a mountain railway which hauled out the logs.

One of the important ancillary crafts associated with forestry was charcoal burning. In the nineteenth century Château-d'Oex became a significant supplier of charcoal for Swiss iron furnaces which had no supplies of coal. No iron stone was available in the western Alps but good quality ore was mined on the far side of the plain in the Jura mountains and the state of Solothurn developed an important iron industry dominated by the firm of Von Rolle. In Château-d'Oex all waste timber, off-cuts from the saw mills, branches from the undergrowth and wood flawed by knots or warping, was securely tied in great bundles. These bundles were then thrown into the river, floated down the valley past the Fribourg saw mills, and eventually reached Solothurn at the foot of the Jura 60 miles away. There they were fished out of the water, dried, and turned into charcoal to fuel the great iron furnaces. The profits to the highland woodmen were not great but in the deeply impoverished nineteenth century every scrap of foreign income was welcome.

The history of local charcoal burning as one of the forest industries of the highland was brought to prominence in an unexpected manner. The most famous craftsman in the history of Château-d'Oex was a charcoal burner called Hauswirth. He was an Alemannic recluse who came from Saanen and lived alone in the forest that separated

Château-d'Oex from the isolated valley of Etivaz. He travelled the
length and breadth of the highland, building his great mounds of
timber, covering them with turf, and then slowly burning them for a
week until the wood had carbonised. During his travels he stayed with
his customers on local farms but was a taciturn man who made few
friends. He repaid farmers for their over-night hospitality with his artistic works made of cut-out paper. Although he had huge fingers and
thumbs he used a tiny pair of scissors to make the most delicate
tableaux. He eventually became, albeit posthumously, one of the most
famous paper-cut artists of Switzerland.

Hauswirth died, remote and alone, in 1871. Over the decades
Château-d'Oex artists and antiquarians were gradually able to build up,
exhibit and publish a small collection of his work. The art of paper-
cutting, sometimes with scissors rather than with knives in the Chinese
style, had old roots in Alemannic forest societies. Hauswirth began his
artistic career by making conventional black on white mirror-image
cut-outs of complex Alpine scenes. These showed columns of cows
climbing up to the high pastures accompanied by pigs, goats, cats and
the cauldron porter. He later experimented with coloured cut-outs,
using toffee papers to make delicate miniatures. After that he embarked
on collage, assembling immense and intricate pictures by combining
many tiny scenes and by using a multiplicity of vivid colours. The
traditional mirror-image remained the base of his tableaux but individual items of the collage were single cut-outs which enabled him to
include more motifs in each picture. The hallmark of each genuine
piece of Hauswirth art was a cottage gate, always shut, and always with
himself on the outside looking in. His life was undoubtedly a sad one
but his genius inspired successive later generations of cut-out artists
who flourished in Château-d'Oex. One of them, Louis Saugy of the
saw-mill hamlet of Gérignoz, created a fine collage on the logging
industry, and another, Marianne Ginier, became the custodian of the
Château-d'Oex museum and its collection of cut paper art.

One of the great questions of the nineteenth-century history of
Château-d'Oex concerns the failure of cottage industries to take root
in the highland. Château-d'Oex did not become a centre for small-
scale local manufacturing and did not receive significant piece work
farmed out by entrepreneurs in the Swiss cities. Elsewhere in apparently comparable communities across Switzerland nineteenth-century
industrialists exploited sweated labour and soaked up the underemployed hours of the rural poor. The industries were based on the finishing of textiles, the handmaking of fine metal parts, or the crafting of

wooden objects. All attempts to graft such activities on to the work practices of Château-d'Oex failed. Even crafts relating to the labour-intensive use of wood made little progress though they might have seemed to have the greatest chance of success in view of the available local skills and materials. The closest that the highland came to developing a truly local cottage industry was in the creation of black lace bonnets with highly individual flower motifs. Women were said to work at them in the cow sheds where the warm breath of the cows kept their threads damp so that they would not snap. Many bonnets were sold on the Friday market in Saanen and then carried over the mountain to the bishop's fairground at Sion. The industry reached a peak in 1830 but then declined and finally collapsed with the rise of Swiss machine-made lace in the 1880s. In the highland women expected to be buried in their finest bonnets when they died and few examples of the style survive.

In contrast to Château-d'Oex, which stuck to cheese, beef and timber, neighbouring valleys took drastic steps to create new forms of employment during the depressed years which followed the Napoleonic wars. In the valley of Frutigen, 50 kms away, a cottage industry based on sweated labour reached a peak of exploitation in wood craft. The local carpenters had developed a distinctive style of oval wooden box made of thin shavings of wood. Each box was glued, clamped, dried and had its lid decorated with painted flower motifs. Traditionally boxes were used for storing clothes, hats, or jewellery. Larger boxes were presented as betrothal gifts and smaller ones were packed with perfumed soap. Light-weight wood-shaving boxes for transport were designed for use on the long-distance footpaths by postmen, by travelling herbalists, by rice merchants, by pedlars of wooden toys. In 1850 an effort was made to extend the industry and alleviate poverty in this wood-craft village by creating employment for the Alpine hordes of child beggars who distressed upper-class visitors. An allegedly philanthropic entrepreneur introduced to Frutigen the production of tiny boxes designed to hold handmade sulphur matches. Such was the acuteness of Alpine deprivation that families woke their children at four in the morning to begin the long box-making day and earn a pittance. A family with five children aimed to produce 10000 handmade oval matchboxes per week. The 'philanthropic' entrepreneur paid 70 Swiss cents per thousand boxes, the boxes to be collected each Thursday. Any family which missed the collecting schedule had to carry their boxes down to the plain on their backs. To make matters worse, child wages in the matchstick industry were constantly pushed downwards by competition from machines in the towns. To cap it all the health of the workers, especially the children, was ruined by the effects of the sulphur used to coat the matchheads. Such degradation contrasted with the merely relative poverty of the Château-d'Oex highland of Vaud where people were not driven to the depths of depravity encountered in neighbouring villages of the Oberland of Bern.

The problem of child begging was nevertheless a symptom of highland poverty in Château-d'Oex which exercised Dean Bridel. He addressed himself to the subject in a talk he gave to the Olten Association, a somewhat pretentious annual gathering of literary patriots. He linked the problems of Château-d'Oex to a reduction in the poor law tax on farm land. His much admired *ancien régime* had raised four francs per thousand for poor relief, but the new Vaud republic, needing tax money for war purposes, had cut the poor rate levy by half thus causing, in Bridel's opinion, an increase in child begging. The pastor also complained of the attitude of the rich folk of Château-d'Oex who preferred to give food to children on their doorsteps rather than pay taxes to the borough and thereby alleviate the suffering of all poor people. In the long run, however, Bridel understood full well that the answer to highland poverty was economic diversification.

The potential for economic growth in Château-d'Oex, Bridel claimed, was good. Most essential artisans were available, bakers, butchers, carpenters, blacksmiths, locksmiths, joiners, cobblers, tailors, weavers, hatters, potters, caskwrights. The striking omission which he noted among the available skills, and which epitomised Château-d'Oex's isolation, was the lack of a wheelwright to make and repair carts or of a saddler to supply harnesses. Bridel, like the later philanthropist of Frutigen, was convinced that craft industries should be developed in his parish. He particularly expected to be able to encourage wood crafts and imagined that wooden spoons, bowls, chests, buckets, barrels and utensils of every kind would sell on the plain. The marginal profits, however, were never much better than those in the box-making industry and the canny people in Château-d'Oex found preferable ways of surviving. Farmers continued to make cheeses even if in hard times they sometimes had the exhausting and heartbreaking experience of carrying them over the mountain and down to Vevey market several times before they could find a buyer. The journey down took six hours and was hard enough, but bringing a 30 kg head-yoke of cheeses back up to Château-d'Oex after failing to make a sale took a discouraging ten hours.

Nineteenth-century aspirations to introduce 'modern' industries to Château-d'Oex had their roots in the eighteenth-century economic dreams of Bonstetten. Before the revolution an attempt had been made to create work for the poor of Château-d'Oex by introducing a cotton mill. After eighteen months of trial and error the investors were discouraged by their lack of profit and withdrew. They were defeated, according to Bridel, by the remote location of Château-d'Oex and the excessive cost of highland transport. In addition the mill owner found that prospective workers lived in dispersed hamlets and on remote farms and only came to work at the mill for limited hours on cold, short, winter days. Worse still he found that the price of bread with which to feed the spinners was exorbitant in the highland. Despite this initial failure another attempt to establish a cotton mill was made after the revolution. The now disused lord-bailiff's castle was offered for the purpose but this time the project was defeated by local political opposition. Château-d'Oex statesmen suspected that if they permitted a Vevey textile mill to set up a highland branch factory its owners would soon insist that the cloth produced by the plant should be given a preferential status at the local fairs. Château-d'Oex naturally feared the imposition of a monopoly and pointed out that only competition kept textile prices within range of the reduced incomes of farmers. A more cynical interpretation of the Château-d'Oex rejection of industrial investment might consider whether the civic officers of the borough were land owners who benefited from cheap labour and did not relish the prospect of wage competition from a mill.

The failure of the textile industry to enter Château-d'Oex was matched by a failure of the nineteenth-century Swiss metal industries, and notably the watch industry, to take root in the highland. Vevey had for a time been a clockmaking centre and in 1800 three watchmakers and one clockmaker were working in Rossinière and trading through Vevey. The business did not expand, however, perhaps because Vevey's trade in cheese and wine made it difficult to obtain adequate cheap labour. It was the rival town of Geneva, at the other end of the lake, that became the centre of the watch industry. Geneva was able to farm out piece work to low-cost workers in the Jura mountains. The early roots of success in the Jura watch industry, however, lay in the skills of landless refugees who had fled from France and settled in Switzerland. Protestant immigrants who did not own land had no alternative but to live by craft work, and some of them brought a tradition of skilled metal-working with them. In Château-d'Oex, unlike the Jura, there was little space for refugees, either Huguenot Protestants from France or Waldensian Protestants from Italy. The village was marked more by emigration than by immigration. The watch industry did, however, have an indirect impact on Château-d'Oex. As cottage piece work gave way to factory assembly work in the hills north of Geneva, the Jura farms became starved of seasonal labour. Château-d'Oex cowmen, as has been seen, took to walking across the plain each summer to hire themselves out as cheesemasters on the farms surrounding the watch factories of the Jura.

The short hours of daylight in a village hidden behind high rocks where the winter sun rose late may have discouraged the opening of workshops in Château-d'Oex. Good light was essential for the fine work of assembling watches. Furthermore watchmaking was not the only fine industry which failed to gain a foothold in Château-d'Oex. Embroidery was the other great craft industry which generated Switzerland's exports. The centre of the embroidery industry was in Zürich and the city generated piece work for the mountain peasants of the northern Alps. Even if the people of Château-d'Oex had had the skills and the inclination to take up the ill-paid piece-work of embroidering ribbon, their highland village would have been too far from Zürich to make the prospect viable. Instead the women of Château-d'Oex continued to hand-knit stockings. The town of Burgdorf, near Bern, fostered commercial links with Château-d'Oex and in the nineteenth century regularly advertised there for female piece workers. Before the revolution of 1798 Château-d'Oex women had knitted up to 2000 pairs of linen or cotton stockings a year and some women continued to knit for a factory agent from the plain. In the main, however, Château-d'Oex remained a village of butchers, foresters and cheesemongers and did not fall into the orbit of either the Geneva watch industry or the Zürich embroidery trade.

8
Education and Social Change

Education in Château-d'Oex opened the way to social change, new opportunity and the escape from poverty, but only slowly over a long time span. As in most of Europe the Reformation brought an acceleration of the recognition that education and literacy were beneficial to society and that Christians ought to be able to read the Bible. When Calvin, an immigrant from France, wrote to his travelling ministers in the Alps he did so in Latin. Gradually, however, French replaced Latin as the *lingua franca* of Château-d'Oex and as the language of its written records. A large influx of French Protestant refugees, both in the sixteenth century before toleration was granted through the Edict of Nantes, and in the seventeenth century, after the edict's revocation extended the use of French across western Switzerland, though few if any Huguenots seem to have reached Château-d'Oex except as parish pastors. By the eighteenth century most children were being taught some French in the five hamlet schools and two village schools of the borough. Samuel Henchoz, in his old age, purchased seven complete bibles from a printer in Lausanne as a gift to each highland school. The borough treasurer was authorised to incur the expense of binding each bible in leather to ensure that the old cheese farmer's bequest might endure for successive generations of children.

In Château-d'Oex education came to be a distinctive feature of social policy and of attempts to mitigate the scourge of poverty. The limited financial capacity of the borough to staff, heat and equip rented schoolrooms in the hamlets was supplemented by the action of charitable foundations. One such endowment had been set up in 1777 for the education and training of female orphans. It had been established by Esther Tannaz in a bid to emancipate highland girls from their cycle of economic hopelessness and give them skills deemed appropriate to their station. Esther Tannaz was descended from fifteenth-century Château-d'Oex land owners rejoicing in the names of Mermetus and Umbertus. By the eighteenth century, however, the family had fallen on such hard times that Esther herself had been a pauper and was raised at the expense of the poor chest. She subsequently moved from the highland to the plain where her lot improved so dramatically that she eventually married into the nobility. She then undertook to repay her debt to Château-d'Oex society and endowed a bursary fund for orphan girls. The beneficiaries were to be taught singing, writing, religion, virtue and the 'Osterwald catechism'. They were also to be trained in the crafts appropriate to their sex, namely lacemaking, sewing, knitting and most particularly spinning on a large spinning wheel. The charitable school was initially placed under the supervision of the lord-bailiff of the castle but when he was swept away by the Swiss revolution of 1798 the justice of the peace became the school's trustee. He was responsible for investing the one hundred-sovereign trust fund and paying the teacher a salary of one French sovereign per month.

In the nineteenth century a second benefactor, Suzanne Marie Descoullayes, added 4000 German florins to the capital of the orphan school. Classes were to be held daily from eight until noon, except on market day. The mistress was to be someone who spoke fluent French, which was now the spoken as well as the written language of the middle class. The Romanic vernacular which was the oral language used by farm girls was not to be spoken in school. A framed copy of Dame Esther's benefaction was to hang in the schoolroom lest any pupil forget her generosity. When funds permitted prizes were to be awarded as incentives for application and achievement. The endowment was not aimed at feminist liberation but rather at the training of good wives and mothers who could impart domestic skills and crafts to their daughters and so raise the economic level of their self-reliant subsistence. The orphan school may have raised the standard of Château-d'Oex housework, or enabled women forced to emigrate to find a better class of domestic employment on the plain, but it did not create new employment, other than home spinning, and most highland women remained closely integrated into the cycle of the farming year. After a century of endeavour the fund for girl orphans was wound up in 1871 and its assets appropriated by the men who managed the borough's financial affairs. By then the Victorian tourist industry had begun to create new female jobs, albeit low-grade ones, in the service industries. Girl pupils in the village school began to apply for leave-of-absence to serve as ball girls on the new English tennis courts. On leaving school they graduated to indoor employment as chambermaids. The breaking of stereotypes for female labour, and the granting of a political voice to women, had to wait another hundred years in Château-d'Oex, as it did in the rest of Switzerland.

The education of boys also benefited from a charitable benefaction in Château-d'Oex. In their case the village politicians managed to get permission to alter the terms of a medieval charitable institution and use the income to pay the wages of schoolmasters. The ancient charity had initially been set up to care for men and women suffering from leprosy but the disease disappeared while the income from the endowments continued to be available until the nineteenth century by which time it had been converted to educational purposes. In 1809 the borough used over five hundred 'Helvetian francs' from the leper chest to pay the wages of six schoolmasters. The leper fund was also called upon to pay for the ceremonial banquet that was offered at the end of each year to the professional men of the village who were appointed to serve as school examiners. In 1817 the fund held assets of 10 028 francs invested at five per cent. Since, however, the now independent republic of Vaud had become responsible for schooling, Château-d'Oex's municipal councillors saw no merit in preserving an education fund of their own. They won permission to absorb the leper chest into the general borough revenue, thus easing the pressure of taxes on property owners and rate payers. Spending on education was poorly regarded in a community that was struggling to survive and the old charitable foundation disappeared after more than four centuries of existence.

Early in the nineteenth century Château-d'Oex was endowed with a new charitable bequest that was intended to challenge the antagonism towards school spending and improve the standards of scholarship in the borough. The initiative was taken by two brothers who had left Château-d'Oex in the eighteenth century to seek their fortunes on the plain. Their first business ventures were in the textile town of Burgdorf, but in a life time of commerce and banking they moved first to the city of Bern, then to the market town of Vevey, and finally to the metropolis of revolutionary Vaud at Lausanne. The brothers were part of one of the Henchoz clans to which almost a quarter of all Château-d'Oex families belonged. From their business premises on the plain they continued to maintain a direct interest in the affairs of the highland. When indebtedness drove small farmers to bankruptcy and exile the Henchoz brothers stood ready to buy vacant plots and consolidated their land holdings. The highland estates which the city brothers bought and rented out far exceeded those of their country cousin, Samuel Henchoz, who was a practising farmer as well as a small-scale landlord. From their city vantage point the two Henchoz merchants recognized that Alpine farmers, like Welsh or Scottish ones, needed trained skills if they were to survive even in the highland let alone on the plain. Since neither brother had any direct heirs both decided to bequeath their highland estates to Château-d'Oex with instructions that the income be used to found an academic school.

The Henchoz school project met with a hundred years of difficulty before its value was finally acknowledged. The first objection came from the many Henchoz families who had hoped that their own personal poverty would be alleviated by the bounty of their urban cousins. The second objection came from local politicians who said that the borough had so many debts relating to orphans, geriatrics, the unemployed and the insane that the least of their priorities was rarefied scholarship. A third objection came from the farmers whose struggle for survival depended heavily on child labour and who would not contemplate the release of herd-boys, or even of their own sons, during school hours. For 30 years a bequest worth 3200 francs a year, six times that of the leper foundation, lay dormant. The post-Napoleonic restoration of 1815 came and went, as did the Liberal revolutions of 1830. It was only after the Radical revolutions in 1848 that education acquired a new political priority. On 1 December 1849 the president of the state of Vaud signed the legal instrument which created the Henchoz Institute.

The objective of the Château-d'Oex institute, known as the college, was to give vocational schooling from the age of 12 to boys intending to take up an industrial career. Academic training for boys aspiring to a scientific or literary education was to be offered from the age of ten. The college aimed to provide for common study in religion, French, German, geography, history, arithmetic and singing. The academic section would also teach Greek, Latin and mythology while the vocational section would includes trigonometry, architecture and agricultural science. Each of two proposed schoolmasters would teach 33 hours a week and receive 1200 francs a year together with a free apartment and a kitchen garden. Any vacancy for a teacher could be advertised in Switzerland and abroad and candidates would be tested through specimen classes and essays written on subjects chosen by the random drawing of lots. Clergymen of the Church of Vaud would be given preference though appointment was by the ministry of education in Lausanne. Each teacher would be sworn in by the Château-d'Oex burgomaster, and the parish minister would serve as the school director responsible for staff discipline.

Prospective pupils in the new grammar school were expected to have a reasonable grasp of French spelling, though it is unlikely that by 1849 the children would yet have considered French to be their mother tongue. School places were to be allocated to Château-d'Oex children before being offered to those of distant boroughs for a fee of 40 francs per annum. The deserving poor were to be given scholarships for books, quills and stationery. Classes were to begin at nine in winter and seven in summer. Pupils scoring 60 per cent in the annual examination would progress up the school provided they were clean, well-dressed and obedient. Those scoring 80 per cent would receive a prize at the Easter end-of-year festival. In addition to the summer break a two week holiday was to be given in October, to bring the cows down, with a one week holiday at New Year and Easter.

The Henchoz Institute became a remarkable corner-stone of village society and for a hundred years it was the only rural secondary school in French-speaking Switzerland. When its centenary was celebrated in 1949 the school was run by a remarkable team of scholars. The headmaster, Robert Werner, was an Anglo-Swiss theologian of the Free Church and a distinguished local historian. The German teacher, Donald Morier-Genoud, held the awe-inspiring rank of major in the Swiss militia and at ten o'clock each morning orchestrated school gymnastics, an activity which the army had introduced into schools when it realised how physically unfit its prospective recruits were. The botany master, Marcel Gardel, was a well-known water-colour artist who also accompanied the school choir on his violin. But the most revered teacher of them all in the centenary year was the old teacher of mathematics and physics, known throughout the village as Mr Albert, a member of the Morier-Genoud clan. He was the cultural heir of Dean Bridel, a patrician who taught his pupils to rejoice in the crafts, customs, dialects and scenery of the mountains and who travelled home to lunch on a small toboggan, tipping his hat to startled pedestrians in the high street.

The Château-d'Oex college did not reach its glorious centenary without traversing decades of doubt and difficulty. The two initial classrooms were supplemented by a make-shift annexe in the pigeon loft above a laundry room which doubled as a soup kitchen. The space intended for the library suffered from endless damp caused by blocked drains. Even when a stove was lit twice a week mildew attacked the books and the management committee decided that a library was an unnecessary expense and sold off the Henchoz collection. Finding a qualified schoolmaster proved difficult as the committee searched for applicants willing to teach for a modest salary in a close-knit highland community. No teacher could be found in French-speaking Switzerland and the first recruit came from England, soon to be followed by equally temporary teachers from Alemannic Switzerland. A refugee from Prussia did some part-time teaching while serving as the village pharmacist. Only in 1860 was the first native-speaker of French appointed to the staff.

Finding pupils for the new school turned out to be as daunting a task as finding masters to teach there. The reluctance of Château-d'Oex farmers to send their children to school meant that the college opened with only 16 and the roll soon fell to seven with erratic attendance. Even the Favrod-Coune family, one of the richest professional families in the village, would not permit young Charles-Victor, later to become the Château-d'Oex burgomaster and a member of the Vaud parliament, to attend school while the second crop of hay was being harvested and in August 1863 the college threatened to expel him for truancy. The school management committee agonised long over whether the vacant school benches should be filled with girl pupils many of whom had proved themselves more assiduous than boy pupils in primary classes. For years the school turned its face against mixed education but in 1879 it finally decided to admit, as its first female pupils, two fee-paying Alemannic girls from the Simmental. The experiment was later extended to local girls but on the understanding that they would not qualify for prizes, would not receive grants to buy school materials and would not be given places for which there were male applicants. The school also decided that no female child should be admitted who had reached the age of 16. Despite the restrictions the female demand for school places caused the male establishment constant embarrassment and between 1904 and 1910 girls were confined to the vocational wing of the school. The confidential minutes of the governors also reveal that covert discrimination was practised and that the segregated entry examinations for girls were more demanding. In time female pupils were permitted to compete for school prizes and by 1925 the borough actually began to take a pride in its school when scholarly standards were pronounced excellent by the Lausanne inspectorate. Distinguished citizens who served as school examiners were entertained each spring to a banquet in one or other of the eight sumptuous Victorian hotels that had sprung up in Château-d'Oex to cater for the luxury tourist trade.

A modest, independently-funded, primary school was founded at about the same time as the college by the Château-d'Oex Free Church which had emerged from the Vaud religious crisis of 1845. Children who had been taken out of the National Church by their dissenting parents were severely bullied in the village elementary school which most children had been expected to attend since the 1720s. The congregation deplored the detrimental effects which ostracism was having on the moral character of its young people after Free Church teachers had been sacked from state schools. The elders decided to create a schoolroom in the building which served as their chapel and invited David Roch, one of the dismissed teachers, to hold classes once benches could be found for the 14 children who enrolled. The syllabus evolved to include half an hour of Bible reading by the pastor, three hours of French taught by Mr Roch himself and two hours of arithmetic taught by a Mr Lüthy on the days when he was not engaged in market duties. Lessons in Swiss history and geography were given on Monday, Wednesday and Saturday afternoons and in natural history on Tuesday and Friday. The acting teachers were paid a mere 180 'old Helvetian francs' in the first year. For the school's second year a full-time post was advertised at 320 'new federal francs' and a pastor who had lost his living in the Vaud revolution of 1845 was appointed schoolmaster. He proposed to include German in the syllabus but the elders felt hymn-singing to be a greater priority and the new teacher soon gave in his notice to be replaced by a 19-year-old French adolescent from Besançon, in Burgundy, whom the elders kept on a tight rein lest he should show 'negligence or immorality'. At the end of the school year prizes of 40 'new federal cents' were given to four boys and five girls who obtained grades above 50 per cent. Consolation prizes, taking account of singing and good behaviour, were given to one girl and six boys whose grades fell below 19 per cent. Falling school rolls forced the school to close temporarily in 1877 and permanently in 1912 when the more rigid 'brothers' of the Free Church refused to apply for state assistance lest their ideological autonomy be contaminated.

Education does not seem to have seriously alleviated the poverty of nineteenth-century Château-d'Oex. Indeed children who did gain an education were liable to adopt the strategy of highland scholars everywhere and move to the plain to become church pastors, schoolmasters or in rare cases schoolmistresses. This was the élite end of a pattern of migration which had for generations been Château-d'Oex's economic and demographic safety-valve. By the eighteenth century the highland, with a population of 4000 people in the three boroughs, had no land for more people yet births regularly exceeded deaths by about ten a year and an outlet for excess population had to be found. In the decade from 1754 to 1763 100 men and 30 women left the highland without returning. In the nineteenth century emigration to serve in overseas mercenary regiments declined sharply, though Britain was reported to be recruiting in Vevey in the 1850s and taking volunteers to be trained at Dover castle for service in the Crimea. The main escape from poverty was into civilian service on the plain and Château-d'Oex family names became familiar in the towns around the lake as far as Geneva. The least fortunate disappeared into the anonymous crowd as housemaids and labourers, fending for themselves or seeking to escape further afield to Europe and the colonies.

Emigration from the highland to the Swiss towns was not a wholly secure means of evading poverty. During the nineteenth century, and even as late as 1938, any Swiss pauper was liable to be deported from his or her place of residence to his or her ancestral borough of origin and citizenship. If necessary the victims of poverty were loaded on the poor wagon with their children and transported under police escort to their often hostile 'home village'. The policy was catastrophic for boroughs such as Château-d'Oex. They were a source of cheap labour for the towns in prosperous years and a dumping ground for the unemployed during recession years, a pattern of labour oscillation not wholly dissimilar from that practised on labour reserves in British colonies. Inter-state emigration was beneficial to Swiss urban industries which retained the more productive of the highland migrants and shipped back those who were burnt out or incompetent or unemployed. The policy minimised the social security costs incurred by towns but put intolerable burdens on village taxes. Château-d'Oex struggled throughout the nineteenth century to fund its work house, its asylum and its infirmary, and to pay maintenance for the old, the lame and the returnees from the plain. Many paupers were farmed out to families who needed the pittance which the municipality offered by way of maintenance in order to subsidise their own meagre household budgets. In the most extreme cases Château-d'Oex paid for the unemployed, and especially for delinquents, to emigrate to the Americas. The borough treasurer chose to have pauper families escorted to Atlantic steamers in Le Havre or Marseille at public expense rather than harbour them at home as a drain on the exchequer.

Voluntary rather than forced emigration was an old and continuing means of escaping from poverty. Those who were driven out of the highland by hunger, or by social pressure, sometimes went as far as southern Russia in search of survival and employment. One member of the Bornet family was reported as being indigent in Odessa. Elisa Martin was found barely surviving in a Kiev hospital and the Swiss consul at Vienna arranged to have her repatriated to Château-d'Oex, though she never did succeed in fully recovering her expenses from the borough treasurer. The scale of overland emigration to the East may not have been large but it did demonstrate the intensity of demographic pressure. The Château-d'Oex women found in Russia may have been indirectly associated with an overland column which had set off from Vevey in covered horse wagons in 1822 and which reached the Black Sea after an eventful journey across Europe lasting 103 days. Tsar Alexander I had given the trekkers a neglected lake-side vineyard, but when the overland column arrived they found it already occupied by Russian squatters. Survival was precarious, horses were scarce, cows and pigs were stolen, wives were difficult to attract, share-croppers who came to work for the Swiss settlers expected one third of the harvest, drunkenness became rife, and in the absence of boats wheat could only be taken to the market when the lake was frozen over. In 1829 plague struck the Swiss colony. Russia was not to become an Eldorado for the poor of the Château-d'Oex highland though the last Swiss settlers witnessed both Lenin's revolution and Hitler's invasion before being repatriated to Vevey by the Nazis in 1944.

After the Vaud flirtation with Russia, those who chose to migrate in the later nineteenth century turned their attention more seriously to the Americas. Brazil attracted many Swiss migrants over time though the pioneering colony of Catholics at New Fribourg, like the Protestant overland migration to Russia, had its problems and survivors trickled home to the Alps. By the 1880s it was Canada which was being opened up by railway builders and Mr Hauswirth, of Saanen, let it be known through the Château-d'Oex newspapers that emigrants wishing to go to Manitoba should seek particulars of land grants and employment opportunities from his wife while he himself went to Liverpool to negotiate passages for migrants. He reported back that the steamship *America* was due to sail on 1 May and the *St Lawrence* on 29 May. Advertisements were also placed in the local press inviting migrants to embark at the Rhine port of Basel *en route* to Chile where the government had offered 40 hectares of land to any Swiss family of colonists. Fares were heavily subsidised. An even more exotic destination than America was tropical Africa and in 1901 Mr Ramseyer gave the Château-d'Oex public a lecture about his life of missionary adventure in Ashanti on the Gold Coast. Some highland families responded to such appeals and certificate-holders from the Château-d'Oex grammar school provided Christian personnel for the Swiss missions in Africa.

Neither the slow growth of opportunity through education, nor the escape by means of emigration, was enough to lift the Swiss highlands in general, nor the Château-d'Oex highland in particular, out of the long nineteenth-century cycle of poverty. Institutional change of a more radical kind was brought about by the needs of a wider society which, on the plain at least, was undergoing the process of industrialisation. The cities and their factories, even more than the farmers and their cheeses, needed an open economic climate in order to flourish. The changes which the townspeople sought began to take place in 1848 and were orchestrated by political parties which called themselves Radical and which had gained power in several states of the plain, most significantly in Vaud. Thus it was that although Château-d'Oex was a conservative, agrarian, highland society, it was transformed by its attachment to one of Switzerland's more progressive states. Vaud was one of the republics which favoured closer Swiss union, even the creation of a federal government with specific, if circumscribed, authority over all 22 of Switzerland's nations. Château-d'Oex did not, by and large, share Vaud's federal aspirations, but between 1848 and 1994 no less than six of the seven governors appointed by Lausanne to rule the highland were members of the Radical party.

The unification of Switzerland to which the Radicals aspired began at an almost purely economic level. The greatest of the problems that had been faced by the Swiss restoration régimes of 1815 was that each state was largely dependent for its income on customs revenue levied at all its border crossings. Since few of the Swiss republics were more than 30 km across, all trade was subjected to endless delays at successive customs posts and all prices were inflated by the cumulative charging of multiple customs revenues. Efficiency of transit seemed to require a single market, a *zollverein*, with the free movement of goods throughout Switzerland's economic space. The Radicals, however, wanted to go further than a customs union. They also aspired to create a federal post office and, more controversially still, a single currency. In the panic which followed the Swiss civil war of 1847 the Radicals were able to benefit from the wide-spread desire for mutual security and to achieve all of their initial economic objectives. Inter-state customs posts were demolished. A Swiss post office was established from which only one state, Schaffhausen, sought an opt-out clause. And a federal franc was instituted so that in 1850 Switzerland slowly began to issue its own coins. Over the next 30 years these federal coins replaced the cosmopolitan and provincial array of coins to which the Swiss were accustomed and in 1890 Switzerland established a central bank with a monopoly on the issue of bank notes.

The changes of economic structure were undoubtedly beneficial to Château-d'Oex, particularly the abolition of the Fribourg customs post at Montbovon. Smuggling, intimidation and bribery had created constant chicanery on a border through which most of Château-d'Oex's external trade passed, notably the out-going cheeses and the in-coming wines. Eight kms in the other direction Château-d'Oex peddlers appreciated the closing of the Bern customs post which had hitherto restricted their access to the Saanen fairs. Removing such immediate barriers to free trade, however, did not entirely allay highland conservatism and local suspicion of big government, particularly of supranational federal government, remained marked during the first 100 years of Swiss unification. The federation had been founded with a staff of only 50 civil servants, accommodated in the now partially eclipsed city of Bern, but the Swiss attitude to this minimal bureaucracy was largely negative and during the nineteenth century the union government of Switzerland gained in scope, if not in popular esteem. One Château-d'Oex farmer put the matter bluntly when told that the new federal telegraph would be able to give advance weather forecasts before the hay was cut and proclaimed that if the information came from Bern then surely no one should trust it.

Free trade, a single currency and a union post office were not enough to protect Château-d'Oex from the catastrophic recession which hit Switzerland, and Europe, in 1885. The crisis was so severe that it almost destroyed the fabric of highland society. It also brought about a most virulent confrontation between the Château-d'Oex progressives in the Radical party and their conservative rivals in the Liberal party. As the local economy imploded farmers who had been less than prudent in the use of scarce resources went bankrupt. Even successful farmers who had generously guaranteed loans for their neighbours and relatives were crippled when banks made them liable for the debts they had underwritten. Local newspapers carried pages of farm bankruptcies. When artisans and retailers had no farm customers to buy their wares they in turn became insolvent. Meetings of credit holders soon found that the assets they had seized were worthless as there were no buyers with money to purchase confiscated businesses. Bargains went unheeded and crops of hay were sold standing in the fields while debt holders stood idly by unable to harvest them. In a single year

Château-d'Oex witnessed the auctioning of no less than 113 farm properties of bankrupted families who were then driven from the highland by economic necessity. Equally dramatically 571 households throughout the highland had all their mobile property, furniture and livestock seized for debt. Despair led to a dangerous increase in alcoholism, already a serious plague in the highland, but efforts to curtail the home distilling of gentian gin and cherry brandy were largely abortive. Taverns also continued to sell quantities of white wine, but since wine was the mainstay of the economy of the Vaud plain curtailing production and consumption would have been politically sensitive. As poverty bit ever deeper into the highland the Radical borough government became intensely unpopular and one of its leaders was charged with embezzlement. In 1889 a municipal election brought the long rule of the Radical Party to an end in Château-d'Oex and the Liberal Party, with a different set of social priorities, returned to power for the first time in a generation.

The revival of the Château-d'Oex Liberal Party pre-dated the economic crisis which had brought such urgent demands for political change. Politics had taken on a sharper edge with the founding in 1881 of an opposition newspaper, the *Journal de Château-d'Oex*, which stridently challenged the Radical paper, *Le Progrès*. The semi-establishment organ of the 'red aristocracy' had been founded in 1877 as a handwritten sheet owned by Isaac Schümperlin, the Alemannic schoolmaster, and Dr Rosat, the local tax collector. The editor of the new Liberal newspaper was David Morier-Genoud, a gentleman farmer and college schoolmaster whose ardent objective was to use his editorial axe to 'fell the Radical tree'. He had a mordant turn of phrase, describing the modernising state which the Radicals had so painfully created for the Swiss as a cattle manger where bureaucrats lined up to feed. The Liberals were not only opposed to the state, and to interference from Lausanne, but were also ardently anti-federal. They orchestrated a campaign to prevent the union government of Switzerland from creating a schools inspectorate, insisting that education should remain a parsimoniously-funded borough responsibility rather than become any part of an expensive national vision of social change for the future. So strident was the tone of the Liberal newspaper that it frequently lost libel actions and on one occasion the editor was even challenged to a duel. Its persistent complaints about electoral fraud, voter impersonation, or free drinks for Radical supporters contributed to the 1889 Liberal victory.

The conservative burghers who came to power in 1889 were dominated by the middle-class professional and farming family of

Favrod-Coune. Charles Victor became the new burgomaster and ruled as chief executive for 19 years. His brother Jules was elected speaker of the new borough parliament while continuing to serve as the village doctor and remaining, according to his friends, bountiful in his treatment of the poor and good humoured in his care of political opponents. The new ruling family took upon itself the editorship of the Liberal newspaper, though journalistic quills remained charged with brimstone and the new editor was described as a 'featherless condor' who had been educated in the *beau monde* of the plain. The vitriolic spasms of democratic confrontation died down as the economy recovered from its battering, and the press became more noted for its social commentary than for its political pungency as leisured foreigners began to discover Château-d'Oex during the *belle époque* of the 1890s. As prosperity grew the Favrod-Coune family became benevolent patrons of their highland borough, sponsoring the refurbishment of the church carillon, building a new civic centre on the site of the old prison tower, constructing a village hall on land donated from their own front lawn, and opening an elegant new primary school with a spire and a public clock.

While free-enterprise conservatives administered Château-d'Oex with benevolent if selective largesse, the representative of the state in the highland was a member of the Radical party which customarily dominated the Vaud parliament in Lausanne. His official title was 'Prefect of the Highland' and, like the Lord Lieutenant of an English shire, he combined ceremonial, administrative and judicial roles. As the reach of the state grew, the role of the highland governor came to include the swearing into office of dozens of elected or appointed office holders. The governor maintained a paternalistic eye over the proliferation of institutions that impinged on the lives of proud, independent-minded, and sometimes resentful, mountain citizens. The highland was divided between judicial circuits, church parishes, electoral constituencies, military companies, forestry sections, registries of births, inspectorates of artisans, police units of the quasi-military gendarmerie, road repair services, water supply fraternities, controllers of bee hives, game wardens, medical services and veterinary inspectorates, most of them operating within local boundaries which did not coincide with one another. Attempts to rationalise traditional procedures and synthesize them with new bureaucratic functions continued to meet with hostility though some change did take place, as when the high court of the highland was amalgamated with the high court of the Rhône and relocated at Aigle. In a small society, with a limited number of professionally qualified people, the duplication of office holding was often pronounced. The Château-d'Oex town clerk was not precluded from serving as member of the Vaud parliament and the burgomaster was likewise free to stand for election to the union parliament in Bern. When it was suggested that appointment to the post of governor should debar the holder from elective office the people of Château-d'Oex voted against the proposal in a plebiscite, but they were overruled by the much more numerous voters on the plain. Even the separation of the judiciary from the legislative and executive branches of government, one of the great ideological features of the American Revolution, was not implemented in Château-d'Oex. Yet Vaud politicians greatly admired the American constitution, on which the Swiss one had been modelled, and when Lincoln was assassinated the Vaud parliament sent the American congress a message of condolence, imperiously sweeping aside the objection that Vaud was no longer a sovereign nation since it had transferred responsibility for foreign relations to the Swiss confederation in 1848.

Many of the duties of the highland governor concerned the ceremonial commemoration of approved political anniversaries. The choice of public holidays was always controversial in Switzerland. The Catholics commemorated the anniversaries of saints appropriate to each state while Protestants celebrated New Year, Ascension Day and Whit Monday. Political commemorations were more problematic and traditionally they often took the form of fast days rather than feast days. One such fast day had been called in early 1756 when news of the Lisbon earthquake reached Switzerland and frightened people wanted action. In Vaud the federal fast instituted in 1832 to pray for peace between Swiss Protestants and Swiss Catholics continued to be celebrated as a bank holiday on the third Monday of September. Château-d'Oex preserved the custom of not cooking on the fast day and of eating cold plum tart that had been prepared the day before. The borough may have remained ambivalent about the political holiday celebrated on 24 January, the anniversary of the Vaud rebellion of 1798, but it did celebrate the day during both world wars and, at least until the end of the nineteenth century, it continued to recognize the national independence of Vaud as celebrated each year on 14 April.

The governor of the highland at the turn of the century was Auguste Cottier, a lemonade manufacturer with a degree in law who had been one of the early pupils of the Château-d'Oex grammar school. Cottier reigned over his highland kingdom like an uncrowned monarch for no less than 46 years. Cottier's own predilection was for personal contact with his subjects and he had little time for paper work. One of his duties, however, was to report annually to the government in Lausanne on the year's weather, the success of the harvest, the yield of the rather stunted orchards and the quality of the mountain flowers on which the dairy herds grazed. The great pro-forma ledgers that he maintained had a certain folkloric quality about them which accorded well with the quasi-royal nature of his office. Cottier's style was autocratic, but his constitutional duties required him to protect democracy, an ideology which he understood having been elected to parliament at the age of 29, two years before his astonishingly youthful appointment to the post of governor. Although a member of the Radical party associated with the modernisation of government, Cottier was in many ways a romantic who cherished the traditions of his mountain subjects. He was a keen horse rider, cavalry officer and hunter who became responsible for enforcing the game laws which had come down to him from those old medieval forest guardians, the counts of Gruyère.

The hunting of wild game may have originally been designed to protect barnyard animals but by the late nineteenth century the main predators which attacked hens or lambs were foxes and eagles. Bears and wolves had been hunted to extinction in Château-d'Oex though wolves still roamed the near by Valais and several bears were shot each year in the Engadine, Switzerland's remote eastern province. Cottier became concerned that the hunting of foxes with guns was too dangerous a business to be left in the hands of angry young farmers but his ban on fox shooting naturally caused a great outcry, partly because of the damage that foxes would cause in the chicken coops and partly because of the loss of sport which the ban entailed. A more important sport, however, was the noble art of chamois stalking. The huntsmen organised themselves into a society under the patronage of Diana, the Greek goddess of the hunt. Each September, at the opening of the season, they met on a mountain farm to celebrate with feasting and singing accompanied by an accordion. Licences to 'bag' chamois were carefully shared out and game wardens patrolled the high crags at dawn to apprehend poachers. The season for the shooting of each of several types of highland game was strictly limited to a few autumn weeks. On 13 December 1907 Cottier fined young Charles Favrod-Coune, the village lawyer, ten francs for hunting out of season and using a dog to track and shoot a chamois. In addition to chamois the valley sportsmen hunted deer, badger, ermine and marmotte. In the mid-twentieth century Cottier's successors re-introduced ibex into the highland as a game animal. At the same time, however, nature protection gained support and ecologists imposed new restrictions on hunting. A wildlife reserve was created below the great rocks on the south side of the valley where tourists could watch shy chamois grazing the margins of their wilderness. It was these tourists, rather than the social, economic and constitutional changes wrought by Radical politicians, which brought the greatest change to the face of Château-d'Oex in the second half of the nineteenth century.

9

The Romance of the Alps

The transformation of Château-d'Oex from a society whose economy was almost exclusively based on farming to one in which farming was complemented by an income derived from foreign holidaymakers occurred over the course of the nineteenth century. The early roots of the Château-d'Oex tourist industry are to be found in eighteenth-century Lausanne. Members of the wealthy leisured class of England, who spent their winters on the Côte d'Azur, discovered that during the hot summer months they could withdraw to the shores of Lake Geneva and enjoy Lausanne society. During the nineteenth century the fashionable attractions of western Switzerland grew and the mild lake shore at Montreux, sheltered from the north wind by the Château-d'Oex mountains, developed as an all-season resort. In summer the visitors hired guides to explore the idyllic mountains which Jean-Jacques Rousseau, in his novel *The New Héloïse*, had peopled with imaginary lovers and which Dean Bridel had extolled in reams of sentimental verse.

One of the first of the new tourists to describe a walk over the mountains to Château-d'Oex was the composer Mendelssohn. He arrived from Italy in 1831, relieved at his escape from misery, beggars and bureaucrats, and hoped to find an inexpensive guide to take him to Château-d'Oex. A guesthouse matron kindly explained to him that in mid-summer the men were sometimes too busy harvesting to accept a tourist assignment. She did, however, tentatively suggest that her maid Pauline might be available to lead him over the mountain. Surprised but charmed the musician set off for the Jaman pass with the young lady carrying his sack and chatting all the way up the steep stony path on a blazing August morning. She told him of the dance she had attended the previous Sunday when she had set out from home at midnight, arrived on top of the mountain before dawn to make coffee for the boys, danced all day, and then returned home in the evening ready to start work again on Monday. The next dance, she said, would be on the far side of the lake, in Savoy, but her mother was afraid of the water and would therefore not allow her daughter to attend it. She would, however, be going to the dance of the cherry pickers and also to the milking festival in the high cheese dairy. Mendelssohn, brimming with sentimentality, wished that he had been a highland peasant as he climbed through the stupendous scenery. On top of the Jaman pass the guide met her cousins making hay and they sang and yodelled and gossiped in dialect before she escorted him down to the cattle trail on the far side. There he took his leave of the innocent damsel and, refusing the portering services of an importunate old man, pursued his adventure carrying his own sack. At La Tine the innkeeper who served luncheons of roast lamb was a cabinetmaker by trade and he proudly showed travellers and customers the tables, dressers and chairs that he made. In the evening the German hiker reached Château-d'Oex, with its church perched on a mound of green velvet, but his candlelight letter to his sister in Berlin dwelt as much on the charms of his vivacious young guide as on the picture-like qualities of the village and its spectacular mountains.

Romantic musicians like Mendelssohn were not the only leisured travellers to visit Château-d'Oex. An alternative tradition of Alpine travel had been established by persons seeking the curative waters of mountain springs. The salt baths of Bex on the Rhône had long been popular with wealthy travellers and the resort hotel there had been extolled not only by Rousseau but also, as noted, by that other French literary giant, Alexander Dumas. On a much smaller scale Château-d'Oex had its own cure resort and the sulphur baths at Etivaz attracted some visitors from the plain. The Swiss archaeologist Dompierre, accompanied by a governess, took his six-year-old son to the Etivaz baths in 1821. The party changed horses at Fribourg, ate a frugal meal of fish and eggs at Bulle, and arrived by nightfall in the great chalet-tavern of Montbovon. The smoke-darkened rooms told of the risk of fire and filled them with trepidation, but they slept well after an excellent supper of coffee, butter, milk and cream for which they were charged only ten pence. Next day the travellers crossed the thundering gorge at La Tine on foot and in Rossinière rented a horse with a well-constructed saddle for the governess and hired a porter to carry the luggage. On arriving at Etivaz the guests weighed themselves in and jocularly offered to pay the bathkeeper according to the weight they managed to put on during their mountain cure. She declined the bargain with good humour although her meals of mutton, beef and veal, served with beans and salad, were ample and cheap. The baths were so generous in size that young Theodore could almost swim in them once his father had made sure that the water was not too hot. When not bathing the pair took the mountain air, climbing for four hours and then tumbling back down in 20 minutes. Father and son happily ignored the more conventional cure guests one of whom was the very formal mayor of the city of Vevey.

Despite the enthusiasm of bathers and walkers, holiday travel to Château-d'Oex remained a rarity in the first half of the nineteenth century. In 1840, however, 23 years before Thomas Cook organised his first tour of Switzerland, Elizabeth Strutt arrived in Rossinière from

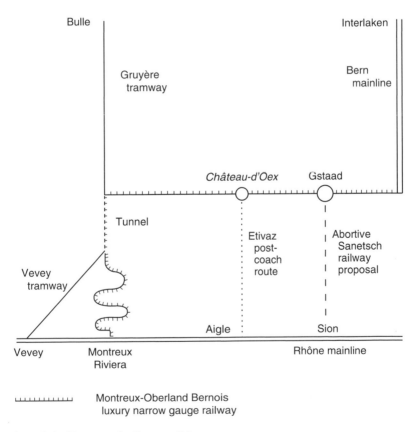

Figure 9.1 Diagram of railway politics

England and subsequently published an account of her highland vacation. Her husband had been commissioned to paint a portrait of Dean Henchoz, the now venerable friend of Dean Bridel's student days. Mrs Strutt arrived on the stagecoach, to the gaping amazement of the local farm lads, and had her Victorian travelling chests taken to the inn. When she ordered dinner it was her turn to be astonished at the frugality of the local diet of vegetable soup, hard cheese, occasional slithers of dried beef and plum cake. Mrs Strutt settled in while her husband worked and enjoyed listening to village tales of how the postman had escaped from the wolves on the Jaman pass or how the herdboy had lost a goat on the mountain. Her pioneering account of highland life attracted more English visitors and guesthouse accommodation began to improve, eventually creating both summer and winter holidays for affluent and leisured visitors.

The second half of the nineteenth century saw the institutionalisation of the Château-d'Oex tourist industry. The local inns could no longer cater for the influx of visitors and boarding houses were opened that offered full board to long-term foreign residents seeking mountain scenery. A few members of the farming community began to benefit from the fashionable city belief in the curative power of Alpine air by opening their houses to child visitors. While the men were away in the mountains making cheese and herding bullocks the women took in as paying guests children from the plain. The practice became lucrative and purpose-built homes for children were opened to meet the demand, though one of them was later burnt down with a tragic loss of child life which cast a lasting pall over mountain children's homes. Although children were accepted as guests to improve their health Château-d'Oex took care to emphasize in its brochures that it was not a resort for invalids. Clients who wanted to cure their tuberculosis in the mountains were expected to go to the neighbouring borough of Leysin, in the Ormont valley, which specialised in building sanatoria. One partial exception to the Château-d'Oex ban on medical facilities was made in 1910 when Dr Delachaux was granted permission to build a huge health clinic, later known as the Soldanelle, where fitness devotees would be given diets and exercises.

The Château-d'Oex tourist trade gradually developed a luxury branch. Hotels were built of masonry in the French style, their pastel-coloured walls rising to four stories capped with slate roofs. By 1879 some 500 holidaymakers spent the summer in Château-d'Oex escaping from urbanisation and industrialisation, especially English industrialisation. The thirst for 'uncontaminated nature' seemed insatiable and in 1896 the borough established a tourist office to widen its publicity campaign and attract yet more visitors to its new hotels. The last and largest of the great hotels, the Grand, was built in 1905 on the crest of a wave of Edwardian prosperity. For 60 years this hotel was the centre of upper-class society. While common folk held dances in the village hall, built on land graciously given to the borough by the Favrod-Coune political dynasty, the *haute bourgeoisie* held balls in the Grand Hotel. To entice a foreign clientele the hotel built courts on which lawn tennis could be played in summer and ice hockey in winter.

During the *belle époque* of the naughty 1890s the limited relations between peasant society and bourgeois visitors sometimes showed signs of strain. After an incident at a road-side inn Cecil Minod was compelled to withdraw the defamatory remarks he had made about a Miss Olimpe Geissenhof, probably a foreign guest, and publicly recognize that she was an honourable and worthy girl in every particular. Local prejudice against foreigners was, and long remained, ingrained in peasant attitudes despite the money which visitors brought to the highland. Farmers, accustomed to working at all hours of the day and never enjoying weekends or holidays, tended to assume that leisured foreigners had very loose morals and they were not above trying occasionally to benefit from the assumption. Suspicion was sometime reciprocated and visitors were fearful, as Mendelssohn had been, of being overcharged, importuned or cheated. A Miss Wilkinson was particularly distressed to find that someone had stolen the postage stamp from a personal letter addressed to her and, worse still, the miscreant had mislaid two of the precious pages. The English Miss placed an advertisement in the local newspaper hoping to recover her *billet-doux*.

The intrusion of the modern world was not widely welcomed in Château-d'Oex. Farmers were much exercised when the interfering union government of the federation decided that Château-d'Oex should adopt standardised Central European Time and move all its clocks forward by half an hour. Rather than expect its children to rise half an hour earlier by sun time the community resolved to change the school opening hour from seven to half past. As the traditional pace of life gave way to modern bustle, parking became a problem in the village and the town clerk announced that in future no person was to hitch a horse in front of the town hall for more than one hour. The threat from bicycles travelling dangerously down hill was curbed with fines for speeding. Worse still traffic became increasingly congested in the high street. It was decided in 1912 that instead of each vehicle making a free choice as to how to negotiate with any other vehicle, be it cart, sledge, or motor, all should pull over to the right when meeting on-coming vehicles. This rule of the road, let it be noted, did not apply to bugle-playing mountain post-coaches which, despite being now motorised, continued to hug the rock-cliff while leaving private vehicles to negotiate the dangerously open rims of the gorges. Motors were perceived as a serious nuisance in Château-d'Oex, spreading the smell of burnt motor spirit and raising great clouds of dust despite the regular watering of the village street. When two of the expensive monsters had an accident while navigating a hairpin bend on the mountain it was reported with awe that both had suffered damage to their front off-side wheels. It was claimed that as many as 30 motor cars were attempting to cross the mountain each day and the borough council was tempted to ban motor vehicles from public roads altogether, as Zermatt was to do. Opponents of the new vehicles pointed out that very few vacationers came by motor car and that those who did tended to be 'tourers' who did not stay long enough in Château-d'Oex to be an attractive economic proposition.

At the turn of the century newspapers carried extensive advertisements for services which reflect life in late-Victorian Château-d'Oex. The lemonade factory at Rougemont requested that its customers return empty syphons as a matter of urgency. In Vevey one Jean Fray offered infallible correspondence cures for alcoholism, assuring his clientele that only half his fee was payable in advance. In Rossinière the Great Chalet, now an hotel, advertised billiards, croquet, hot baths and milk diets. It was later noted that one of the hotel's guests was Mrs Alfred Dreyfus who had brought her husband there for a long rest-cure in the Alps after his incarceration in the notorious Devil's Island prison. At Etivaz the sulphur baths boasted new premises. In Château-d'Oex the pharmacist, Mr Chappuis, sought to acquire a plot of land suitable for flooding as an ice rink. Two young ladies describing themselves as 'pretty damsels of the yellow race' appealed to the genteel class of refined residents for positions as ladies' companions, claiming that they were from the Canary Islands and drawing attention to their musical skills. To avoid upsetting guests of distinction and sensitivity the municipal council decreed in February 1888 that all begging should be outlawed in Château-d'Oex.

Despite the welcome supplementary income which visitors brought to the Château-d'Oex economy of beef, cheese and timber, the small nineteenth-century tourist industry was not enough to bring real prosperity to the highland. The politicians of Chateau-d'Oex, Radicals and Liberals alike, therefore set about modernising the Alpine mode of production and generating new income. One of their most enterprising ventures was to tunnel through the mountains and build a long-distance pipeline all the way to Lausanne to supply the city with pure mountain water as an alternative to filtered lake water. In the long term an even more fundamental innovation was to abandon the inefficient old watermills and use the highland's abundant water power to generate the electricity which was becoming a source of energy for the Swiss industrial revolution. As the modern age encroached Château-d'Oex's local peasant democracy had to decide whether or not it wanted to move into the era of electricity and hydrological engineering.

The question of using water to generate electricity for Château-d'Oex came to a head in 1894. Favrod-Coune, the Liberal burgomaster, summoned a public meeting to debate the merits of the innovation. Hoteliers were in favour. They claimed that their English customers would soon expect electric lighting in preference to paraffin lamps. It was pointed out that in Charmey, a near-by Catholic village, water-driven electric power was already available even though Swiss cities were still lit by gaslight. A businessman at Les Avants, a near-by Protestant village, was willing to generate electricity for Château-d'Oex. He had already bought the old watermill at La Chaudanne and claimed that if 200 customers subscribed to one lamp each from his electric light service he could install a generator within eight months. The project was accepted and the first consumers began to store away their oil wicks and candleholders. Villagers were astonished to be able to light a room before entering it rather than stumble round in the dark looking for the lantern and the matches. Two public electric lights, one of 16 candlepower and the other of 25, were placed on angle-brackets at the corners of the town hall while the Bear Inn installed an electric bulb above its double-sided entrance stairs. The socially-minded even suggested, albeit abortively, that the electricity supply might be run as far as the grammar school.

The affairs of the highland electricity company did not run smoothly. The conduit carrying water to the turbine sprung a leak and subscribers were plunged into darkness without warning. After many local mishaps Château-d'Oex subscribed to a more reliable electricity source from across the Fribourg state boundary at Montbovon. There the local Catholic congregation had long been anxious to replace its solid old church tower with a fashionable new church spire. A sharp-witted electrical entrepreneur bought the old church and used the historic stones from the tower to dam the Sarine river. He then installed a hydro-electric turbine which was larger and more reliable than the one adapted from the old Château-d'Oex flour mill. The Montbovon electricity company, although large by the Swiss standards of the day, initially had difficulty in meeting demand and in hot weather, when the Sarine river ran low, the power supply to highland villages like Château-d'Oex was liable to be curtailed. Later, however, electricity supplies gradually improved and the river was dammed again to provide stored water that could be sold to Montbovon through an underground pipeline. Later still, in the 1960s, Château-d'Oex became the site of one Switzerland's largest and most unusual hydro-electric projects when the valley of the Hongrin stream was dammed by a huge concrete wall. Instead of filling the reservoir from the highland springs, however, water was pumped up the mountain daily from Lake Geneva using off-peak electricity, some of it purchased from nuclear power stations in France. In the day time the water was released back down the pipes and the full force of the 1000 metre drop operated giant generators near Vevey.

Bringing Château-d'Oex into the modern age to make it more attractive to foreign visitors and more efficient for local farmers required more than the construction of an electric supply line. The highland also required improved communications and transport. The federal post office did its best and in the 1890s advertised an improved timetable of diligence services. The ten o'clock stagecoach was scheduled to connect at Aigle with the Rhône valley railway in order to get passengers to Lausanne by 6.48 pm. The timetable even advertised an onward connection to Geneva the same night. The coach fare over the mountain was expensive, however, and one dissatisfied postal passenger who had paid eight francs complained of being taken over the high pass seated on a packing case strapped to an open horse sleigh. Passenger services down the valley used the old eighteenth-century cart track which had been partially upgraded. The 2.30 p.m. coach through Gruyère was timed to connect at the old horse fair of Romont with the night train to Bern. But improved though the coach services were, Château-d'Oex politicians were convinced that to enter the modern age they needed a railway service of their own through the mountains. Bringing Château-d'Oex into rapid communication with the plain, however, involved immersion in the world of finance and engineering. The politics of building a railway to Château-d'Oex became complex, partisan and confrontational. A one-time federal member of parliament wryly summed up the highland railway debate when he reported that he had actually seen the Radical governor, Cottier, speaking to the Liberal burgomaster, Favrod-Coune, but when he awoke he found that the negotiations had been a dream. No less than three highland railways were planned, and even partially constructed, leading towards Château-d'Oex. The Bern railway from Lake Thun brought manufactures from the industrialised Swiss cities into the Alps along the Simmental, using standard gauge track, but the line never went beyond the head of the valley and stopped at Zweisimmen, 20 km short of Château-d'Oex. A Fribourg railway project, favoured by the Château-d'Oex Radical party, proposed the building of an electric tramway which would bring street cars and cattle wagons up from the corn and cattle market at Bulle to a terminus only one mile short of Château-d'Oex, a point where the road became too steep for tram-cars. This railway was also partially built but it never crossed the Fribourg state boundary and stopped at Montbovon where the electric light company supplied it with power for the overhead wires. The Vaud blueprint for a highland railway would have linked Château-d'Oex to the lake-side cheese market and industrial centre of Vevey on a very steep narrow-gauge line but this railway was also never completed and only reached the foot of the Jaman mountain pass. It was therefore left to a fourth, rather different, company to design and build a railway which successfully tunnelled through the mountain and dramatically opened Château-d'Oex to the world.

The Château-d'Oex Liberal party, unlike the farmers of the Radical party, favoured an ambitious railway proposal directed at the leisure industry. A private company, calling itself the Montreux–Oberland Bernois, suggested building a line which linked Château-d'Oex directly to the elegant lake-side resort of Montreux. The scheme, in which some Château-d'Oex Liberals may have invested money of their own, aspired to run 'international' trains from the Vaud riviera to the lakeland of the Bernese Oberland, a journey that was later widely advertised as the Golden Mountain service, though without drawing the attention of foreign passengers to the fact that they would need to change gauges, and therefore trains, at Zweisimmen. Junctions on the line were built at Montbovon, where farmers and their cattle could change for the Gruyère line on their way to the markets of the plain, and at Chamby, where cheesemongers and buttermaids could catch another train down to Vevey. No through trains ever ran to either commercial destination for the convenience of the agricultural community.

The building of the Montreux railway involved feats of audacious engineering and the piercing of a major Alpine tunnel under the Jaman mountain over which the old cheese path climbed. Swiss engineers, and the Italian navvies working on the project, also had to construct several railway spirals in the sheer hillside behind Montreux in order to gain altitude before they entered their 3 km Jaman tunnel. They tunnelled again on their approach into Château-d'Oex thereby circumventing the road's steep gradient, and also avoiding giving offence to powerful property owners who did not want to sacrifice prime agricultural land. The chosen route, however, involved by-passing the saw mills at Les Moulins. The angry mill owners were forced to cart their timber to railway sidings on the far side of the river in order to avail themselves of a rail service which clearly gave preference to tourists rather than to foresters.

The first train reached Château-d'Oex in 1904 and a prestigious new railway station was built on the site of the old cattle market. A few years later the old primary school building was converted into the station hotel and restaurant. Although the railway did carry sawn timber, beef cattle and market women, its distinctive cachet was always the luxury trade in foreign guests. The company ordered a firm of coach-builders in Paris to design four unique narrow-gauge dining cars. Since the cars were too heavy to haul regularly up and down the spiralled slope from Montreux the company stabled them at the summit, near the mouth of the Jaman tunnel, and served meals, three sittings for lunch and one for dinner, as the trains plied back and forth through Château-d'Oex. In 1907 the price of a meal was three shillings and six-pence in British sterling. After a hiatus during the Great War of 1914, luxury traffic to Château-d'Oex rapidly revived and the company ordered Pullman-type luxury coaches in the dark blue-and-gold livery favoured by the Compagnie Internationale des Wagons-Lits. By the time these coaches were delivered, however, Wall Street had crashed and Pullman travel declined sharply. During the Second World War the line was used by the Swiss federal army, but in 1945 tourists returned, among them Field-Marshal Montgomery of Alamein. By then, however, Château-d'Oex had been partially eclipsed by Gstaad where a bigger and more luxurious complex of hotels had been built next to the old farming village of Saanen.

Although the luxury branch of the tourist industry had dwindled with the onset of the world depression of the 1930s, a diminished expatriate gentry hung on in Château-d'Oex. There were some 400 semi-resident British citizens in the community during the inter-war years. Some had come from the empire, preferring the crisp air of the Alps to the mellow mists of the English shires after a life-time of colonial service in India. Others were visitors, many of them from a semi-privileged *débutante* tradition which sent young ladies to finishing schools in Château-d'Oex to learn French and good manners or to perfect their tennis and skiing prior to marriage. One such short-term visitor in the post-war era was a future Princess of Wales, Diana, and another who had passed through on the luxury train was her future mother-in-law, Elizabeth II. A few of the young English ladies flirted daringly with local farmers and some, often to the chagrin of their families, married and settled in Château-d'Oex. The British expatriate community included a number of working residents such as matrons and teachers. They helped to evolve a philanthropic culture which occasionally interacted with local society. The sale of works in aid of the infirmary was developed along lines familiar in English vicarages and became a tradition, along with the parish jumble sale, which survived the virtual disappearance of resident expatriates. The English church also survived, though with a tiny do-it-yourself congregation, and its chapel was used by the local community for concerts. In 1921 the world famous organist, Albert Schweitzer, gave a recital to raise money for his mission hospital in Central Africa. One institution did not lend itself to local needs, however, and in the early 1950s the last expatriates were forced with heavy hearts to sell the books of the British library to a pulp factory.

The rise and fall of the Château-d'Oex tourist industry was closely connected with the evolution of winter as well as summer sports. Before the invention of artificial ice rinks Château-d'Oex became an ideal place to make open-air natural rinks. The winter was usually cold enough to freeze flooded tennis courts or even a whole football field. The weather was often sunny and open-air skating attracted the Victorian hotel guests. The art took on a growing elegance and music was provided for men and women who wanted to indulge in the fashion for ballroom dancing on ice. The Scottish sport of curling, a form of bowls in which the stones were slid on polished ice, was adopted by the more elderly foreign residents. With natural ice rinks cheaply available the local population also took to skating and Château-d'Oex established an ice hockey team with help from the sports-minded British. So good did this team become that the Château-d'Oex club was able in the 1920s to win the Swiss championship. The return of poverty to the village meant, however, that the club was unable to defend its title since team members could not afford the rail fares to attend championship matches.

In the long run ice rinks became less important than snow slopes for the development of winter sports. Château-d'Oex never built a bob-sleigh run but some of the mountain trails were ideal for tobogganing. Day trippers and weekend visitors came up from the foggy Swiss plain by train carrying their wooden toboggans and spent crisp sunlit days climbing the mountains and hurtling down the slopes. For affluent sightseers horse-drawn sleighs were on hire from which they could view the scenery wrapped in furs and rugs. Tobogganing gradually gave way to sheeing, or skiing, as the preferred winter sport. Men in knicker-bockers and women in long skirts negotiated the elementary slopes of the village fields balancing themselves with a single long pole, like acrobats, in the years before twin ski sticks became the mode. For the more adventurous Château-d'Oex built a ski jump in the inter-war years. It was reached by foot across a suspension bridge held high above the river on two long cables. On the mountain above the ski jump a trail led steeply up through woods to open meadows that were ideal for downhill skiing. The most effective way of climbing the slopes was to fix seal skins to the undersides of the skis. So good were these snow fields that in the 1960s a cable car was built spanning the valley and linking the railway station to the shoulder of the opposite moun-tain. Some years earlier, in 1945, a more rudimentary type of hoist had been built up the hill above Les Moulins. Enthusiasts abandoned their seal skins and were hauled to the summit by short ropes clamped to a moving cable. This ski slope became internationally famous in 1956 when one of the local farm-girls, Madeleine Berthod, achieved the Olympic gold medal for downhill ski racing. Château-d'Oex's reputa-tion as a ski resort was not, however, to last. By the 1980s new invest-ment and new technology had opened higher fields in the Alps where snow fell more reliably and the season was longer. Château-d'Oex, unlike some other Alpine resorts, had to cling to farming as its eco-nomic mainstay though it still sought to blend farming with a modest level of involvement in the tourist industry.

During the first two-thirds of the twentieth century a summer farm-ing industry with a slack winter season could, in theory, release labour to staff the winter sports industry. Farmers who could not earn enough from cheese and beef alone, and who were reluctant to engage in dan-gerous and ill-paid winter logging with horses, could supplement their income by attaching skiers to cable hoists, by serving meals and hot drinks in mountain restaurants, or by rescuing accident victims with ambulance sledges. The most popular ancillary work was the teaching of skiing, but a potential conflict between farming and tourism could emerge as happened in the resort of Villars across the mountain. There young farmers found that ski-teaching in the day time could be congenially complemented by *après-ski* socialising and drinking with foreign visitors. The adult sons and daughters-in-law of the Villars farmers began to resent the evening chores of winter milking and feeding and sought to escape from agriculture, as did the young in many other mountain boroughs. Château-d'Oex, in marked contrast, saw its dairy industry survive and grow despite the potentially demoralising appeal of the dance floor or other tourist distractions. Young men, usually with fully working farm wives, remained committed to farming and cheesemaking and so preserved an Alpine culture with its own social appeal and a slightly superior moral disdain for the foreigners who passed through. Although many farm children did leave for the plain to seek employment, others remained in the highland, won cups at the shooting championship in the spring, went chamois stalking in the autumn and joined the male voice choir in winter.

The survival of farming was partly a necessary function of the limits of tourism in Château-d'Oex. In the 1930s the resort had precociously boasted a cinema and a swimming pool and in the 1940s its antagonism to motor cars gave way to Alpine rally racing and later to a huge annual jamboree of Volkswagen 'beetles'. In the later twentieth century the village developed white-water rafting down the cataracts once used for floating logs, and mountain-bike racing over the highland cattle trails. Alpine ballooning, initially encouraged by David Niven who had been the hero of the film 'Around the World in Eighty Days' became such a successful enterprise that attempts to circumnavigate the world in a hot-air balloon were launched from Château-d'Oex. In March 1999 the Breitling 3 balloon took off from Château-d'Oex piloted by Bertrand Piccard and Brian Jones and in three weeks won the race to undertake the first non-stop flight around the globe. But despite all the efforts put into tourism only 14 per cent of employment was tourist related in the 1980s and some of the jobs were undertaken by guest workers from abroad rather than by highlanders trying to keep a foothold in their mountains. Ancillary services, boutiques, galleries, workshops, museums, were all limited in their economic impact. More fundamentally the nature of the hospitality sought and offered in Château-d'Oex changed during the last third of the twentieth century. Traditional hotels and boarding houses now accounted for only 700 of the available tourist beds. Visitors developed a new tradition of self-catering holidays in tents, caravans or the youth hostel and these generated little employment. More dramatically Château-d'Oex was cautiously opened to the building of secondary homes, a development which created temporary architectural and construction jobs but not necessarily much employment for local highlanders. Farmers were ambivalent about the building programme, resenting the loss of the sunniest hay slopes which were the ones most desirable for building plots yet valuing the influx of short-term wealth as the housing stock doubled with a rash of weekend pseudo-chalets imitating the traditional architectural style. In the long-term, farming continued to dominate the Château-d'Oex economy.

As Château-d'Oex straddled its two economic sectors, farming held its own in a modest new round of consolidation. The richest farmers even assembled herds of cows which they owned outright instead of cobbling together a herd with the animals of neighbours or with cows hired for the season from stockmen on the plain. Whereas eighteenth-century farmers had sought to accumulate enough summer cows to be able to produce one whole Gruyère cheese each day, some twentieth-century farmers made two or even three whole cheeses per day. The milk yields of the new cross-bred Simmental–Holstein cows were double those of their Simmental mothers and production reached 4000 kilograms of milk per cow per season. The Château-d'Oex dairymen not only sold their Alpine Gruyère, now commercially known as 'Etivaz Cheese', but also sent daily tankers of milk to the plain as well as selling annually three hundred tonnes of beef. Beef cattle no longer went to market on the hoof, or by mountain railway, but were delivered door-to-door by road hauliers in exchange for imported fodder. By the 1990s 70 working dairy farms epitomised the successful recovery of the highland cheese industry. The average size of Château-d'Oex farms remained small, however, each having about 20 cows on about 20 acres. Half the acres on a medium farm were owned by the farmer himself, but half were rented from a neighbour or from an absentee landlord. Making a living in the highland remained a struggle.

In the postwar decades the Château-d'Oex farming industry had at first tried to minimise its costs and maximise its profits by a policy of hiring immigrant labour which was cheaper than the Swiss labour which had been seduced away by city wages. Historically migrant workers in Château-d'Oex had been 'Sardinians', subjects of the king of Sardinia who ruled both the Savoy and the Piedmont flanks of the southern Alps. Most of these Italian migrants had been seasonal stone-breakers but a few gained residence rights, established families and set up business as cobblers, decorators and greengrocers. Some worked alongside the itinerant Catholic cowmen from Fribourg who followed the transhumant herds up from the plain. A later generation of oscillating labour, sucked in when needed and squeezed out when redundant, came from the Catholic regions of Iberia, Spain first and later Portugal. Although some of the new migrants worked in the farming industry, most found their niche in domestic work, in the hotel trade and in the service industries. Conservative Protestant farmers managed, though not without difficulty, to adjust to the cultural expectations of their Catholic migrant workers, but soon Iberian labour costs rose and a new generation of migrant workers were recruited from among Muslims of the Balkans. Some were Turkish or Bosnian *gastarbeiter* accustomed to working in Germany but others were peasants from Albania, Europe's poorest and most isolated country. Their problems of communication and harmonisation were so severe that Château-d'Oex farmers relied on them only to herd heifers and bullocks on the remotest alps. In the dairy industry farmers turned to mechanisation as an alternative to cheap labour.

At the end of the Second World War motors were virtually unknown in the Château-d'Oex farming industry. Men, women and horses still provided virtually all the energy used for milking, churning and carrying. Electricity provided rail transport, village lighting and the small proportion of domestic cooking and heating that was not done with wood. Petroleum fuelled the post bus, the vet's jeep and two doctors' cars, but the fire engine was still man-hauled and the chimney sweep did not acquire a motor car until the 1950s. Within a generation this situation had been revolutionised. Labour saving of every kind came to be based on train loads of imported fuel oil and on the huge Hongrin hydro-electric storage dam built in the 1960s. Horses virtually vanished from the farming scene though a few survived in the tourist industry. In the new mechanical age the scything of hay was replaced by machine mowing with hand-held, single-axle tractors. Land Rovers, and occasionally even helicopters, were used to ferry the biggest cheese cauldrons up to the highest Alpine dairies. Portable, diesel-driven, milking machines doubled the productivity of cowmen and generator-operated cauldron paddles took some of the muscle ache out of cheese stirring. Motorisation, however, was not enough to make farming economically attractive. The capital required to buy automatic hay loaders, fan-operated grass silos, and tractor-driven muck spreaders remained beyond the reach of any farmer dependent on the profits derived from mountain cheese.

Market forces were not propitious to the preserving of Alpine farming in postwar Château-d'Oex. The survival of highland farming came to depend on the politics of agricultural loans and of subsidies offered by the state of Vaud and the federal government. Farmers had to become skilled at measuring the costs of soft loans and the benefits of subsidies when farming steep, or inaccessible, or high-altitude land. Switzerland was unwilling to allow its mountain farmland to revert to wilderness and Swiss farm subsidies overtook those in the rest of Western Europe, outstripping by 50 per cent the controversial subsidies which the European Union paid to its farmers and peasants. In 1997 it was said, with almost as much truth as humour, that the average Swiss cow was subsidised to the tune of one thousand dollars per hoof. Farm support from the federal government had its most dramatic effect on transport. Between 1960 and 1987 Château-d'Oex was enabled to build 100 km of farm access roads with all-weather concrete surfaces. The new roads enabled hay, straw and fertilizer to be moved quickly, milk to be delivered to the dairy daily and staff to be deployed to any part of the highland. The perceived disadvantage of road construction was that some of the cost fell on the farm user, some scarce farm land was sacrificed, and badly surveyed roads in unstable terrain caused danger-ous erosion. Roads, however, also did much to restore the integrity of family life since herdsmen and loggers, who had formerly lived for days if not weeks in their mountain shelters, could now drive home to the village each night. Alternatively families could move up to the mountains. The isolation of old style summer farming with all-male production teams was ended and dairying became a family industry in which supermarket shopping by car replaced self-reliant catering based on potato biscuits and cottage cheese.

The politicians, both in Lausanne and in Bern, tried to find ways of minimising the cost of preserving mountain farming. They particularly tried to persuade small farmers to share their motorised equipment, offering cash subsidies to those who jointly bought mono-axle mowing machines and agreed to cut their hay in rotation using a single machine. The policy had limited success since good haymaking weather was relatively rare in the highland and a farmer who could not profit from it because it was his neighbour's turn to use the tractor was disadvantaged. Moreover the farmers played a strong hand when driving their bargain with the politicians. Land that was not farmed rapidly became subject to ecological decay, erosion and flooding. Good farming practice, moreover, enhanced the picture-book attraction of the highland and brought seasonal foreign visitors who earned the government foreign exchange. The interdependence of farming and tourism met one persistent difficulty, however, when tourist revenues were constantly threatened by the rise of the Swiss franc which, in half a century, moved steadily up from one twentieth of a pound sterling to half a pound sterling. This harmful strengthening of the federal currency gradually whittled away traditional British tourism and only partially replaced it with domestic tourism or with tourism from Germany and the Netherlands where late twentieth-century currencies were strong. By the 1990s the foreign visitors on the now refurbished 'panoramic' trains of the Château-d'Oex railway often came from Japan.

10
Patriotism and the Shadow of War

Over the course of 800 years Château-d'Oex belonged to three different nations, the principality of Gruyère, the city–state of Bern and the republic of Vaud. In each case the village had come to acquire a loyalty to its sovereign rulers, be they aristocratic, oligarchic or democratic. Identifying with a new national culture took time, but by the middle of the nineteenth century Château-d'Oex's integration with Vaud had become a reality. So loyal had Château-d'Oex become, indeed, that when in 1848 Vaud became a member of the embryonic Confederation of Helvetia the village showed little inclination to switch from its local loyalty to the state with the green-and-white flag to adopt a wider federal identification with the new Switzerland. The development of a patriotism which embraced all of the Swiss languages, cultures and religions grew only slowly. It spanned the hundred years from the signing of the initial federal charter in 1848 to the postwar demobilisation of the federal army in 1945. Belonging to a single, federated, Swiss army had been one of the factors responsible for bringing about closer patriotic union.

The nineteenth-century Swiss states were initially quite unwilling to surrender their military autonomy to a federal super-state. The inaugural structure of the confederation included a parliament that was responsible for foreign affairs, a common currency and a union post office but it did not include an integrated federal army. Instead each state was required to supply a proportion of its militiamen to serve the needs of common defence. These militia units had their own style of weaponry, their own regimental command structure, and their own fiercely patriotic loyalty to their homelands. For 20 years the Swiss union remained a largely economic one and each state retained sovereignty in matters of law and was partially autonomous in matters of defence. By 1870, however, the old constitution of 1848 could no longer stand the strain that was put upon it by the changing European world.

The second stage in the unification of Switzerland, and the creation of a Swiss national army, was triggered by the final stages of the adjacent unifications of Germany to the north and Italy to the south. When the king of Italy entered Rome in 1870 and made it his capital city the Pope shut himself into the Vatican palace and declared that he might no longer have any temporal authority over a state, but that in matters of doctrine his word was infallible and could not be challenged by faithful Roman Catholics. The effect of this on the Swiss was immediate alarm among Protestants. They remembered clearly the war of the Catholic League in 1847 and feared that loyalty to the Vatican might take precedence over loyalty to the confederation if the Swiss union were not strengthened. Proposals to strengthen the central institutions of the federation were put forward. Château-d'Oex, although traditionally isolationist and suspicious of big government, was also strongly Protestant and therefore feared its ultra-Catholic neighbours both north and south. By itself, however, the crisis over papal infallibility would probably not have been enough to persuade the Swiss to accept a strengthening of their federation.

A second impulse towards increasing the power of the centre followed hard on the heels of the first. The unification of Germany had even more disturbing consequences for the Swiss than the unification of Italy. When the army of the new German empire captured Alsace, and defeated the army of the crumbling French empire, thousands of French soldiers sought refuge on Swiss soil. The confederation had no troops of its own either to repel the French or to prevent the Germans following in hot pursuit should they so choose. The impact of the Franco–German war was felt as far from the frontier as Château-d'Oex. Disarmed French soldiers fleeing from the war struggled into the highland in search of sanctuary. They brought with them a plague of cholera. Even parochial politicians who opposed any transfer of new powers from the individual states to the confederation recognized that some improvement in national defence might serve the common good. A new constitution was drawn up in 1872 but it went too far for the traditionalists. It took two further years of bargaining before the structure of a federal army, and a matching constitution, could be agreed and accepted by plebiscite. The attitude of voters in Vaud to the proposal was sweetened by an offer to locate a proposed Swiss supreme court at Lausanne.

Creating an army was not in itself sufficient to create a sense of patriotic solidarity among the Swiss states. The citizens of Château-d'Oex, although only attached to the state of Vaud and to the metropolis of Lausanne since 1803, were nonetheless ardent defenders of Vaud rights. Attempts to soften their provincial patriotism and create a wider federal loyalty to a red flag with the white cross met with only limited success. Once petty disputes over the exact shape and design of the federal flag had been resolved, the federal government tried to launch a grand appeal for national solidarity in 1891. Their efforts were not always felicitous or sensitive. They chose the date of 1891 for their nationalist crusade because it represented the seventh centenary of the founding of the city of Bern. But to many Swiss the city of Bern, seat of the federal government, was not the pride of the federation but its problem.

The federal celebrations of 1891 were crafted so as to embrace the old lake-side states of central Switzerland by giving prominence to the August treaty of 1291, one of the many treaties that had facilitated the growth of the self-governing oligarchies of the central Alps. A previously favoured 'founding charter' of 1315 was superseded as the symbolic document of Swiss nationhood by the newly-revealed treaty of 1291. This treaty was now deemed, without much evidence to support the claim, to have been sworn on the first day of August, a day thereupon chosen to commemorate freedom and unity by becoming a 'national' independence day for all of the Swiss states. Château-d'Oex took little notice of this new August feast day but continued to celebrate independence on 14 April, the day on which Vaud had become a free republic in 1803. A hundred years of federal propaganda still did not establish the new August bank holiday though in 1991 Château-d'Oex did build numerous mountain-top bonfires to celebrate the seventh centenary of the pact of 1291 and when the working day was over the bonfires were lit and spectacular fireworks were let off.

Another strategy aimed at forging a Swiss national identity in the late nineteenth century had little more success than the August fireworks in inspiring the people of Château-d'Oex or of Romanic Switzerland. This initiative involved the re-invention of William Tell as Switzerland's founding ancestor. The legend of the archer who had been cruelly forced by his lord and ruler to shoot an apple balanced on his son's head had spread through Europe from the Norse countries after the twelfth century. One hypothesis suggested that it had been brought to the Alps by Swedish bishops who regaled their colleagues with Nordic folk-tales in Swiss taverns while attending the Council of Basel around 1431. A Swiss variant of the legend, in which the oppressor was a wicked lord-bailiff, was written down in 1472. Stories of the mythical resistance hero circulated in the war camps when the Swiss regiments defeated the army of Charles the Bold of Burgundy in 1476.

For nineteenth-century mythmakers William Tell was a fickle figure to conjure with. To some he was the champion of liberty, the defender of the weak against the arrogant, of the poor against the powerful. In some accounts Tell not only stood up to a wicked ruler who had unjustly forced him to put his son's life at risk, but had then taken his just revenge by murdering the lord-bailiff. This 'Robin Hood' variant of the Tell legends had little appeal to politicians trying to build a disciplined and orderly confederation among the 'ungovernable' Swiss. Indeed one would have expected William Tell to send shivers down the spine of any statesman who recalled that Tell had been a hero of the Jacobins who had carried the French revolution into Switzerland in 1798. The fathers of the federation looked for another variant of the Tell legends and found the 'Joan of Arc' version.

In the hands of the inventors of tradition William Tell became a patriotic hero and the wicked lord-bailiff became a foreigner. The story was richly embroidered. In one variant William Tell was not only Swiss but had actually been present in the field of Rutli, on the bluff above Lake Lucerne, where the charter of 1291 had allegedly been sworn. The charter was transformed from a temporary agreement about mutual security during an unexpected interregnum in the reigning Swiss family of Habsburg into a nationalist challenge to the now foreign Habsburgs who had become Austrians. William Tell's challenger was neatly turned into an oppressive Austrian. The hero's weapon anachronistically became the crossbow used by a later generation of Swiss warriors. Had the nineteenth-century masters of propaganda wanted a genuinely historic figure they could have adopted the pacific hermit, Nicholas of Flue, who had saved the Swiss from fratricidal war in 1481. But a reticent oracle mediating in a shameful civil war was not an adequate patriotic folk hero for 1891 and so a carefully tailored rendering of the Tell legends was adopted to give Switzerland a 'national' hero. Thus it was that Tell the slayer of tyrants and defender of liberty was replaced by Tell the loyal and obedient Swiss patriot. His image was put on the union postage stamps and the federal coins. His crossbow was adopted as the hallmark of Swiss industry. Not until the dark days of 1940, when Switzerland was surrounded by Hitler's armies and the Nazis had banned performances of Schiller's revolutionary play about

Tell, did the Swiss remember that their national hero was the hero of freedom as well as the hero of political obedience.

Attempts to create a sense of Swiss national identity with a new folk hero, a new flag and a new August bank holiday had only very limited impact on the people of Château-d'Oex. It was the outbreak of the First World War that brought home to them with dramatic effect the significance of their new national loyalty to the federation. The long-established neutrality of the Swiss union was threatened by the sudden spread of war through Europe. On 1 August 1914 the federal army of Switzerland was mobilised for the first time. The call came exactly 40 years after the constitution of 1874 had unified the 25 armies of the member states of the union. The old provincial armies had proved inadequate to guarantee the armed neutrality which the Congress of Vienna had imposed on Switzerland and now the ability of the new union army to protect that neutrality and independence was about to be tested. The first day of August was suddenly etched into Château-d'Oex folk memory by the trauma of mobilisation. Ironically it was the very day which the federal government had been trying, with so little success, to establish as a feast day on which to celebrate unification. In 1914 Château-d'Oex men of military age were given only a few hours notice to don their uniforms, pick up their rifles, leave their families and join their units at Aigle in the Rhône valley. Many of them remained conscripted under federal colours for four years and four months. Women, children and grandparents were left to haul the hay and milk the cows.

The August crisis of 1914 hit the Château-d'Oex cheese industry adversely albeit momentarily in the middle of the milking season. Swiss farmers throughout the union were quick to point out that by mobilising cheesemakers the federal authorities would jeopardise one of the country's most valuable sources of food and of export revenue. The army chiefs-of-staff met representatives of the dairy industry and agreed that any cheesemaker certified as indispensable by his borough authority would be released from military duty as soon as his call-up papers had been verified. The cheesemasters of Château-d'Oex returned to their dairies within days of being mobilised. Equally significantly the army agreed to rescind the mobilisation for army use of any horses that might be required for dairying. In Château-d'Oex the order to conscript horses and carts had been issued on 31 July and 52 horses had been sent over the mountain to the military depôt at Aigle. A few days later the horses were sent back to the highland. Meanwhile, however, the reserved men of the first company of Château-d'Oex fusiliers, who had not been conscripted to serve outside of the highland, were summoned to present themselves for local duty on 6 August at 5 p.m. They were instructed to bring with them enough food of their own to last them for two days while the army sorted out its supply logistics.

Food for a federal army that was being conscripted for the first time presented the quartermasters with long-term planning problems. On the plain, cereal farmers who were about to embark on the harvest emulated cheese farmers in seeking exemption from military service. They protested that mobilisation of all male labour before the harvest was liable to endanger the national supply of bread as well as army rations. Their plea was rejected. The politicians were sure that when pressed the cereal farmers would be able to bring in the harvest using the unskilled, the unemployed, surplus women from the town and men unfit for military service. Even on the cheese farms it had only been the craft specialists who had been exempted from call-up. In Château-d'Oex the borough authorities agreed emergency measures to ensure that the second crop of hay, a particularly good one, should be safely brought to the barns. Any farmer's wife needing assistance was invited to apply to an emergency agricultural committee presided over by Charles-Victor Favrod-Coune, still a member of the Vaud parliament sitting for Château-d'Oex. In the heat of the emergency peasants were impressed when members of the English community, who normally lived a leisured expatriate life supported by their stocks and shares, rolled up their sleeves and helped bring in hay before the fine weather broke.

The outbreak of war led to panic buying, to the stockpiling of food, to speculative profiteering by shopkeepers and to immediate artificial shortages, particularly of sugar and flour. Although the panic was less acute among farmers than it was in Lausanne, Auguste Cottier, the now venerable governor of the highland, nevertheless issued orders restricting food sales and ordering shops to post their prices outside their doors. He also demanded that bars and cafés should close at 9 pm. One symptom of the crisis was a shortage of coins. Shops quickly ran out of change and could not get new supplies from the local savings banks. The federal government eventually issued banknotes in five franc denominations to partially replace familiar gold coinage for the duration of the war. Government suddenly became much more interventionist, milk prices were fixed at 20 cents a litre, bread was restricted to a single 'national' quality of loaf sold at 40 cents a kilogram and the price of butter was reduced from 2 francs to 1.80 per metric pound.

When the federal government mobilised its army it naturally anticipated that highland farms would be able to help feed the troops. The

Château-d'Oex town clerk, V. Turrian, was appointed to the post of war-time commissioner responsible for buying meat. As a consequence rumour and panic swept through the valley. One woman, managing her absent husband's farm, was told by a travelling butcher that the army would confiscate all livestock on the hoof without compensation. He urgently pressed the woman to sell her cow to him for a derisory price before she was too late and the government had come to seize it. The army retaliated against such sharp practice with racist warnings to villages that 'Jewish merchants' were scouring the country in search of livestock for the meat trade. On 21 August 1914 Cottier advised his government in Lausanne that no 'Jewish' profiteers had yet been reported in Château-d'Oex. Ten days later, to limit the growth of the black market, the army posted the prices it would pay for meat, offering 85 francs per metric hundredweight for goat's meat and 115 francs for best beef. This open strategy backfired, however, when farmers immediately expected that they would obtain premium army prices for any elderly breeding cows or lean bullocks they cared to offer. The army did nonetheless manage to buy 32 suitable head of cattle from Château-d'Oex for 20 000 francs. A war-time process of price escalation began and eventually put substantial incomes into the pockets of highland farmers. At the Château-d'Oex autumn fairs 300 beasts were on offer in 1914. The fair also did a brisk trade in fruit and vegetables for preserving but there was little demand for consumer goods or clothing during the uncertain early weeks of the war.

The effect of the outbreak of war on the cheese market was as striking as it had been on the meat market. No cheese was available during the month of August since the old season's cheese had already been sent to market and the new season's cheese was still being salted in the dairy cellars. What little cheese the retailer Desquartiers had available in his grocery was 'foreign' cheese imported from a factory at Bulle. On 2 September the army tried to buy 6000 kilograms of cheese in Château-d'Oex but the canny owner of the dairy advised it that no cheese was yet available for consumption. Producers clearly hoped that by the time the current season's cheeses had matured war-time shortages would have raised the price of dairy products. By February 1915 these hopes were being realised as merchants from the plain began to offer premium prices for immature cheeses that were still only half salted. These cheeses were later sold to war-time profiteers from France. The traffic created such a scarcity in Château-d'Oex that normal households could no longer afford to buy their accustomed staple of mature cheese in order to satisfy their protein requirements.

The Swiss government intervened and granted a cheese export monopoly to a cartel of cheese merchants. The dairies, which had gained from escalating prices, protested strenuously that the newly-licensed export barons were now profiting from speculation and the government was forced to stabilise cheese prices for domestic consumers. In 1916 they fixed a price at 204 francs per metric hundredweight for best Gruyère. A different problem arose, however, when restricting exports to satisfy home demand interfered with the raising of revenue needed to pay for essential war-time imports. Cheese scarcity therefore continued, consumers were deprived of protein, prices rose yet further, dairymen grew rich and Swiss cheese exports reached ten million francs a year.

During the war many items of food came to be rationed in Château-d'Oex including potatoes, rice, pasta and bread as well as meat and cheese. Overall the price index rose three-fold during the war severely hitting a society accustomed to stable prices and zero inflation. Cheese prices had been kept to a two-fold increase but beef had risen four-fold. Potatoes and eggs had risen fastest in price and there were bitter complaints about the poor quality of imported German potatoes. By 1917 some 26 hectares of Château-d'Oex's prime hay meadow had been dug up to grow local potatoes, though no other crop such as oil-seed or wheat was attempted in the highland during the emergency. On the Swiss plain the food crisis was matched by an equally severe coal crisis. Château-d'Oex was partially immune from this since it relied on local wood for cooking and heating and on hydro-electricity for rail transport. When fuel prices on the plain reached exorbitant levels Château-d'Oex sought ways of making a profit from the crisis and the village tried to find seams of coal which it could mine and sell to the plain. Some local investors even set up a colliery which offered shares to the public and advertised for a craftsman who knew how to dig a mine but it never extracted any coal.

The combined food and fuel crises caused acute anxiety to government. Fearing popular protests from cold and hungry citizens it issued orders banning public demonstrations. Any Château-d'Oex innkeeper found selling alcohol to a customer deemed to be 'in a state of exaltation', or in other words hostile to the authorities, was to be denounced to the police. Publicans were also warned that all persons in receipt of social security were banned from buying alcoholic beverages. At the same time the opening hours of chocolate houses and drinking saloons were restricted. Furthermore any shopkeeper accused of profiting from war shortages, or condoning the hoarding of paraffin oil and candles, was liable to have his or her premises closed. Harassing wealthy foreigners who brought foreign exchange into the village was strictly prohibited despite the climate of patriotic xenophobia which prevailed.

The degree of panic that the outbreak of war created in one remote village surrounded by mountains may seem surprising. An early decree required the village to report by telegraph any outbreak of smallpox, typhus, cholera or plague. Louis Struby, the Château-d'Oex chief of police, remained more fearful of subversion than of infection. He drew up a rota of citizens who were required to mount a night watch in the village from 9 p.m. to 5 a.m. Sightings of strangers were to be reported to the authorities particularly, it was specified, if they were suspected of coming from Russia. Russians had probably been symbols of popular fear since a Russian army had entered Switzerland in hot pursuit of Napoleon one hundred years earlier. The warning, however, seems to have been a self-fulfilling prophecy and later in the war four 'Russians' were arrested in a field at Etivaz. They claimed to have escaped from a prisoner-of-war camp in south Germany and to have walked across Switzerland for 36 days in ragged clothes and leaking boots. The phenomenon of war panic in the first days of the war caused one schoolmaster, at Les Granges, to set up a neighbourhood watch but his volunteer guardsmen soon disbanded their rota when war fever waned. Later in the war the same people claimed that they had heard the big war-guns firing in Alsace 100 km beyond the mountains.

One early war-time fear in Château-d'Oex was that the railway would be disrupted by saboteurs. Railway personnel on the remote mountain line were required to carry weapons and ammunition to protect their trains from unspecified dangers. For a few days Château-d'Oex citizens were even forbidden to walk within 200 paces of the railway track such was the level of hysteria. Normality soon returned but train services were curtailed, the noon-day express was cancelled and all restaurant-car services were suspended for the duration of hostilities. The bourgeoisie was also incommoded by restrictions on the sale of motor car fuel and by a ban on the sale of motor tyres and engine spares.

Château-d'Oex found many ways of adapting to the inconveniences of war-time austerity. A women's union tried to make life easier for the soldiers who had been sent to protect Switzerland from Germany along the Rhine by knitting them woollen socks before the winter set in. In practice, they later realised, the greatest enemy of the Château-d'Oex conscripts was not physical deprivation but homesickness. Back in the village the women's union organised a rota of young girls willing to do cleaning, mending, sewing and cooking when farm wives took over the heavy agricultural work. Schoolteaching had apparently remained a largely male occupation and the mobilisation of one grammar schoolmaster disrupted secondary classes in the college. In the village elementary school women took to organising the cooking of soup for children from poor families. The children themselves grew the potatoes to make the soup. Charity was tinged with puritanical resentment, however, when middle-class philanthropists noted that children who had run all the way to Château-d'Oex from their hamlet classrooms for the soup were later seen gathering outside the sweetshops and pastry parlours in the high street.

Sugar deprivation was acutely felt by the poor but austerity also affected the rich. At the beginning of the war the annual confectionery sale in aid of the infirmary was cancelled when it was said that 'no one will buy meringues when there is no cream to go with them'. In 1916 the government tried to cut down on flour consumption, as well as save sugar, by ordering that all cake shops should close on Thursdays. There was a public out-cry throughout Vaud and pastry cooks held a protest meeting at Yverdon. Much more serious than the craving for sweet food was the low nutritional level overall. One of the surprises of the mobilisation in Château-d'Oex had been the realisation of how poor the health of farming children was. So many youths were rejected as unfit for military service that the government organised sporting events as a national means of improving fitness and health. The initiative was so successful that competitive gymnastics became one of the great patriotic activities of Switzerland. It was perhaps appropriate that the Olympic movement decided to locate its headquarters at Lausanne.

The war brought new sights and experiences to Château-d'Oex. Crowds turned out to see a unit of the Valais army which came over the mountain from the Rhône. Although the Valais army had been a part of the new Swiss army since 1874 the soldiers with their long procession of pack mules were still exotic and caused much excitement in the village. After a short night's rest the strange conscripts set off to cross the northern pass at La Verdaz and descend the steep stone-carved steps down the mountain to the old castle at Montsalvens before walking to Fribourg. Another troop movement brought 3000 men and 160 horses to Château-d'Oex but they only stayed for one night and disappointed the shopkeepers by spending very little money. They were crudely billeted in schoolrooms, chapels and the village hall rather than in the empty guesthouses. As winter closed in a cycle regiment pushed its bicycles through thick snow over the pass from the Simmental; when the men eventually reached Château-d'Oex they were given the luxury of heated accommodation. The most exciting military event of the war, however, was the arrival on 30 and 31 May 1916 of two train loads of British internees.

The internees were men who had been wounded and captured on the war front and then sent to Switzerland as mutilated servicemen whom Germany could no longer feed in its prisoner-of-war camps despite a system of food parcels organised by Britain and Switzerland. An internment camp was set up for the men in Château-d'Oex under the command of a young Swiss medical officer, Carl Jung, who had a reputation in psychiatry. The liberated prisoners-of-war arrived to a festive reception in Château-d'Oex with garlands, speeches and toasts from a host community which was strongly pro-French rather than pro-German in its war-time political sentiments. This partisanship had caused trouble in Lausanne when a passionate young man had climbed to the roof of the German consulate and torn down the imperial flag. The Swiss confederation felt it not only necessary to apologise to Germany but also, to the great indignation of Château-d'Oex when the news leaked out, to mobilise a secret force which could repress any subsequent signs of anti-German feeling in the Romanic part of Switzerland.

The Château-d'Oex hotels did good business with their new British guests. Local boy scouts ran errands for the mutilated officers and received a letter of thanks from Lord Baden-Powell himself. In Ireland the women of Ulster raised a gift of 300 francs for the children of the poor in Château-d'Oex. In England collections were made to enable the wives of the more privileged internees to join their husbands for holidays in the Swiss Alps. Officers' wives were taken across war-time France in special convoys. The village was initially enthralled by the sight of a Scotsman in a kilt and a Gurkha in a turban. The 'British Internees Variety Company' put on concerts in the village hall to raise money for local charities. The British colonel and his lady held a reception for the former prime minister of France who passed through Château-d'Oex on his way to visit French internees in the hotels of Interlaken.

Coming to terms with the internees was not all a matter of improving lectures and teas with the Reverend Sutherland, vicar of the English church in Château-d'Oex. Attempts to teach English soldiers French were an almost total failure. Farmers who had hoped for additional hands to bring in their hay crop found that the English had no aptitude for mountain agriculture. Even army carpenters and bookbinders did not perform well in the Château-d'Oex workshops. The public works department had anticipated that prisoners-of-war might build the long-planned new road across the river, but soon realised that long demoralising spells of idleness in prison camps had eroded any concept of work discipline. Restlessness set in, drinking became a problem, a black market in British army boots and clothing had to be crushed and the law courts opened a special isolation prison for convicted internees. The official chronicler of the war noted, however, that khaki uniforms had a romantic appeal to the young women of Château-d'Oex whose regular admirers had been away at the front for two years. The courting habits of foreign soldiers caused as much indignation as their drinking sprees. On 11 October 1918 fighting broke out and the British officers could no longer control their men in the last weeks of the war. It was not until 4 December that the internees could finally be repatriated to England. Twenty of them took Château-d'Oex brides with them. By the time the British left American soldiers were stationed in Château-d'Oex, apparently oblivious to the concept of Switzerland's neutrality. The Americans built themselves huge prefabricated barracks on the great meadow at the eastern end of the village.

By the time the war ended the supply of food to Château-d'Oex was genuinely in crisis. Visits by British wives were stopped to preserve stocks. A blackmarket ring in Chalet Iris was disclosed to have been buying up food and smuggling it at great profit to the war-starved Austrian empire. When the authorities tried to restrict the retail price of potatoes the Château-d'Oex greengrocers refused to handle them. Instead the borough managed to buy a whole railway wagon of potatoes from Italy which it sold direct to the public. Later the federal government nationalised all potato stocks and ordered the creation of a national census of potato fields. The co-operative retail society of Château-d'Oex was appointed to be the local potato agency and was permitted to sell farmers 18 kilos of potatoes per month though other customers only got seven. The co-op also issued potato growers with 22 kilos of seed potato per hundred square metres of tilled ground. In addition to potatoes farmers were entitled to buy 500 grams of bread per day while labourers were restricted to 375 grams and all other consumers to 275 grams. Bakers were prohibited from selling their bread freshly-baked and hotels were required to demand bread ration cards from their clients. By then, however, it was recognized that 25 per cent of the population of Switzerland was living in poverty and could not afford to buy even its minimal bread entitlement. Château-d'Oex was ordered to subsidise its registered paupers by making a 58 cent loaf available to them at 43 cents.

In September 1917 Ami Chabloz had been appointed to take charge of food rationing in Château-d'Oex. He was required not only to issue cards to consumers, but also to check the returned tallies from retailers. No task could have been more thankless and he was the subject of so much abuse that he handed the job over to Louis Morier. In March 1918 lard was rationed for all those who did not raise their own pigs and by June even cheese was rationed. In a community whose diet was based on cheese half a pound of Gruyère per month per adult, with none for children, was totally insufficient. Sugar loaves were sawn up into small rationed cubes though beekeepers were entitled to 2 kilos of sugar to feed each straw hive and 8 kilos for each wooden hive. Milk was restricted to half a litre per adult and in order to guarantee the winter supply cheesemaking was banned from October. As winter approached German suppliers trebled the price of coal and Château-d'Oex reacted by prohibiting the export of firewood. So tight did controls become that even the selling of a cartload of hay to a neighbouring village was made subject to official permission. A society of proud and independent peasants had become bureaucratised down to the last ounce of its initiative.

The end of the war brought a new range of problems to Château-d'Oex. Peasants who had complained bitterly about food and fuel rationing had neglected to publicise the exceptional profits being made from cheese and meat sales. The first year after the war was a very wet one, however, and in 1919 hay prices which had been held at 60 cents a cubic foot in 1918 shot up to 100 cents. There was suddenly a glut of livestock and no winter feed. Traditionally in such circumstances Château-d'Oex had exported its meat cattle but in 1919 the value of the Swiss franc remained high while all the surrounding currencies fell. No foreign butchers could afford to buy Swiss meat. Inside Switzerland austerity regulations, with compulsory meatless days, continued until July 1919. Depressed postwar trade conditions, however, were a less grievous form of crisis than the advent of Spanish influenza.

In July 1918 pulmonary influenza had broken out among the English internees in Château-d'Oex. Those infected were quarantined in isolation in the Victoria Hotel but the infection soon spread to the native population and many people died. The borough banned funeral processions and instructed that influenza victims be privately buried. It closed the schools and churches and only permitted religious worship in the open air. Despite these measures the disease carried off active young men in reserved occupations and then spread from the highland to the plain. A Château-d'Oex appeal for poor relief raised

3330 francs for the families of victims. The disease abated in the autumn but the pall of death tempered any desire to celebrate the end of the war and all ceremonies were postponed until after the signing of the peace treaty at Versailles in the following year.

It was on 12 October 1919 that Château-d'Oex finally honoured its 'war veterans'. It was pointed out a little acidly, however, that a federal administration which had been so intrusive during the years of austerity should have been a little more lavish in rewarding its heroes. The local celebratory procession of heroes was led by Sergeant Philippe du Blancscx who was seen as the greatest of all local patriots, a man 'who feared neither the rays of the sun nor the shades of the night'. The old sergeant's service career pre-dated the founding of the still suspect federal government in Bern. He had fought against Fribourg as a member of the Vaud army in 1847. This ancient patriot was followed by the veterans of 1870 who had been mobilised by Vaud to help defend the infant federation during the Franco–Prussian war. They too were well received by the crowd. A more sceptical welcome was given to the modern recruits with their functional steel helmets and drab confederate uniforms of grey-green. The fine coloured costumes of the cavalry officers gave more panache to the proceedings.

The crowning speech of the peace celebrations was given by the old Radical politician, Auguste Cottier, who had been governing the highland since 1883. For Cottier the end of the war had been particularly difficult. The armistice in Switzerland, as in Germany and elsewhere, had been accompanied by potentially serious political unrest. A Swiss general strike broke out immediately the war ended. Liberals and Radicals alike suddenly feared that their nineteenth-century world order might be swept away in a Soviet-style upheaval. The newly-released conscripts, home after four years in the barracks, were hastily re-mobilised. Their officers wanted them on stand-by, ready to repress the aspirations of a people who had suffered four years of austerity and now expected the rewards of peace. In the eyes of Auguste Cottier the worst evil that could befall his highland domain was a revolution that might bring Bolshevik idealism to previously obedient peasants. The Swiss ruling class assumed that subversion was most likely to be found in Alemannic Switzerland and more especially in the cities. Rural troops from Romanic communities like Château-d'Oex were seen as the best potential strike breakers. In an emotive speech Cottier talked of those unpatriotic citizens who dragged the flag of the confederation through the manure. They threatened the unity which had been brought to Switzerland's diverse nations with such difficulty over the half century of his political career. The old highland governor was sure that anyone criticising government was a demagogue who had to be silenced. The strike collapsed and Château-d'Oex's weary soldiers came home for the second time. Their demobilisation caused an even graver tragedy in the highland than the revolutionary crisis had done on the plain. The strike breakers brought back to the mountains a renewed outbreak of influenza. Disease decimated the population of Château-d'Oex once more.

In September 1939, 20 years after the pandemic of influenza had killed so many of the young men of Château-d'Oex, war broke out again in Europe and a new generation of youths from the highland was called up to serve in the Swiss federal army. The Second World War was differently experienced from the first one. Many men were called to arms during the German invasion of France in 1940 and again during the American invasion of France in 1944. On each occasion the confederation sought to protect its heavily militarised neutrality from the possibility of a strategic foreign invasion by armies wishing to take a short cut to their destination, Paris in the first case and Berlin in the second. In between the beginning and the end of the war, however, a widespread demobilisation took place. In Château-d'Oex agricultural life carried on in a more orderly fashion than during the First World War. The bureaucratic cogs were better oiled, the rationing of food was better managed, the digging of meadows to make potato fields was not quite so fiercely resisted, the village never came near to the brink of starvation. Neither, however, did it understand how Switzerland's affairs were being managed as the country trimmed its sails to the winds blowing from Fascist Italy, Nazi Germany and Churchill's Britain. War time brought censorship, propaganda and obedience. It also brought fierce patriotism.

The Second World War was much more clear cut in its nationalising effect than the first one had been. In 1914 the Alemannic Swiss, or at least their officer class, had sympathised with Germany, while the Romanic Swiss had been vocally pro-French. After the first war even Château-d'Oex's conservative newspaper, run by the Liberal party, cautiously voiced a seditious opinion. Had the federal government, it asked, maintained a truly neutral stance during the war? The target of the paper's disquiet had been General Ulrich Wille. The editor said that although he would not go so far as to accuse the Swiss commander-in-chief of treasonable partisanship during the war, he would nonetheless question his patriotic judgement. That judgement had clearly been affected by the general's close integration into

German high society and by his marriage to Clara von Bismarck. In 1912 either a 'lack of judgement', or alternatively a shrewd protective strategy, had been very pronounced when the Swiss colonels proudly showed off their defence capability to the visiting Kaiser Wilhelm. The Kaiser went back to Berlin to tell his officers that the unwitting Swiss would protect his southern flank by not allowing the French through their well-armed neutral territory. Germany, he said, could safely redeploy 300 000 men for an attack on France via Belgium.

In the second war Château-d'Oex took a different attitude to federal military politics. In that war the Swiss parliament elected as its commander-in-chief General Henri Guisan, a man of Vaud. As one of the colonels preparing for the expected war he, like his predecessor in 1912, negotiated with potential aggressors. In 1937 he entertained Marshal Pétain who had come over from France to assess the will of the Swiss to resist should Germany try to invade France via Switzerland. Pétain reported that the neutral hub of Europe would hold firm and that France need not invest in defence on the Swiss section of its border. Guisan may have been partisan in helping France avoid unnecessary defence expenditure, as Wille had been when unwittingly helping the Kaiser in 1912, but as far as Château-d'Oex was concerned Guisan was their hero. Guisan, however, was much more than a homegrown charismatic patriot who was idolised in Vaud. He also became the idol of the Alemannic Swiss who needed a hero to worship during the Second World War. Hitherto the concern of the Swiss states to limit the powers of central government had meant that no leader could use charisma to capture the popular imagination and the chairmanship of the council of ministers rotated annually so that only the most passionate Swiss devotees of politics even knew who their head of state was. Moreover many Alemannic Swiss no longer felt their initial sympathy for pan-German culture and feared another *Anschluss* like the one which had swallowed up Austria. A French-speaking general therefore became a national folk hero who transcended Switzerland's divisions.

In 1939 Switzerland needed political cohesion. A mythical folk hero such as William Tell was inadequate in cementing the nation together at a time when foreign politicians such as Hitler and Mussolini on one side, and Churchill and Roosevelt on the other, were creating mass national loyalties. The newly-elected Swiss general took it upon himself to become the human face of Swiss solidarity. He resuscitated all the most powerful myths of the Swiss treaties of alliance and ordered his senior officers to meet him in the field of Rutli on the famous bluff above the old forest lake. The general turned out to be a politician such as Switzerland had never seen before and although he retired in 1945 his portrait continued to be revered on parlour walls much like that of Queen Victoria in the drawing rooms of the loosely linked states of the British Empire.

Swiss defence strategy during the Second World War was two-fold, a silent strategy and a public strategy. The silent strategy, which only slowly emerged into the light over the years, was to negotiate with Nazi Germany and protect some Swiss freedoms by meeting any foreign demands that could not be resisted. Thus it was that Germany continued to supply coal, food and raw material to the Swiss but the Swiss were required to pay for them with the products of their precision engineering plants. Each year millions of francs worth of chronometers, altimeters and other instruments needed for civilian, military and air force capacity were sold across the Rhine. Switzerland also silently protected itself by avoiding any policies that could offend Berlin, and in particular avoiding any over-provocative assistance to refugees fleeing the pogroms conducted against Jews, gypsies, Poles and dissidents. Guisan was the ideal commander for such a silent strategy of political defence. Although he came from Romanic Switzerland and was seen as a non-Alemannic national leader, he knew Germany well, spoke German and could shrewdly oversee the politics of survival.

The role of Château-d'Oex in the pragmatic maintenance of international business activity during the Second World War long remained shrouded in secrecy. In the early 1940s, however, the Bank for International Settlements had taken refuge in the old castle of the lords-bailiff of the highland at Rougemont. There, hidden within Guisan's alpine fastness and far removed from the risky frontier town of Basel, the representatives of the Bank of England and the German Reichsbank conducted their daily transactions under American guidance. When they were not working, the war-time bankers and their secretaries went hiking together, admiring alpine flowers and mountain scenery. Only in 1944, at the Bretton Woods conference on the future of the world monetary system, was the daily settlement of hard currency accounts between Britain and Germany challenged, but even then Maynard Keynes defended the ultra-secret preservation of war-time banking transactions through Switzerland. The people of Château-d'Oex, however, had apparently remained oblivious to their role in hosting the money merchants of the combatants as gold assets were moved across the battle lines in paper transactions signed in their highland castle.

The public strategy of defence to which Guisan gave select publicity was quite different from the silent strategy and this public strategy affected Château-d'Oex very directly. A military plan named after an officer called Wahlen tacitly admitted that the Swiss army could never resist a German invasion and that in the event of attack it should immediately surrender the plain and the towns to avoid destruction during any campaign of resistance. By contrast, however, maximum effort should be devoted to military resistance in the highlands. The Swiss national heart would continue to beat in the mountains. All access points from the plain to the highlands would be rigorously protected by artillery, by machine-gun emplacements, by mountain troops equipped with skis and rifles, and by a home guard trained in all the villages. Château-d'Oex was one of the highland gateways to the 'real Switzerland' of Guisan's patriotic imagination. Its hillsides and rock cliffs were riddled with military installations and the highland farmers at last felt proud to be Swiss. They gave little thought to the people of the plain who were to be strategically sacrificed in the event of a German conquest. Had anyone wished to speak out for an alternative political agenda, or wondered publicly how the mute towns people felt about the unstated element of the resistance strategy, they would no doubt have quickly found that war did not permit much freedom of speech even in the cherished highland. In the end it was diplomacy, not defence, that enabled Switzerland to survive, first on German terms and then on American ones.

By the time the Swiss army was demobilised in 1945 it had played a key role not only in the forging of Switzerland but also in determining the nature of its society. The Second World War had united people in their opposition to the dictatorships however much they had had to compromise to survive. But military service had also polarised them in their class attitudes to each other. Professional men almost automatically became officers and working-class men almost as inevitably became soldiers. The deferential attitudes required by obedience to military orders were carried over into civilian life. Every year the social distance was reinforced by compulsory training camps for all members of the militia army. Equally emphatically the annual male bonding of military service, both for private soldiers and for ranking officers, reinforced the exclusion of women from Swiss public life. Business and politics were carried out in circles of military classmates.

The effects of the Second World War on Swiss women are still poorly documented. The most striking feature of their experience was that unlike women elsewhere in Europe, notably in France, the peace of 1945 did not bring political emancipation to Swiss women. Votes for women were postponed by 25 years in 'progressive' states and by

50 years in 'reactionary' ones. The Swiss obsession with domesticity and cleanliness was maintained rather than relaxed. During the Second World War less than 30000 women went to work on the land compared to over 90000 during the first war. Women in Vaud who tried to sign up for the armed forces were liable to be instantly rejected in defiance of the federal policy of accepting female recruits. Despite their marginalisation the political awareness of many women was enhanced by the war. Women conscripted into the war industries were better informed than most citizens, and female watchmakers redeployed to armaments were discreetly aware that 60 per cent of their product was sold to the Third Reich. Women living in border regions were often conscious of the pogroms which surrounded them despite the very tight censorship of news. A few humanitarians organised escape routes which secreted refugees across the 15-kilometre free-fire zone from which the Swiss army was ordered to return aliens to their persecutors without benefit of trial. Other women, however, had radically different sympathies and an order of nuns in the Bernese Oberland forfeited half its butter ration to help 'poor Mr Hitler'. One nurse in the Château-d'Oex infirmary recalled how the windows shook when heavy bombers from England took short-cuts across Swiss territory to obliterate Milan and Turin. Over the hill in Leysin the sanatoria received wounded men from both France and Germany to be nursed by peasant girls from the poorest Catholic villages of Valais. Down the valley at Montbovon the grocery was kept permanently open by women and children except for the single hour of mass on Sunday morning. Passing soldiers, including on one memorable occasion General Guisan's driver, stopped to buy cigarettes, sausages and chocolate bars on their way to defending the Château-d'Oex entrance to the Alpine fastness that symbolised Swiss resistance. The woman who owned the Montbovon grocery had constant difficulty in satisfying the bureaucrats of Fribourg by tallying her supplies of sugar, flour and oil with the rationing coupons, but by the end of the war she had made enough profit to invest speculatively in four houses.

In the male domain the inevitability of army service was accepted by the men of Château-d'Oex though not with the same Teutonic seriousness with which it was viewed in Alemannic Switzerland and certainly not with the same sense that army service could enhance a civilian career. It was perhaps no accident that it was the teacher of German at the Collège Henchoz who rose to the rank of major in the Swiss army, thereby accepting a double or even treble commitment of time to service in the militia. To most Château-d'Oex men, largely farmers with minimal elementary education, the army was perceived as a vacation, a hardworking annual holiday of travelling and drinking with army friends. Only in the Darbyite congregation was conformity systematically resisted as the men insisted that they would only join the army in a non-combatant medical or veterinary capacity. After the second war a generation went by before the reflex acceptance of military patriotism began to be challenged. Then graffiti on city walls began to enjoin soldiers to take off their helmets and think for themselves. It was at last being suggested that mindless obedience was not healthy in a democratic society. Such was the extent of the seachange in Swiss political culture that a referendum proposing the abolition of the federal army received almost 40 per cent support in 1989. In Château-d'Oex such an independent-minded challenge to the received order might have seemed unimaginable, but before the plebiscite the local newspaper unexpectedly did carry a plea for pacifism written by Nicholas Tièche. Among the village elders, however, the Radical party and the Liberal party had become almost indistinguishably conservative, divided by family tradition rather than by political ideology. Even their rival churches, the National Church and the Free Church, had amalgamated in 1968. The only remotely distinctive political voice in the village was that of a socialist postal worker, elected to office under proportional representation, though he too served loyally in the municipal 'council of ministers' which governed the borough by consensus.

Outside the highland the Second World War had cast a very long shadow across Switzerland. Material prosperity grew dramatically for half a century but political maturity proved more elusive. Switzerland, although not a member of the Atlantic alliance, or even of the United Nations, was deeply affected by the cold war. Fear of Soviet communism permitted federal politicians to establish a network of internal surveillance over their subjects which was not exposed to democratic accountability until the 1990s. In Château-d'Oex the conservative village leaders would probably not have protested very vigorously at such anti-democratic modes of repression had they been aware of them. Those rare highlanders who held truly independent political opinions, who refused to be unquestioningly herded by patriotism, or who declined to serve even unarmed in a federal militia whose ideals were not their own, left the Alps in search of more liberal countries of exile. Farmers remained on the land and continued to work long and hard. The fruits of their labour were now enhanced by such bountiful subsidies that they could enjoy almost extravagant material comfort and asked very few questions about the basis of Switzerland's affluence.

In the 1990s independent-minded citizens did begin to ask questions about the moral rectitude of policies which had turned Switzerland into the world's richest country. A new generation of youths questioned the morality of Switzerland's role as a large-scale broker in the world marketing of sophisticated weapons while the ecological lobbies raised questions about the cost-cutting methods by which the chemical and pharmaceutical industries disposed of their waste. Even the milk industry was challenged for its marketing strategies in the Third World where dependency on powdered milk was liable to create as many health and nutritional problems as it solved. But the most devastating challenge, and the one most closely linked to the dark shadow cast by Hitler's war, was the challenge to the banking industry. Switzerland's banks had persuaded the world that their laws of secrecy were a sign of moral probity. This stance began to wear thin when it became clear that Swiss banks were storing the ill-gotten gains not only of corrupt politicians but also of the world's leading drug dealers. Worse still it emerged that deposits made by persecuted German investors in the 1930s and 1940s had never been returned to heirs who had survived the war and the holocaust. Not until 1997, when United States banks threatened to boycott Swiss banks, did lists of dormant accounts, many of them Jewish, begin to be published. Switzerland, it emerged, had been cushioned for 50 years by the gold of the Hitler's victims. On the 50th anniversary of the end of the war the federal president apologised for the political timidity of his predecessors in admitting refugees on to Swiss soil. The bankers, however, remained slow to return the money.

The crisis of morality which shook Swiss banking and industry did have remote repercussions in Château-d'Oex. The cold war had, for 50 years, created a satanic enemy against which all could unite, while the profits of banking had helped make possible the subsidies from which all could benefit. In the 1990s the wind in the Alps turned chill and the Swiss were no longer seen as heroes of the cold war, capitalists par excellence who could rely on the benign support of the United States. Worse still the Swiss declined to become members of the European Union, the farmers of the rustic states having out-voted the industrialists of the cities in a referendum on European membership. The prospect of isolation, of trade barriers and of economic recession seemed real, and the Swiss looked on with dismay as Europe's other multi-ethnic federation, Yugoslavia, dissolved into murderous factions as prosperity and security eluded its leaders. In Switzerland a return to the civil wars of the nineteenth century seemed inconceivable and yet fear grew as economic prospects began to falter.

In the era of self-doubt at the end of the millennium the politicians of Château-d'Oex turned for comfort to their golden past. Reassurance was to be found in contemplating one thousand years of highland culture. Had Samuel Henchoz, the old cheese farmer, returned to Château-d'Oex two hundred years after his death he would have recognized many continuities in a mountain society wedded to the dairy industry. On his old farm of Glacière, the frost pocket down by the river, modern farmers had built a huge new barn. It served the local community as a store for imported hay and the world community as the hangar for hot-air balloons. Even more impressively the cheese farmers had formed a co-operative in 1932 to co-ordinate their cheese-selling strategies. They had chosen the bend in the road at Etivaz, below Samuel Henchoz's two largest Alpine estates, as the site for their joint cellar. By the 1990s this cellar had been greatly expanded to cope with the production of 14 000 cheeses a year and it employed a university graduate to manage its affairs. The cheeses had become even bigger and better than those which were so famous in the eighteenth century. Meanwhile a much older Château-d'Oex cheese cellar, the one at Etambeaux belonging to the Henchoz banking cousins, had been turned into a museum of farm life. Samuel Henchoz would have recognized most of the tools on display; carts, sledges, scythes, looms, sausage presses, cheese moulds, shoulder baskets and a cast-iron kitchen range, all articles still in use until the 1950s when the motor revolution reached Château-d'Oex.

Up on the shelf of flat land at Les Quartiers, the home patch of his wife Marie Desquartiers, Samuel Henchoz would no longer have found his beautiful home which had burnt down in the middle of the twentieth century. But surviving houses he had known in the hamlet still had a magnificent view out over the church on the motte that Dean Bridel had rebuilt and refurbished with such energy after the fire of 1800. The carillon of bells still rang out the Angelus at eight o'clock each evening and reminded the whole village to cover its fires before retiring to bed. The motte was no longer crowded with wooden houses, as it had been in 1787 when Samuel Henchoz died, but had become an ornamental garden with bronze chamois grazing among Alpine flowers and shrubs. The houses, now built of stone and slate, were at the bottom of the motte, stretching down the old royal road away from the town hall and the cattle market. The new architecture would have surprised Samuel Henchoz, but had he walked beyond the end of the houses to the new graveyard he would have found that nearly all the names on the stones were familiar ones. Although half of the

50 traditional families of the village had died out or emigrated, the other half remained active and continued to farm the alps of their ancestors.

If Samuel Henchoz had gone into the town hall where he had worked so long as a part-time administrator he would have found more continuity than change. He would not have been surprised that the speaker of the village parliament was a member of the Henchoz clan, though he would have been astonished that she was a woman. He would have been surprised that the town clerk was a full-time bureaucrat, but he would not have been surprised that he was simultaneously the village's member of parliament serving in Lausanne and had even been the parliament's presiding speaker. The old market arches and lock-up shops which Samuel Henchoz had once rented out were gone, but the new town hall, built in 1801 and re-built in 1991, still had the familiar public inn well patronised by dairy farmers. Across the square the Bear Inn, which had supplied wine to his wife in the summer hayfields, was also still in business, though the mounting block at the front door had gone and a new French-style roof had been added during the empire days of luxury tourism.

Perhaps one of the great surprises in the economic field was the nineteenth-century development of two new branches of the dairy industry. Down in the market town of Vevey cheese and butter came to be matched in importance by powdered milk and milk chocolate. The Vevey firm of Nestlé became the world leader in sales of condensed and dried milk. The town's chocolate cafés also pioneered the development of milk chocolate in the form of chocolate bars. In lower Gruyère the family of Cailler built a large chocolate factory within sight of the castle of Montsalvens which had once ruled Château-d'Oex. But the dairy farmers of Château-d'Oex were too isolated in their highland to be able to deliver fresh milk to Nestlé or Cailler and so the cheese industry survived. Only when the electric tram from Gruyère and the railway tunnel from Lake Geneva were built in 1904 did Château-d'Oex acquire a fast and modern system of transport. Samuel Henchoz, for whom it took two days to nurse a cart load of salt up from the plain, would have been truly impressed. He would have been even more impressed, less than a century after the building of the railway, to find that road tankers could now ferry milk to the factories on the plain in one hour.

Eleven years after Samuel Henchoz died the political world was turned up-side-down by the Swiss Revolution and the French wars. For half a century Château-d'Oex was cut off from the city–state of Bern, whose mountain militias Samuel Henchoz had trained and was attached to the cathedral city of Lausanne. When industrial modernisation, and political change in Italy and Germany, triggered off the unification of Switzerland Bern gradually began to influence Château-d'Oex once more, this time as the seat of a federal government. If highland farming would have looked traditional and familiar to Samuel Henchoz two centuries after he ceased to manage his farm estates, it was because the now largely industrial Swiss federation had decided to invest heavily in maintaining the highland dairy industry. The mountain hikers and winter sports enthusiasts who had stimulated the growth of Château-d'Oex before and after the two world wars had now dwindled in number and it was the heavily subsidised Simmental dairy cows who were once more the champions of the highland as their multi-coloured forebears had been in the eighteenth century.

When Samuel Henchoz was an old man he probably went, in 1776, to hear the young governor of the highland, Lord-Bailiff Bonstetten, give his farewell speech to his subjects before leaving Rougemont castle to conduct a three-year enquiry into the finances of the Swiss colonies in northern Italy. Bonstetten advised his 'pastoral people' to remain faithful to their traditions without aping the ways of the town. The plain, he said, had been showered with human blood and they should keep faith with their mountain culture and preserve it from tyranny. Although the highland was poor, he said, its human spirit was rich and the search for another life would lead only to humiliation, a grasping for riches and a neglect of charity. Distinguished families who had preserved highland customs in the harshest of climates should, he said, be honoured by the city in this century of the Enlightenment. Château-d'Oex came very close to following Bonstetten's advice. Although many of its citizens did have to seek work on the plain they commonly retained their links with the mountains, returning to build secondary homes and took part in the great festivals which honoured the history of the highland.

The greatest of the historic festivals was organised in 1994 to commemorate the second centenary of the 'Ancient Abbey' of military sports. Samuel Henchoz, the old drillmaster, would have been thrilled by the pageantry. The great shooting festival did much more, however, than commemorate the prowess of Château-d'Oex's riflemen. It reconstructed the past throughout the valley of the cranes and invited sportsmen from 30 boroughs of the 'Old County' of Gruyère to visit the highland. The rivalries of the great merchant towns of Bern and Fribourg, which had dismembered the ancient principality 450 years before, were forgotten. The religious animosities, which had split the valley into two from the time of Reformation until the ecumenical mellowing of the late twentieth century, were reconciled. Highland unity was once more celebrated with pageantry, banquets and civic pride.

Sources

The genesis of this history of village Switzerland is a chapter of autobiographical accidents. At the age of ten I helped to herd goats which browsed alpine shrubs high above Lake Geneva. During the winter I learnt French at a Protestant dame school in the carnival town of Martigny. I then moved to the village of Château-d'Oex where I studied at the local grammar school for five years. In this sheltered mountain valley, surrounded by the limestone summits of the Alpine foothills, I found out about the folklore of a peasant community. Cowmen reminisced about life on the high pastures and described how, when the day's large Gruyère cheese had been made, they ate a communal meal of potato bread dipped into hot whey. The oldest men still spoke in the Romanic vernacular, a language which had spread up the valley a thousand years ago, but a century of schooling and literacy had gradually made the French of the bourgeoisie the tongue used by farm labourers. Seven miles up the road, however, lay Switzerland's great linguistic divide and children who cycled to the autumn fair at Saanen grew accustomed to hearing people who spoke the Alemannic dialect of German.

While living in Switzerland I became so acculturated that my critical faculties as an outsider were numbed and I failed to perceive that the history lessons I received were informed by a powerful strain of Swiss patriotism. Even when I moved to the city academy at Lausanne no teacher enabled me to understand or explain Swiss history, let alone recognize that much of Switzerland's historical tradition had been 'invented' in an effort to create a federal union out of 25 republics. In 1948, the centenary year of the founding of modern Switzerland, the divisions which had long pitted the Swiss so bitterly against one another were too close to the surface to be safely exhumed. I therefore absorbed the myths that proclaimed Switzerland to be a 600-year-old land of peace and milk chocolate smiled upon by a benevolent general who had guided its fortunes through the Second World War.

In 1954 I left Château-d'Oex and went to Africa where I trained as an historian. My interests dwelt on peasant societies and I raised questions about how farmers made their economic choices, how they drew on the labour of their neighbours and kinsfolk and how they maintained the balance between arable crops and wandering livestock. I became interested in the growth of specialisation in farming communities where innovative entrepreneurs moved from subsistence-oriented trade in surplus foodstuffs to a market-oriented trade in long-distance commodities such as salt and iron. In Africa I found that the great fairs to which merchants walked for days, with or without the help of pack animals and lake barges, became centres of political authority. I also found that in Africa the advent of fire arms, and the drilling of militias drawn up in defensive squares, transformed the old-style warfare of cavalry and bowmen, and the sieges of walled cities. Africa, I also discovered, was deeply changed by the spread of world religions. Religion provided not only the security craved by farmers on the margins of the wilderness but also kindled the ideological fervour that fired local wars. Never once, however, did I realise that the seminal themes of African history were also the seminal themes of an Alpine history that my schooling had neglected.

In 1981 I returned to Switzerland and found a country which had woken to the moral dilemmas of shifting from peasant poverty to urban wealth. The young, deprived as they were of historical training, did not remember their parents' recent past: the heartbreak of forced emigration, the harshness of the great depression, the bread rationing of wartime, and the aching task of carrying hay down from the mountains on the backs of men and women who owned neither mules nor carts. The middle-class discovered that it had too readily accepted a diet of patriotic propaganda which was at variance with the small-scale rivalries and local loyalties that make up the Swiss historical tradition. Rebellious voices went so far as to claim that the Switzerland of the 1980s was little more than a coalition of xenophobic police states which spied on their own citizens, locked up their dissidents and allowed their bankers to function with unsupervised secrecy. Swiss scholars began to question the received wisdoms and the comfortable old certainties were subverted. As the images of Switzerland I had been given as a child began to dissolve, it became a fascinating intellectual challenge to understand the new view of Swiss history.

An Alpine vacation turned into a busman's holiday when the town clerk of Château-d'Oex generously allowed me into village archives that no previous historian had consulted. The curator of the highland museum gave me every assistance in exploring cupboards full of old papers. The staffs of the provincial archives in both Lausanne and Bern helped me to sample a few of the records which had been transferred to the city for safekeeping. Scholars from the Swiss federal polytechnic showed me the ethnographic research on Château-d'Oex mountain society which Unesco had sponsored. The editor of the national dictionary of Swiss history invited me to re-write the history of Château-d'Oex in encyclopaedia format.

A book unexpectedly grew out of these accidental discoveries. Its first aim is to explore peasant history in relation to a community rather better documented than the peasant communities which I have been accustomed to studying. The second objective is to put the history of one particular highland community into the context of the revisionist national history which professional Swiss historians have presented since the 1980s. And the third aspiration is to make Swiss history live among readers for whom Switzerland might not be an obvious case-study for the thematic analysis of historical process.

1   The Valley of the Cranes

A much fuller medieval history of Château-d'Oex than the introductory chapter of this book could be written on the basis of the extensive documentation collected by J.J. Hisley and his collaborator Abbé J. Gremaud. I have used his three-volume *Histoire du Comté de Gruyère* (Lausanne, 1851, 1855 and 1857) to sketch a simple picture of the medieval structure of administration and taxation. Readers with a firmer grasp of Latin than mine will be able to analyse laws and events in the documents reprinted in Hisley and Gremaud, *Monuments de l'Histoire du Comté de Gruyère* (Lausanne, 2 vols, 1867–69). A geographical and geological description of the land which medieval Alpine colonisers tamed can be built up from the *Dictionnaire Géographique de la Suisse* (Neuchâtel, 6 vols, 1902–10). A modern dictionary of the Romanic languages of 'La Suisse Romande', vulgarly known as 'les patois romands', has only reached the letter 'E', but W. Pierrehumbert, *Dictionnaire du Parler Neuchâtelois et Suisse Romande* (Neuchâtel, 1926) provides an admirable glossary of terms that have entered French usage in Switzerland. The etymologies of Celtic and Romanic place names can be looked up in Maurice Bossard and Jean-Pierre Chavan, *Nos lieux-dits: toponomie romande* (Lausanne, 1990).

A detailed source of contextual historical information is the *Dictionnaire Historique et Biographique de la Suisse* (Neuchâtel, 7 vols, 1921–33). A new edition, to which I have contributed the Château-d'Oex entry, is currently in preparation and the first entries may be consulted on the Internet. For the Canton of Vaud, of which Château-d'Oex has formed a part since 1803, the *Encyclopédie Illustrée du Pays de Vaud* (Lausanne, 12 vols, 1970–84) is a scholarly and lively modern reference book. One of its editors, Lucienne Hubler, subsequently published her own concise and elegant *Histoire du Pays de Vaud* (Lausanne, 1991). An important earlier work was Armand Vautier, *La Patrie vaudoise: le pays et ses habitants* (Lausanne, 5 vols, 1903). For detailed reference matter see Eugène Mottaz, *Dictionnaire historique, geographique et statistique du Canton de Vaud* (Lausanne, 2 vols, 1914–21).

Speculation about the early peopling of the highland around Château-d'Oex is found in three local histories of neighbouring boroughs: J.R.D. Zwahlen, R. Marti-Wehren *et al.*, *Beiträge zur Heimatkunde der Landschaft Saanen* (Saanen, 1955); H.-L. Guignard (ed.) *La Vallée des Ormonts* (Lutry, 1994); Moritz Boschung (ed.) *Jaun im Greyerzerland* (Freiburg CH, 1989). The coats-of-arms of the Romanic immigrants to the highland are discussed in Hubert de Vevey, D.L. Galbreath and F.T. Dubois, *Armoiries et sceaux des comtes et du comté de Gruyère*, reprinted from *Archives héraldiques suisses, 1921–1926*. Magnificent pictures of Gruyère castle are in Henri Gremaud, *The Castle of Gruyère* (Neuchâtel, 1965). A popular history of Château-d'Oex at the time is André Gétaz, *Le Pays d'Enhaut sous les comtes de Gruyère* (Château-d'Oex, 1946). An imaginative account of medieval court life in the highland was written by the romantic though well-read Dean Bridel, *Le Sauvage du Lac Arnon* (Vevey, 1837).

The history of Rougemont and its priory records, including P. Aebischer, 'La Pancarte de Rougemont de 1115' and R. Werner, 'Etude sur le "Fasciculus Temporum"' is in Bibliotèque historique vaudoise, *Rougemont: 9e centenaire 1080–1980* (Lausanne, 1980) and a later study by P.-Y. Favez, 'Rougemont' appeared in *Helvetia Sacra*, vol. III, no. 2. The *Journal de Château-d'Oex*, May 1980, ran a special issue on Rougemont's eighth centenary. See also Alain Chesaux, *Rougemont et son église* (Château-d'Oex, 1980). The legacy of Moudon customary law may be seen in Bernard de Cérenville and Charles Gilliard, *Moudon sous de régime savoyard* (Lausanne, 1929), as well as in the works of Hisley, and can be put in context with J.-F. Poudret, *Les libertés et franchises dans les pays romands du Moyen Age* (Lausanne, 1986).

The history of the castle and church of Château-d'Oex has been inconclusively debated, as shown by the pamphlet by Jean-Pierre Monnet, *L'église et la paroisse de Château-d'Oex* (Château-d'Oex, 1977), the article by Emile Henchoz, 'Les cloches des églises du Pays d'Enhaut', *Revue historique vaudoise*, 1961, and the 1935 Christmas special issue of one village newspaper, *Le Progrès*. The most convincingly scholarly interpretation of the archival material remains Maxime Raymond, 'La villa et le Château-d'Oex', *Revue historique vaudoise*, 1935. The history of Château-d'Oex's suzerain, the viscount of Montsalvan, is illuminated by Henri Naef, *Montsalvan: une famille et son château* (Gruyère, c. 1950).

2 Under the Paw of the Bear

The traditional national history of Bern is given in Richard Felner, *Geschichte Berns* (Bern, 4 vols, 1946–60). In the 1980s the history of Switzerland underwent a fundamental scholarly revision and the history of Bern's relations with the old Swiss republics, and of its penetration into the highland, is now best presented in Jean-Claude Favez *et al.*, *Nouvelle Histoire de la Suisse et des Suisses* (Lausanne, 3 vols, 1982–83). A persuasively elegant history of the Swiss was published by the Fribourg scholar Gonzague de Reynold, *La Suisse et son histoire* (Lausanne, 1965).

Since the early modern history of Bern is deeply concerned with military history I have made contextual use of two works on the Swiss tradition of mercenary service, John MacCormack, *One million mercenaries: Swiss soldiers around the world* (London, 1993) and Jérôme Bodin, *Les Suisses au Service de la France* (Paris, 1988). The outstanding historian of military life in Château-d'Oex itself was Emile Henchoz, founder of the Musée du Vieux Pays-d'Enhaut and author of *L'Ancienne Abbaye de Château-d'Oex: Etude d'histoire locale* (Château-d'Oex, 1946). For details of the Château-d'Oex involvement in the wars between Bern and Burgundy in the 1470s I have relied extensively on Marcelle Despond, *Les comtes de Gruyère et les guerres de Bourgogne* (Fribourg, 1925). An important economic essay on the wars is J.-F. Bergier, 'Vie matérielle et politique économique au temps des guerres de Bourgogne' in 'Grandson 1476' a centenary commemorative volume. For the Château-d'Oex military campaigns in the Simmental and Ormont see Hisley, Gétaz, Guignard and other sources cited above for Chapter 1.

The last years of the principality of Gruyère, and the bankruptcy of Count Michael, are discussed in Henri Naef, *L'alchimiste de Michel de Gruyère* (Lausanne, 1946). Some details of the county's financial affairs, including Emperor Wenceslas' license of 1390 permitting the count to mint Gruyère gold coin, are to be found in an inventory of Gessenay [Saanen] documents, layette 325, in the Vaud archives in Lausanne. A note on the legal status of Gruyère-Bern co-citizenship in Château-d'Oex can be found in Claude Cuendet, *Les traités de combourgeoisie en pays romands* (Lausanne, 1979) and a discussion of the issue was presented in the *Journal de Château-d'Oex* of 23 December 1947 by André Gétaz.

3 Tradition and Reformation

The Château-d'Oex historian of the Reformation was Robert Werner, a Free Church theologian who served as headmaster of the Henchoz secondary school. Although he published very little, his research notes are preserved in the attic of the town hall. Among them are typed and manuscript papers relating to the reformers Haller, Farel and Viret including notes on a lecture on 'La Réforme au

Pays d'Enhaut' given in 1933 by Henri Meylan and a lecture given by himself in 1936. His published sources included Anton Tillier, *Geschichte des eidgenössischen Freistaates Bern*; Robert Marti-Wehren, *Die Mauritius Kirche in Saanen*; Henri Vuilleumier, *Histoire de l'Eglise réformée du Pays de Vaud*; Michael Stettler, *Annales* (Bern, 1626–27); Johannes von Müller, *Geschichte der Landschaft Saanen*; and Godfried Aebersold, *Studien der Geschichte der Landschaft Saanen*. A recent English-language article on the theological context of the Swiss reformation is Kaspar von Greyerz, 'Switzerland' in Bob Scribner, Roy Porter and Mikuláš Teich, *The Reformation in National Context* (Cambridge, 1994).

The Church of Bern's supreme consistory, which heard appeals from the Château-d'Oex consistory court, preserved some records which are in the Bern state archives and scholars with a greater facility than I in reading old German longhand will, with luck and patience, come across further material on Château-d'Oex in this treasure trove. Many records of the Château-d'Oex parish administration have disappeared but some surviving registers of baptisms and deaths have been microfilmed by Mormon genealogical researchers and can be consulted in the Vaud state archives while others have been put on a card index in the Château-d'Oex museum. Illuminating comparisons may be found in the social history of Saanen, Christian Rubi, *In der alten Landschaft Saanen: aus dem Leben der Voreltern* (Gstaad, 1979).

The law suit of 1649 over non-attendance at church is in the Vaud archives, file Bda 23/4, and the 1770 case of licentiouness and the 1798 paternity case are in file Bda 23/7. The 1699–1700 trial of Esther Pilet for adultery is in the Bern archives, series A, section V, volume 1174, as are the witchcraft cases from Château-d'Oex in 1696 and from Rougemont in 1712. The local records in Château-d'Oex only survive in a haphazard fashion, many official papers having been destroyed, damaged, or disposed of in the three great village fires of 1664, 1741 and 1800. Some official papers inexplicably survived these catastrophes and, along with some private papers that were subsequently placed in public hands, gradually found their way into the cellar of the municipal annexe, beneath the village hall, into the attic of the town hall after it was refurbished in the early 1990s, and into the museum which eventually decided to convert its old bathroom into a tiny library with a table and chair to work at. It is among these uncatalogued papers that chance reveals records of gambling and fornication along-side the books of draconian but often unenforceable church laws such as the surviving 1746 edition of the *Loix Consistoriales*.

The papers relating to the buying of lottery tickets may have come from the eighteenth-century Henchoz family house in Rossinière before reaching the museum, but the 1771 case of the pig butcher who gambled away six of his herd of swine comes from the Vaud archives, file Bda 23/7. The papers relating to social welfare and charity in the Marmillod family are in the town hall attic and those concerning widow Ramel are in the museum library. A short history of the charitable foundations, including the leprosarium, was published by Emile Henchoz in *Notes sur d'anciennes Bourses administrées aux XVIIIme et XIXme siècles par la Commune de Château-d'Oex* (Château-d'Oex, 1942). Further reference to the care of victims of leprosy can be found in Piera Borradori, 'Histoire d'exclusion et de solidarité; la lèpre au pays de Vaud' in *Revue médicale de la Suisse romande*, 1992. A lively social history of Château-d'Oex under the *ancien régime*, which includes some material on the reformed church and its social control, is Eugène Roch, *Le Pays d'Enhaut au XVIIIe siècle* (Château-d'Oex, 1911). Pictures of the bells in the highland churches, including the Etivaz chapel bell, are in Emile Henchoz 'Les cloches des églises du Pays-d'Enhaut'.

4   The Milk of the Land

Much of the research on the Château-d'Oex dairy industry is based on oral information. It was undertaken with the help of my wife Elizabeth, who has a degree in dairying, and together we walked most of the cattle trails of the Château-d'Oex highland and visited many of the Alpine dairies including Sazième where the medieval summer balls were held on the day of the weighing of the milk. On the alp of Paray, Emile Raynaud, a one-time elder of the Darbyite community and secretary of the Etivaz cheese-farmers' co-operative, gave us not only the full technical information needed to make a Gruyère cheese, but also details of the lore and custom of the highland which his family has farmed for more than 20 generations. Over several years many other Alpine farmers also took time out to lean on their scythes, or rest their axes, while telling us about their meadows, their woodlands, their ancestors, their cattle and the politics of a Swiss highland village.

The key change to early modern farming in Château-d'Oex was the decision of 1585 to enclose and sell the commons. Thereafter detailed records of land ownership and of land tax liability were maintained. One great ledger, drawn up in 1666 by Daniel Gétaz and preserved in the museum, describes every plot of land and public right of way throughout the rural borough. Seventy-odd tomes of land sale records compiled by generations of Château-d'Oex notaries were preserved in Bern and transferred during the nineteenth century to the state archive of Vaud where they can be readily identified in the *Guide des Archives Cantonales Vaudoises* (Lausanne, 1990). The tax survey of all forms of economic production which was compiled on behalf of Bonaparte's 'Republic of Helvetia' in 1798 was rediscovered among boxes of loose papers in the Château-d'Oex municipal archive cellar.

The one Château-d'Oex common which continued to be communally grazed by citizens with recognized entitlements was the Vauseresse. The account book of the committee of management, 'Reconnaissance des Paquiers de la Montagne dite la Vauseresse rière Château-d'Oex faites le 31 Mai 1776 avec les arrêts ou Réglements faites en suite par les Compartionniers de dite Montagne' survives in the museum library. It was drawn up on the orders of Captain Samuel Henchoz, then serving as the chatelain of Château-d'Oex. Other records of land use, cattle management and peasant indebtedness are to be found in the boxes of uncatalogued papers in the attic of the town hall. The reference to early cheeses being used to pay feudal taxes in 1328 comes from Hisley, 1851, and the account of Anthony of Gruyère participating in the milk festival at Sazième in the fifteenth century from Bridel's *Etrennes*, cited below.

The written record which, more than any other, provoked the writing of this village history is the eighteenth-century account book of Samuel Henchoz who kept a ledger containing details of all the loans he made, and debts he incurred, over a 40-year period from 1745 to 1787. This meticulous accountant, whose papers were found in one of the museum cupboards, may have been the same person as the captain-of-militia who served as chatelain in 1776 though this is not certain and in 1780 it was his nephew, another Samuel Henchoz, who was serving as chatelain. The senior Samuel Henchoz was not only a cheese farmer but also a land owner, a money-lender, a trader, an administrator and a cavalry officer. His life history permeates this book and was the subject of an article in *History Today* in February 1991. Only in 1998 did I realise that he and his wife, Marie Desquartiers, had been patrons of the arts and that the murals which had decorated their bedchamber had, by good fortune, been removed before their house was destroyed by fire and survive on the ceiling of one of the museum display rooms.

The references to the famine of 1780–81 is from the *Etrennes Helvetiennes* of 1791 edited by Dean Bridel. It may have also been Bridel who first translated the song of the cowman into French, and reprinted it in *Le Conservateur Suisse* for 1813, though it appears to have been known to Rousseau earlier and has since generated an extensive bibliography including Guy Métraux, *Le Ranz des vaches* (Lausanne, 1984). For another sample of Romanic poetry see Fernand Ruffieux, *Les Armaillis de Colombettes: lè j'armalyi di Colombétè* (Bulle, 1951). Bridel published a widely used *Statistique du Pays-d'Enhaut Romand* (Lausanne, 1807) which can be supplemented by archival statistics cited in Georges-André Chevallaz, *Aspects de l'agriculture vaudoise à la fin de l'Ancien Régime* (Lausanne, 1949).

The classic work of Charles Victor von Bonstetten, 'Lettres sur un peuple de bergers en Suisse' was published in French in the commemorative volume, *Rougemont 1080–1980* (Lausanne, 1980). His farewell speech to the highlanders, 'Discours prononcé dans l'assemblée d'un peuple pasteur des Alpes du canton de Berne par un Membre du Conseil Souverain de cette ville' appeared in a German edition of his letters published in Bern in 1793. The first volume of a new German edition of his works, *Schriften*, was published in Bern in 1997. Reference to the work of his contemporary, Thomas Malthus, on the demography of near-by communities will be found in Pier Paulo Viazzo, *Upland Communities: Environment, Population and Social Structure in the Alps since the sixteenth century* (Cambridge, 1989).

5 Fairs and Markets

The history of Château-d'Oex cheese trading is not only illustrated by detailed local evidence, but also by an important scholarly work on the Gruyère cheese industry, Roland Ruffieux and Walter Bodmer, *Histoire du Gruyère en Gruyère du XVIe au XXe siècle* (Fribourg, 1972). This book provides leads into the international and financial dimensions of the trade and the crises of currencies, coins and tariffs affecting the Geneva and Lyon markets. It also highlights the significance of Vevey for the cheese trade. A short and popular history of the salt industry is presented in a guide to the Bex salt mines, J. Clavel (ed.), *The Mines and Salt Works of Bex* (Lausanne, 1986) which contains details of the Alpine dam built in 1695 to transport timber. The details of the 1725 controversy over the alleged finding of local salt in Château-d'Oex by Lieutenant Desquartiers are recorded in the Bern archives, series A, section V, volume 1171.

Annotated almanacs which provide the structured cycle of dates for markets and fairs in Château-d'Oex and abroad survive in the museum library at least for the years 1721 and 1749, after the official transition from the old Julian calendar to the new Gregorian one in 1700. The more popular Vevey almanac, the *Messager Boiteux*, was founded in 1708 and its 290th edition was issued in 1997. Even closer to home the *Etrennes Helvetiennes et Patriotiques* were written in Château-d'Oex by Dean Bridel during the years of the French occupation, 1798–1803, and contain local information as well as patriotic legends which blend the myth and the history of the Swiss past. A complete set of the *Etrennes*, 1783–1815, is kept in the museum library and much of the information was republished later in *Le Conservateur Suisse*. For a recent history of Swiss markets see A. Radeff *et al.*, *Foires et marchés de Suisse romande* (Morges, 1992). The 1991 *Michelin* reference to the Vevey *fête des vignerons* says 'this is the greatest folk festival in Europe and ends in a display in honour of Bacchus, the god of wine'. Liliane Desponds, *Vevey à la belle époque* (Geneva, 1994) has pictures of the old butter market.

The material culture of highland society and the trade in cloth, clothing and household possessions is visually illustrated by the displays in the museum. The 1772 household and commercial inventory of widow Martin was discovered in a box of loose papers in the town hall attic, along with books of regulations on uniform designs. A published work of great local interest for material culture and market routine is Ruth Usteri, *La vie des femmes au Pays d'Enhaut* (Paris and Leipzig, 1940). This not only gives an account of dress conventions and household customs recovered during research in 1931, but also describes highland language on the eve of its disappearance. For illustrations of old costumes see also Heinrich Hauswirth, *Trachten des Saanenlandes einst und jetzt* (Gstaad, 1989). Trade in metalware and manufactured goods, as well as in salt, is recorded in the account book of Samuel Henchoz. Colin Martin has published widely on the complex currencies in circulation under the *ancien régime* as well as providing evidence for a simplified table of Bern values. A useful table of pre-revolutionary coinage is also given in Chevallaz, cited above.

The wealth of the eighteenth-century cheese trade had a profound impact on the vernacular architecture of the highland and many eighteenth-century farmhouses still survive at the end of the twentieth century. Emile Henchoz, in association with V.P. Kitchin, published an illustrated account of house design and decoration, *Art rustique du Pays-d'Enhaut romand: inscriptions de maison* (Société suisse des traditions populaires, 1929). He also wrote a manificently illustrated history of the seventeenth-century 'Maison de la Place' at Rossinière in *Revue historique vaudoise* (March 1964), and a biographical essay on Jean-David Henchoz, who built the eighteenth-century 'Grand Chalet', in the *Journal de Château-d'Oex* (September 1948). Christian Rubi, *Das Simmentaler Bauernhaus* (Bern, 1980) is a study of the Alemannic architectural traditions some of which influenced Château-d'Oex.

6   The Green Flag of Liberty

The European revolutionary upheavals of 1789 to 1815 which detached Château-d'Oex from Bern and attached it to Lausanne and the new republic of Vaud is the subject of the standard histories such as Paul Maillefer, *Histoire du Canton de Vaud* (Lausanne, 1903), the Society Vaudoise de Histoire et d'Archaeologie, *Cent cinquante ans d'histoire vaudoise* (Lausanne, 1953), volume four of the Vaud encyclopaedia, cited above (Lausanne, 1973) and volume two of the *Nouvelle Histoire*, cited above (Lausanne, 1983). Robert Centlivres, *L'église réformée vaudoise de 1798 à 1803* (Lausanne, 1975) provides a religious background and Maurice Denuzière, *Helvétie* (Paris, 1992) a fictional view of the French invasion.

The best documented aspect of the revolutionary years in Château-d'Oex is the foundation of the 'new' military society described by Emile Henchoz in his scholarly monograph, *L' ancienne abbaye de Château-d'Oex*, cited above. The revolutionary period also generated extensive correspondence now housed in the Vaud archives. Details of the war in Ormont are in file Bda 23/7. The story of Madeleine Isoz's shares in London is in file Bt 16. The Rossinière attitude to the French revolution is recorded in loose papers in the Château-d'Oex town hall attic, and the Christmas issue of *Le Progrès* in 1931 was devoted to the pro-revolutionary Dean Henchoz.

The attachment of the highland to Vaud in 1803 is the subject of extensive debate surviving in the Lausanne archives. The Rossiniere petition to join Vaud, and the Château-d'Oex discussions on sovereignty, are in file Hc 59. The crisis over military recruitment in the highland is in file Hc 58 and questions of taxation and local hostility to the 'Canton of Léman' are in files Hc 59 and H 265 Q. Secondary evidence comes from an article by Eugène Mottaz on the appeals of *vice-préfet* Favre in the *Gazette de Lausanne* of 6 October 1935 and one by Emile Henchoz, 'Le Pays-d'Enhaut et les événements qui précédèrent 1803', in *Le Progrès*, April 1940. In 1941 the rival *Journal de Château-d'Oex* carried a patriotic article by Major Donald Morier-Genoud to commemorate the anniversary of the Vaud revolution of 24 January 1798.

In the current absence of any local parish archives, the religious turmoil which affected the highland in the conservative years of the European 'restoration' from 1815 to 1848 has to be conjectured from accounts of what was happening on the Vaud plain to which Château-d'Oex was now permanently attached. One source is J. Cart, *Histoire de la liberté des cultes dans le canton de Vaud 1798–1889* (Lausanne, 1890). A significant community of 'Darbyite' Brethren took root in the highland by the middle of the nineteenth century but the current leader of the congregation, the florist Louis Duprex, has no written records relating to the first gatherings of Brethren in the more remote hamlets and the Château-d'Oex village congregation was not formalised until 1922. Background to the beliefs of John Nelson Darby's followers will be found in Harold H. Rowdon, *The Origins of the Brethren 1825–1850* (London, 1967). The absence of any local archives relating either to the Darbyite Brethren or to the National Church of Vaud is in marked contrast to the surviving records of the Free Church of Château-d'Oex which was founded in 1845. When the Free Church was dissolved in 1968 its archives and minute books temporarily vanished but in 1993 Marcel Henchoz was able to locate them for me in Rougemont and they are now preserved in the museum's archival collection.

For one contemporary account of the disorders that led to the Swiss 'civil war' of 1847 see Henri Zschokke, *Histoire de la nation suisse* (La Chaux-de-Fonds, revised edition, 1860). For a recent scholarly analysis of that war see Joachim Remak, *A Very Civil War: the Swiss Sonderbund War of 1847* (Boulder, 1993). One of the best single-volume histories of Switzerland, emphasizing diversity before the union of 1848, is Fritz-René Alleman, *Vingt-six fois la Suisse* (Lausanne, 1985). The standard work in English is Jonathan Steinberg, *Why Switzerland?* (Cambridge, second edition, 1996).

7 Butchers, Bakers and Candlestick-Makers

The history of the partial transformation of Château-d'Oex's economy from dairy farming to meat fattening can be reconstructed from a number of official reports such as Edouard Décombaz, *L'économie alpestre dans le canton de Vaud* (Lausanne, 1908). The everyday problems of livestock raising are more vividly brought to life, however, in the nineteenth-century records of the Château-d'Oex police constable which are preserved in the basement of the municipal annexe. It is among these papers that details are found of the goats who came over the mountain from Lessoc to steal hay, of the sheep who broke into rich pasture on their way down to the plain, and of the cowmen who were fined for smoking in cattle-byres regardless of fire regulations. The details of haymaking on the steepest frontiers of the borough are given by Edouard Zulauf, 'Le foin de rocher: vallon des Mérils-Cray' in the local literary journal *Vent des Amonts* (cutting undated).

The controversial history of bread baking and corn milling generated large quantities of litigation. The records of the flour mill of Les Moulin are in the Vaud archive file F 214 and those of the dispute over the Gérignoz mills in the Bern archives, series A, section V, volume 1175. Mill regulations were cited from the museum at Le Locle in the Jura of Vaud. Pierre Delacrétaz, *Les vieux fours à pain* (Yverdon, 1979) is a general, illustrated, history of communal bread ovens.

Some of the most interesting archival documents in Château-d'Oex reflect daily working relationships in the village during the construction of a new town hall after the fire of 1800. The role played by each member of the community, with their 'revolutionary' titles of 'citizen president' or 'citizen bursar', include fully itemised payments made to each labourer and craftsman. The activities of Dean Bridel in energetically helping the village to get back on its feet can be traced through entries in his own *Etrennes Helvetiennes* as well as in his 1807 economic account of the highland, cited above. Bridel's attitude to job creation and economic diversification can be compared to the boxmaking practices in Frutigen described in *Der Schachtelmacher*, an eight-page leaflet of the Swiss national open-air museum at Ballenberg. Details of the black lace bonnet industry of Château-d'Oex are illustrated in Ruth Doepfner-Wettstein, *Dentelles du Pays-d'Enhaut* (Gammelby, 1994). One of the many books on fine paper cutting is Charles Apothéloz, *Deux Imagiers du Pays d'Enhaut: J.J. Hauswirth, L. Saugy* (Paudex, 1978) and smaller paperback books of replicas have been published by Claude Allegri. Some rare originals are in the museum where the custodian, Marianne Ginier, is herself a highly talented *découpage* artist.

8 Education and Social Change

The history of education in Château-d'Oex before and after the French Revolution can, like the history of the Reformation, be partly pieced together from the unpublished research notes of Robert Werner. The enforcement of compulsory primary education was tightened in 1720 and Werner's notes contain a typescript of the archival legislation as well as extracts from Charles Archinard, *Histoire de l'instruction publique dans le canton de Vaud* (Lausanne, 1870) on actual educational practice. Werner also wrote an article on the highland's eighteenth-century 'Latin School' for the *Journal de Château-d'Oex* of 28 December 1945. Further details are given in Bridel, *Satistiques*, and Roch, *Château-d'Oex au XVIIIe*, both cited above. The details of the Esther Tannaz bequest for a girl's school, and the use of the Leprosy Chest for paying schoolmasters, are spelled out in Emile Henchoz, *Bourses*, cited above. The family papers removed from the Rossinière 'Grand Chalet' to the Château-d'Oex town hall attic include, among other educational matter, eighteenth-century exercise books of Hebrew homework and lessons on Swiss geography prepared by the Henchoz children.

Debate over the appropriate syllabus for a primary school is contained in the administrative minutes of the Free Church. Details of the last years of the hamlet schools, as mid-twentieth-century families moved out from the mountains to settle in the villages, is contained in Sonia Rosat 'Les mutations socio-economiques de trois vallées périphériques du Pays-d'Enhaut' (Lausanne mémoire de licence, unpublished, 1985). The slow and reluctant progress of the secondary school in Château-d'Oex is fully documented in the municipal archives. The minutes, including the confidential minutes, of the school's committee of management have been preserved and the records of the municipal bursar are so precise that they even document my own school fees of 60 francs per term, five pounds sterling, in the school's centenary year. The centenary history of the school was published as a special issue of the *Journal de Château-d'Oex* in 1949, expanding on a feature article which appeared in *Le Progrès* at Christmas 1934.

The museum holds complete bound sets of both of the village's newspapers in the storage space under the eves of the roof. These newspapers provide the best evidence for the heated ideological debates that inflamed both the conservative Liberal Party and the progressive Radical Party during economic crisis years in the last quarter of the nineteenth century. Gabriel Morier-Genoud, since 1995 the curator of the museum, has published an illuminating five-part history of the Château-d'Oex press (*Journal de Château-d'Oex*, December 1981) which is also the life story of the village from 1881 to 1981.

On the question of poverty, demography and emigration Maria Schoch, *La population du Pays-d'Enhaut sous l'ancien régime* (Lausanne, 1980) is the most detailed study and has a thorough bibliography of works concerning Château-d'Oex. Lucienne Hubler, 'Emigration civile at émigration militaire à travers le rencensement bernois de 1764' in *Gente Ferocissima*, a 1997 Festschrift for Alain Dubois, shows subtle ways of interpreting demographic data. The extraordinary history of Vaud emigration to Russia is illustrated in Olivier Grivat, *Les vignerons suisses du Tsar* (Chapelle-sur-Moudon, 1993) and notes on Château-d'Oex migrants are taken from the 1995 series of newspaper articles on nineteenth-century Château-d'Oex by André Jacot, later re-edited as a pamphlet entitled *Chroniques à la lumière des registres communaux*. Advertisements for assisted passages to both north and south America appeared regularly in the village press.

9   The Romance of the Alps

The history of the Château-d'Oex tourist industry has its roots in the eighteenth century when Rousseau romanticised the Alps between Vevey and Château-d'Oex by making them the back-drop to his romantic novel, *La Nouvelle Héloise*. This romanticism was taken up by Dean Bridel who as a student frequented the literary salons of Lausanne, including the private library where Gibbon wrote part of his *Decline and Fall of the Roman Empire*. A hundred years later Gonzague de Reynold wrote a literary biography of Bridel, *Le Doyen Bridel (1757– 1845) et les origines de la littérature suisse romande* (Lausanne, 1909) for which he received a Sorbonne doctorate. Bridel's passion for literature, linguistics, geology, botany and folklore might have overshadowed this book had limits not been imposed and the reader is referred to Gonzague de Reynold, himself a leading light of twentieth-century Swiss literature, for a comprehensive bibliography of Bridel's works.

The accounts of Mendelssohn in Château-d'Oex, and of Dompierre and his son at the Etivaz sulphur baths, are culled from undated newspaper cuttings in the archives. The highly perceptive observations on the Swiss of Elizabeth Strutt were published in her two-volume *Domestic Residence in Switzerland* (London, 1842). The revival of the tourist industry from the 1870s is illustrated by news items and advertisements in the local press and at the end of the century a tourist information office was issuing publicity brochures some of which survive in the museum library. A history of the post office, and of the diligence coach services that brought early visitors, is D. Ruchet *et al.*, *Histoire de la Poste du Pays-d'Enhaut* (Monthey, 1990) which can be supplemented by the richly coloured Arthur Wyss, *La Poste en suisse: 2000 ans d'histoire* (Lausanne, 1987). The first Cook's tour of Switzerland, *Miss Jemima's Swiss Journal* (London, 1863) did not include Château-d'Oex but gives a flavour of early Alpine travel. The *belle époque* in Château-d'Oex itself is celebrated in M. Henchoz and G. Morier-Genoud, *Château-d'Oex et son district au début du siècle* (Geneva, 1990) a collection of one hundred Victorian and Edwardian picture postcards.

The history of the Château-d'Oex railway attracted the attention of British railway enthusiasts including the watercolour artist Paget-Tomlinson who published a book on the subject in 1985. Among the popular, technical and illustrated books on the line's history one of the most useful is the company's own anniversary volume, *75 Jahre Mob* (Montreux, 1976). Political disputes over the railway among the ruling Liberals can still be collected in oral memories and the hostile attitudes to the railway of working folk can be gauged from law court records, recently given to the museum, in one of which the federal government persuaded the railway company to desist from prosecuting a carter who, in 1907, had been charged with damaging a locomotive by driving a horse and cart 'carelessly' over the crossing at Les Bossons. The history of electricity in the highland is lavishly illustrated in another 75th anniversary volume by Nicole Zimmermann, *Entreprises électriques fribourgeoises* (Fribourg, 1990).

While the railway was built to attract wealthy foreign vacationers, quite different forms of investment were needed to rebuild the Alpine farming economy. Two published studies give background and statistics: Edouard Décombaz, *L'économie alpestre dans le canton de Vaud*, cited above, was published on behalf of the Société Suisse d'économie alpestre, and Andreas Werthman and Adrian

Imboden, *L'économie alpestre et pacagère en Suisse* (Bern, 1962) on behalf of the federal government. As subsidies became the basis of alpine renewal one can find some of the financial records of Château-d'Oex mountain farming, including applications for grants, in the Vaud archives. By 1997 *The Economist* newspaper claimed, on 16 August, that Swiss cows were subsidised at 1000 US dollars per hoof and the *Journal de Genève* claimed, on 23 August 1994, that at 77 per cent Swiss farm subsidies were as high as those of Norway and 50 per cent higher than those of Brussels.

The *Association pour le développement du Pays-d'Enhaut* has built up an extensive library of published and manuscript materials on agriculture, tourism and the relationship between the two in its rooms above the Château-d'Oex tourist office. The Swiss federal polytechnic, using sponsorship from Unesco, ran a long-term research programme on man and the environment in the Château-d'Oex highland and the findings were synthesised in Erwin Stucki and Françoise Lieberherr, *Sur nos monts quand la nature ... Le Pays-d'Enhaut tourné vers l'avenir* (Château-d'Oex, second edition, 1988). A wider comparative analysis, Jost Krippendorf, *La-haut sur la montage ... Pour le développement du tourism en harmonie avec l'homme et la nature* (Bern, 1987) gives the darker side of 'tourism as a plague'. An important local description of farming, with photographs by Jean Lugrin, is Claude Quartier, *Le Pays-d'Enhaut: les fromagers et l'avenir des Alpes* (Lausanne, 1980). Some of Lugrin's best photographs appeared in G.-A. Chevallaz, *Château-d'Oex et le Pays-d'Enhaut* (Neuchâtel, 1974).

10 Patriotism and the Shadow of War

The history of Swiss national unification and the creation of a Swiss army to match the union post office and the single currency is a subject that can now be studied in the revisionist textbooks of the 1980s and 1990s such as the *Nouvelle Histoire de la Suisse*, cited above. The story of William Tell, the invented hero of Swiss patriotism whose historic status the Gruyère historian Hisely was still energetically trying to defend in the nineteenth century, is well presented in the Uri museum dedicated to his legendary role. The diversity of roles played by Tell is vividly illustrated by Lilian Stunzi, *Quel Tell? – dossier iconographique* (Lausanne, 1973). The radical re-interpretation of early Swiss history is pushed furthest by Werner Maier whose travelling exhibition on the origins of Switzerland was accompanied by a book entitled in French, *Nos Ancêtres les Waldstetten: la Suisse centrale au XIIIe siècle, mythes et histoire* (Lausanne, 1994). A good illustrated history of Switzerland, written to accompany a British Museum exhibition to mark the seventh centenary of the pact of 1291, was published by Peter Barber, *Switzerland 700: Treasures from the British Library and the British Museum* (London, 1991).

The history of the First World War in Château-d'Oex was commissioned by the borough from a local school teacher, André Paillard. His handwritten report, 'La Mobilisation à Château-d'Oex', was apparently filed away in the municipal archive without ever being published and was not seen again until I found it more than 70 years later. The horror of a community of women, children and grandparents living on the verge of starvation only to be decimated by two plagues of influenza and threatened by a Soviet-style revolution was hardly the stuff of patriotic nation-building. The dark years of Switzerland's past began to be captured and put in context in an enlightened work of historical synthesis disseminated by the Migros Foundation, *La Suisse de la formation des Alpes à la quête du futur* (Zürich, 1975). More polemical works concern Switzerland's military leadership, Nicolas Meienberg, *Le délire général: l'armée suisse sous l'influence* (Geneva, 1988) and the revolutionary threat of the general strike, Marc Vuilleumier *et al.*, *La grève générale de 1918 en Suisse* (Geneva, 1977).

The Second World War was, with hindsight, no less controversial than the first war but in Château-d'Oex it appeared less so, sheltered as it was behind a mountain fortress defended by its own general, Henri Guisan. An alternative view of militarised society was given in Max Frisch, *Livret de Service* (Vevey, 1977). An English-language account of the way in which annual military discipline affected the class system, the business networks, and the exclusive male bonding of the Swiss was published by John MacPhee, *La place de la concorde suisse* (London, 1985). Fifty years after the war the radical questioning of wartime politics and their moral repercussions was led by Jean Ziegler, a socialist in the federal parliament who had previously blown the whistle on the laundering of drug money, *La Suisse lave plus blanc* (Paris, 1990). Kaspar Villiger's presidential apology for the political turpitude of his predecessors during the Nazi years was publicised in *L'Hebdo* weekly of 11 May 1995. An early domestic exposé of banking malpractice, ten years before it became an international issue, was Werner Rings, *L'or des Nazis: la Suisse, un relais discret* (Lausanne, 1985).

In Château-d'Oex a history of the village which the antiquarian members of the Club du Rubly had published as *Château-d'Oex et le Pays-d'Enhaut vaudois* (Château-d'Oex, 1882) was reprinted under the auspices of the museum. In a rather different vein the borough's most famous citizen, the former federal president Georges-André Chevallaz, published his controversially conventional *Le gouvernement des suisses ou l'histoire en contrepoint* (Lausanne, 1989). Dominique Henchoz celebrated the seventh centenary of the pact of 1291 with a pamphlet, *Le livre des bourgeois de Château-d'Oex* giving the glossy versions of the coats-of-arms of the 35 traditional families which survive in the highland. In 1994 the *Ancienne Abbaye* of military sports celebrated its bi-centenary with four days of pomp and a copy of the menu for the gala dinner found its way into the museum archives.

Notes on archives

1   Château-d'Oex

As will be clear from the chapter notes above there has never been any attempt to collect and catalogue the archives of Château-d'Oex and research can only be conducted thanks to the patient generosity of officials who hold the keys to the various repositories.

2   Bern

The archival relationship between Château-d'Oex and Bern is fiendishly complex since half of the bailliwick was transferred to Vaud in 1798 and half was not. Much material on Château-d'Oex is therefore mixed in with the records of

Saanen (also known as Gessenay). The state archive is, however, rather well indexed and material is to be found in Series A, Section V, volumes 1168 to 1182. Financial papers are in Series B, Section VII, volumes 1704–28 and geographical material in Series A, Section I, volumes 897–901. Some material which should have been transferred to Lausanne is still in Bern.

3 Vaud

Material which was transferred to Lausanne, or was generated after 1798, will be found in the Vaud state archive. Unlike many rural boroughs, however, Château-d'Oex did not regularly avail itself of opportunities to transfer records to the state repository. Possible sources, some of which have been explored for the purpose of writing this book, are listed below.

A Savoy and the bishopric archives

Aa 112 vols of transcriptions of ancient acts
for example Aa 6 two vols of Chd0 records 1341–
Ab Savoy papers to 1536
Ac Lausanne bishop, chapter, cathedral, castle
Ah foreign relations (including Gruyère)
Ai catalogues of records in parishes and communes
for example Ai 48 Saanen inventory

B Bern records (with possible references to Gessenay and Château-d'Oex though they were not administered by the Welsch-Seckelmeister *but by the treasurer of the Bern home provinces)*

Ba decrees
Bb administration
Bc commissionnaires and bannerets
Bd church and academy
for example Bda consistory records (many subsequently destroyed)
Bda 23, 1–7, concern Chd0, tome 7 on 1770–98
Bdb Vaud records of the five church deaneries
Bf customary laws (Moudon, 1577) and statutes (Bern 1616)
Bg, Bh, Bi, justice
Br 36 occasional papers
Bt 16 private papers
Bv mines and salt workings

C parchments

for example
C VII includes papers on the priory of Rougemont
C XX 17th c. records from Chd0 in sections 323–5

Dq notebooks of notaries in PdE

1. Pierre Bertholet of Rougemont
2. Vincent David Byrde 1803–37 (6 boxes)
3. Moyse Chappalay 1662– (12 vols)

4. Jacques Cottier, 1687, Abraham Cottier, 1688, etc
5. Samuel David Descoullayes 1780–1801 (1 box)
6. Joseph Favre 1788–1834 (1 box)
8. Gabriel Henchoz 1697–1737 (2 boxes, Rossinière)
12. Lt David Isoz 1709–16 (damaged)
13. David Isoz 1760–1803
14. Jean David Mange 1796–1824
17. Jean Samuel Marmillod 1730–73 (1 box)
25. Nicolas Massard 1560–
26. 1714–24
29. David Raynaud 1771–1818 (5 boxes)
30. Louis Rosat 1829–37

F   *terrier land records seized by Bern 1536 and recovered in 1798*
for example
Fc Aigle, Ormonts, PdE and Gessenay from 1253
Fc 1–5, 1300–50
Fc 14– 15th c.
Fc 161–Fc170 1558
Fc 185–Fc196 1592–1609
Fc 219 1666

G   *maps and plans*
for example Gc roads, mines, baths, rivers

H   *Helvetian archives of Canton de Léman 1798–1803*
for example
   5 public safety
   6 military affairs 1798
   7 taxes, tolls, salt
  16 1798 legislation (for example on cattle disease)
  25 correspondence (for example with Talleyrand)
  26 decrees (for example banning *colportage*)
  58 letters to Chd0 1799–1802 (for example urgent requests for troops)
  59 ditto 1803 (for example treasonable approaches to Bern)
  77 lieutenants and municipalities
  79 tribunals
  90 French occupation
  94 sous-préfecture de Chd0 (passports 1799)
 142 Aigle campaign to Ormont 1798 (notes)
 145 arbres de liberté
 153 elections
 162 archive burning
 173/4 Valais campaign
 176 French occupation
 212 financial accounts for PdE 1798–1803
 228–231 abolition of feudal dues
 252–259 laws on 'dimes', 'censes' and 'laud'

264 1803 table of prices
265Q PdE taxes
286 hunting, mining, quarrying
289–319 military affairs
321–356 police, censorship

J   *Vaud domestic and foreign affairs 1803 to 1848*
for example J 224 religious debates

K   *Official archives*
for example
K VI prefects records (of which many destroyed or missing)
K XI coinage and postal systems
K XII agricultural (including cattle)
K XIII education
K XIV the Church of Vaud
K XV the military department (until 1874)
K XVIII tribunals 1798–1911 (many missing)
K XIX justices of the peace (many missing)

P   *Private papers inventoried by commune*

Microfilms of Chd0 births, confirmations, marriages and deaths:
EB 23/ 1–4 Baptisms 1571–1605 and 1605 1702
 Marriages 1605–1702 (164 Family Names)
 Confirmations 1704–1751

ED 23/ 1–2 Births and Baptisms 1821–1862 (60 per annum)
 4 Marriages 1821–75
 5–6 Deaths 1821–1875 (causes not given)

Index

Aargau 117
adultery 48
Africa, emigration to 151–2
Aigle, castle of 28, 30
alcoholism 120, 154
Alemannic Swiss xiv, 3, 41, 201
  in world wars 190, 191
Alexander I of Russia xii, 110, 151
almanacs 82, 84, 207–8
Alsace, war with 27–8
Amadeus V of Savoy 13
Americas, emigration to 150, 151
'Ancient Abbey' 102–4, 199–200
Anthony of Gruyère 5, 24, 71
archery 33
archives 134–5, 205, 214–17
armies
  conscription into 9–10, 27–8; and
    French invasion 105, 108; in
    First World War 189, 190–1
  federal 176–7, 180, 181–2, 193
  uniforms, 18th-century 86
  of 1490 (Zürich) 25–6
  see also mercenaries; and military
    history under Bern and Gruyère
Austria 102, 108, 110
avalanches 77, 86

bakers 127
ballooning 171, 197
banking 89–90, 192, 196
bannarets 7
baptism: after Reformation 43
bartering 74–5, 122
Basel 31, 116
Batz xv, 94
Bear Inn 165, 198
beef-rearing 119–20, 122–5, 172, 182
beekeepers 131
begging 139, 140, 164
bells/bellringing 55–6, 88, 197
Bern xiv, 19, 118, 178, 204
  and Burgundy 28–30

and Château-d'Oex, in 14th–16th
  centuries 19, 20–1, 36; and
  Gruyère sovereignty 18, 24,
  28, 29, 30–1, 35; in 18th–19th
  centuries 102–5, 198–9
expansionism xi, 19–24, 28,
  30–2
and France 32, 90, 104–6, 108
and Gruyère 18, 23–5, 28, 29, 31;
  partition xi, 34–5
military history 18, 19–25, 28, 29,
  30–2, 204
and Reformation 36, 37–9, 40, 41,
  46, 49
and Rhône salt mines 91–2, 93
senate: and Gérignoz mills 129–30
and 1291 treaty 21–2, 178
and Vaud 101, 108
Bernese Oberland 22
Berthod, Madeleine 170
betrothal: customs 47–8, 49
Bex 91–3, 160
Blancsex, Philippe du 189
Bonaparte, Napoleon 101, 108, 110
bonnets, lace 139
Bonstetten, Charles Victor von 65,
  76–80, 87–8, 130, 199, 207
box-making 139–40
Braye valley 51, 75
Brazil, emigration to 151
breadmaking 127–30
Bretton Woods conference 192
Bridel, Dean 131
  almanac 82, 84, 208
  on contemporary life 88, 119,
    120, 125, 140
  on medieval life 6, 71, 203
  and rebuilding after fire 133, 135,
    197, 210; bells replacement
    56, 88
  and revolution 102, 104–5, 106,
    108, 110
  and tourism 159, 212

'British Internees Variety Company'
186
Bulle xv, 132–3
bundling 47
Burgundy: and Bern 28–30
butter: sales 86
Byrde, Justice 103, 106–7
Byrde, Madeleine 48

Cailler family 198
Calvin, John xi, 40, 41, 143
Canada, emigration to 151
candles 130–1
Cart, J. 111
cart tracks 96, 97, 121
castles: of Gruyère 4, 5–6, 17, 24
Rougemont 35, 110
catechism classes 44
Catholics 36–7, 117, 156, 172–3,
177
and Reformation 37–43
cats 95
cattle farming *see* beef rearing; cheese
industry; dairy industry
cereal farming 78, 181
Chabloz, Ami 188
Chabloz, Esther 64–5, 136
Chabloz, Louis David 126
Chabloz, Marie Madeleine 49
Chamby: railway junction 167
chamois-stalking 157
chapalet 48–9
charcoal-burning 137–8
charities 53–5, 143–6
charivari associations 46
Charles the Bold: of Burgundy 28,
29
Charmey 165
chatelains 7–8
Chatelard: castle 28
cheese industry
and Bern expansionism 23
cheesemaking 57, 66, 180; process
59–60, 71–3, 74; seasonal
employment 124–5, 142
coopering 87
farming xi, 66–8, 71, 73
in First World War 180, 182–3
19th-century decline 119, 140

trading xi, 80, 81, 86–7, 90, 207;
in 20th century 182–3, 197
child begging 139, 140
children's homes, mountain 162
Chile, emigration to 151
Chillon, fortress of 16, 31
chocolate production 198
Church
medieval: in Gruyère 14–16
in Vaud 111–18, 195
see also Catholics; Protestants;
Reformation; St Donat's
'civil war,' Swiss (1847) 116–18, 152,
209
Clarens 88
clockmaking 141–2
clothing: in 18th century 85–6
coal crisis: in First World War 183
coats-of-arms
of Bern 19
of Château-d'Oex 7
of Gruyère 1
Henchoz (Rossinière) 56, 97
cobblers 122
coffee 71, 87–8
coinage xv–xvi, 93–4, 152–3, 208
cold war: and Switzerland 195, 196
colonisation: of highland x, 1, 3,
203
communal land use
in Rossinière 60–1, 65–6
in Vauseresse 62–5
communion attendance 44–5
conscription 9–10, 27–8
and French invasion 105, 108
in First World War 180–1, 189
co-operative retail society 187
coopers, cheese 87
corn milling 127–30, 210
cottage industries 138–40, 141–2
Cottier, Auguste 156–7, 181, 182,
189–90
cotton mills 141
courting customs 45–6, 47–8
cow bells 67
craft industries 138–40, 141–2
crane, heraldic 1
crossbows 26, 33
crown (coin) xvi, 94

cultivation: of land 95
  Bonstetten on 77, 78–9
  in First World War 181, 183, 187
curling 169
currency *see* coinage
customs posts 86, 96, 152, 153

dairy industry
  and foot and mouth disease 120,
    122
  pre-enclosure 57, 59–61
  in 18th century xi, 61–2, 65–77,
    79–80
  in 19th century 113, 119
  in 20th century 172–4, 199
  see also cheese industry
dams 92, 166, 173
dancing: after Reformation 45–6, 70
Darby, John Nelson 112–13
Darbyites 113, 195, 209
David 'the German' 129
de la Harpe, Frédéric-César 110
denier (currency unit) 94
Descoulayes, Bombardier 103, 106
Descoullayes, Suzanne Marie 144
Desquartiers, Lieutenant 91
Desquartiers, Marie 100, 207
Desquartiers sisters 126
Diana, Princess of Wales 169
diet
  of farmers 119, 73–4
  in First World War 182–3, 185,
    187–8
diseases: of cattle 120, 122
dogs 95
Dompierre François Radolphe
  (archaeologist) 160–1
Donat, St: church 14, 38
  bells 55, 56, 88, 197
Dreyfus, Alfred 164
drinking songs 51–2
Druey, Henri 112
Dufour, Guillaume (General) 118
Dumas, Alexandre 93, 160

Echallens 111
ecology 158, 196
écu (coin) xvi, 94

education 143–9, 154, 210–11
electricity 165–6
Elizabeth II of England 169
embroidery industry 142
emigration 149–52, 211
Emmental cheeses 23
enclosure, land 57, 60–2, 97, 206
environmentalism 158, 196
Etambeaux: museum 197
'Etivaz Cheese' 172
Etivaz (valley) xv, 75, 113, 124, 197
  church bells 55–6
  funeral customs 42
  sulphur baths 160–1
Etrennes Helvetiennes et Patriotiques
    82, 84, 208
European Union: and Switzerland
    196
evangelism: in Vaud 111–13,
    114–16, 209
  see also Free Church
expatriates, British 168–9, 181
exports 80, 84, 87, 119–20

fairs 20, 89, 96
  Château-d'Oex 82, 84–6, 119–20
Farel, Guillaume 40
farmers/farming
  early/medieval 4, 11, 20
  and 1885 recession 153–4
  taxation 11, 61, 73, 78, 140
  in 20th century: mechanisation
    173; and military service
    194–5; in First World War
    180–3; subsidies 174, 195
  and tourism 163, 170–1, 172,
    174–5, 213
  see also beef-rearing; cheese
    industry; dairy industry;
    enclosure; haymaking
Favre (vice-governor) 107
Favrod-Coune (family) 148, 155, 163
Favrod-Coune, Charles 157
Favrod-Coune, Charles-Victor 148,
    155, 165, 181
Favrod-Coune, Jules 155
federalism xii, 152–3, 176–8
  1891 celebrations 178–80
feudalism: in Gruyère 3–16

Feutersoey 47
firearms: introduction 33
fires: in Château-d'Oex 9, 131–3
 and recovery 56, 88, 133–5, 210
First World War *see* World War I
florin xv, 93–4
flour milling 127–30, 210
food *see* diet
foot and mouth disease 120, 122
forestry 61–2, 69, 135–7
fox-shooting 157
franc xvi, 94, 152–3, 175
France/French
 and Bern 32, 90, 104–6, 108
 and cheese trade 87, 90
 invasion by 61, 104–6, 108–10
 language 143, 147, 201
 Revolution 101–2
 war with Germany 177
Francis I of France 32, 34
Francis I of Gruyère 5, 13, 25, 28
Free Church, Château-d'Oex 114–16,
 149, 195
Fribourg 31, 79, 118, 126
 customs/tolls 86, 96, 153
 and Gruyère 34, 35
Frutigen 139
funeral customs 42, 86

gambling 52–3
game hunting 157–8
Gardel, Marcel 147
gatelet 73–4
Geneva 37, 89–90, 118, 141
Geneyne family 38
Gérignoz mills 129–30
Germany 177, 192
gin, gentian 52, 88, 120, 154
Ginier, Marianne 138, 210
girls *see* women
Glacière 74, 197
goats 65, 126
Golden Mountain service 167
Gothard pass 22, 25
governors, highland xv, 155–7
Graffenried, Captain von 105
Graffenried, Hans-Rudolph 39
Graffenried, Nicholas von 92
Grand Hotel (Château-d'Oex) 163

Grandson, battle of 29
Grandvillars: church 38
'Great Chalet' (Rossinière) 99–100,
 164
Gruyère xiv, 1, 2, 132–3
 and Bern 18, 23–5, 28, 29, 31; and
 partition xi, 34–5
 feudalism 3–16
 and Habsburg invasion 16–17
 house of x, 5, 17–18, 24–5
 military history 2, 16–18, 24–5,
 27–9, 30–1, 34; castles 4, 5–7,
 17, 24
 see also cheese industry; *and named
 princes*
Gstaad 168
Guisan, Henri xii, 191–3
gymnastics 185

Habsburgs 16–17, 21, 29, 117, 179
Haller, Jean 39–40
Häne, J. 26
Hauswirth, J.J. 137–8
haymaking 68, 77, 79, 125–6, 174
Helvetia xiv, 106, 110, 118, 176
hemp 78
'Henchod, Honestum Henricum' 97
Henchoz (family: Rossinière) 56,
 97–100, 102, 130
 see also Henchoz, Gabriel (Dean)
Henchoz, Abraham 97
Henchoz, David 56
Henchoz, Emile 205, 209
Henchoz, Gabriel (Dean: son of
 Jean-David) 100, 102, 107, 162
Henchoz, Gabriel (Judge: 1675–1752)
 97–8, 102
Henchoz, Jacques-Louis 129
Henchoz, Jean-David 98, 99–100
Henchoz, Joshua 75
Henchoz, Moses 74–5
Henchoz, Samuel 74–6, 85, 93, 122,
 197–9, 206–7
 and currency 93, 94
 and horses 95–6
 philanthropy 54–5, 143
Henchoz brothers (merchants) 145–6
Henchoz Institute 145–8, 211
holidays, public 156, 178

Holy Roman Empire   21
Hongrin dam   166, 173
horses   95–6, 136, 173, 180
house tax   9
hunting   157–8
hydro-electric power   165–6

ice-hockey   169
illegitimacy   49
immigration   1, 3, 141, 172–3
influenza epidemics   188–9, 190
inheritance tax   12, 23
International Settlements, Bank for
   192
internees, British   186–7, 188
iron industry   137
Isoz, Madeleine   101
Italy   25, 172
   Alps: cheese industry   87, 95

Jaman pass   86, 105, 159–60
Jaman tunnel   96, 168
Jaun valley   5
Jesuits: and education   117
John IV of Montsalvens/I of Gruyère
   5, 7–8
Jones, Brian   171
Journal de Château-d'Oex   154, 155,
   190
Jung, Carl   186
Jura   124–5, 141, 142

'kiltgang'   47
knitting   69, 142
Kreutzer   xv, 94

lace-making   139
Laupen, battle of   21
Lausanne   xv, 4, 17, 132–3, 159, 165
   and Bern   29, 30, 32, 37–8
   and Gruyère   16–17, 29
   Henchoz sons' education   98, 102
   and Vaud government   110, 112,
      114
leather industry   122
Léman   109
Lenoir, Abraham   127
Lenoir, David   103, 104, 106–7, 110
lepers/leper fund   54, 145, 205
Leysin: sanatoria   162, 194

Liberal party   153, 154–5, 167, 190,
   195
'Liberty Trees'   109
livre   xvi, 94
logging industry   *see* forestry
lotteries   52
Louis of Gruyère   5, 28, 29
Louis d'or (sovereign)   xvi, 94
Louis IV of Bavaria   21
Louis XI of France   90
Louis XIV of France   92–3
Lucerne   117, 118
lumberjacks   *see* forestry
Lüthy, Mr (teacher)   149

McCormack, John   26
Madeleine, St: feast   70–1
mainmorte   12
Malthus, Thomas   77
Marignano, battle of   32
markets   4, 20, 81–2, 119
Marmillod, Josué   55
marriage customs   46–8
Martin, Widow: inventory   84,
   208
Massard, Daniel   69
Massard, David   122
matchbox-making   139–40
meat industry   119–20, 122–5, 172,
   182
Medici Bank (Geneva)   89, 90
Mendelssohn, Felix   159–60
Mercator, Nicolaus   86
mercenaries   28, 32–4, 57, 93, 150
Meril valley: haymaking   125–6
Messager Boiteux   82, 84, 208
metal industries   33, 84–5, 88, 137,
   141–2
Michael of Gruyère   5, 34, 88
Milan   25
military club   102–4, 199–200
military history
   of Bern   18, 19–25, 28–9, 30–2,
      204
   of Gruyère   2, 16–18, 24–5, 27–9,
      30–1, 34; castles   4, 5–7, 17, 24
   see also armies; mercenaries; wars
military service   193, 194–5
   see also conscription

milk 57
  processed 196, 198
  weighing 70
  see also cheese industry; dairy
    industry
milling, corn 127–30, 210
Minod, Salomé 45, 85
monasteries: in Gruyère 14
  Rougemont 14–16, 39, 41, 60
money *see* coinage
Montbovon 165, 166, 167, 194
Montreux 159, 167–8
Montsalvens castle 4, 5–6, 17
Morat, battle of 29
More, Thomas 27
Morier, David 122
Morier-Genoud, Albert 147
Morier-Genoud, David 154
Morier-Genoud, Donald 147
Morier-Genoud, Gabriel 211
Morier-Genoud, Jean 130
motors 164, 171, 173
Moudon: customary laws xv, 13,
  35
Moulins, Les 128, 168
  tavern 52–3, 127

Nancy, battle of 29
Napoleon *see* Bonaparte
Napoleonic wars 101, 104–6, 108–10
National Church (Vaud) 111, 113,
  114, 195
Nazism 170–80, 192
Nestlé 198
Nicholas of Flue 179
Niven, David 171

Ogo 3
  dean of 14
Olten Association 140
Ormont valley xiv, 18, 30, 31
Oudorico-the-German 15

pack animals 95
Paillard, André 213
paper-cutting 138, 210
Paquier Gétaz 68
Paray Charbon 68
pelt tax 8–9

Perronet, Marie 100
Pétain, Henri (Marshal) 191
Peter, prior of Rougemont 5, 41
Peter of Savoy 16
Peter II of Gruyère 5, 16, 17
Peter III of Gruyère 5, 18, 20
Peter IV of Gruyère 5, 20
Piccard, Bertrand 171
Pilet (family: Rossinière) 52
Pilet, Esther 48, 88
Pilet, Joseph 52–3
Pittan, Joseph 126
Plymouth Brethren 112–13
police duty: under feudalism 9
potatoes 73–4, 78, 96, 127
  in First World War 183, 187
poverty
  post-First World War 187
  in 18th century 69
  in 19th century xi–xii, 140,
    149–52, 153–4
printing: in Gruyère 16
Progrès, Le 154
prostitution 49
Protestants/Protestantism 156
  in Château-d'Oex 36, 41–56
  French refugees 141, 143
  and public holidays 156
public holidays 156, 178

Quartiers, Les 197

Radical party 114–15, 152
  in Château-d'Oex 153, 154, 155,
    195
railways 161, 166–8, 184, 212
Ramel, Widow 54–5
Ranz des Vaches (song) 57, 59, 207
Raynaud, Emile 67–8, 206
Raynaud, Jean 100
Redboldus of Gruyère 15
Reformation: and Château-d'Oex
  xi, 36, 37–41, 70
  social effects 41–56
religion *see* Church
republics x–xi
  and Bern xi, 21–2, 29
  and Gruyère debts/sale 34–5

revolutions
  French 101–2
  Swiss 104–10
  in Vaud 112, 114, 116, 117
Rhône (area) 30
  salt mines 91–3
roads: construction 174
Roch, David 149
Rochat, Charles 112
Romanic Swiss xiv, 190
  languages 3, 201, 203; and
    Reformation 40, 41, 44
Romont: horse fair 96
Rosat, Pierre 51
Rossinière 24, 37, 102
  communal land use 60–1, 65–6
  'Great Chalet' 99–100, 164
  and Vaud 107, 110
Rougemont 203
  castle 35, 110
  in middle ages 8–9, 24, 28
  monastery 14–16, 39, 41, 60
  in 18th/19th centuries 50, 103,
    108, 132
Rousseau, Jean-Jacques 159, 212
Rudolph III of Gruyère 5, 16
Rudolph IV of Gruyère 5, 12, 13
Rudolph of Habsburg 16, 17, 21
Russia/Russians 151, 184

Saanen 1, 39–40
  in feudal era 8, 10, 14, 23
St Bernard pass 16, 23, 25, 32
St Donat's church 14, 38
  bells 55, 56, 88, 197
St Gothard pass 22, 25
salt 81, 90–3
Salvation Army 112
sanatoria: in Leysin 162, 194
'Sardinians' 172
Saugy, Louis 138
Saugy, Madeleine 50
Savoy 16, 17, 18, 23
Sazième 70–1
Schinner, Matthew 31
Scholl, Pastor 116
Schweitzer, Albert 169
Schwytz 21, 116

secondary homes 172
Second World War *see* World War II
séré 74
serfdom 11
settlement: of highland x, 1, 3,
  203
Seventh Day Adventists 112
sexual offences: penalties 48–9
sheep-farming: in Vauseresse 62–5
shooting 102–4, 157–8, 199–200
Simmental (valley) xiv, 1
  cows 123, 199
  and Gruyère expansionism 18, 20
Simmental-Holstein cows 172
Simplon pass 16
skating 169
skiing 77, 170–1
slurry, spreading 123–4
Smith, Adam 79
Soldanelle 162
Solothurn 33, 41
sol/sou (currency unit) xv, 94
sovereign xvi, 94
sports 157–8, 169–71, 185
  military 102–4, 199–200
stockings, knitting of 69, 142
Struby, Louis 184
Strutt, Elizabeth 161, 162
suicide 42
Sunday observance 43–4
Swiss Revolution 104–10
Swiss Society for Alpine Economy
  123

taille 11
Tannaz, Esther 143–4
tanning 122
taxation
  agricultural 11, 61, 73, 78, 140
  border 86, 96, 152, 153
  feudal 4, 8–9, 11–13, 23
  on milling 128–9
  and poor relief 140, 150
  on salt 90, 91
Tell, William 178–80, 213
textiles 78, 85, 141
Thirty Years War 87
Tièche, Nicholas 195
timber *see* forestry

tithes 11, 73, 78
tobogganing 170
tourism xi–xii, 144–5, 155, 158,
  159–70, 212
  and farmers/farming 163, 170–1,
    172, 174–5, 213
traffic, road 163–4
transhumance 4, 67–8, 79
transport
  of cheese/salt 86, 91, 95–7
  and farm subsidies 174
  see also cart tracks; railways
treaties
  of 1291 21–2, 178
  Bern–France 32
  Vienna 110–11, 117, 118
Tribollet, Lord-Bailiff 48, 51

Ulrick of Gruyère 15
unification, Swiss *see* federalism
Unterwald 21, 39
Uri 21, 22, 25, 32–3

Valais 117
  army 185
Vanel 2
  castle 6, 24
  gorge 3
Vaud xv, 118, 140, 177, 209
  and Château-d'Oex xii, 106–8,
    110, 176, 178
  and meat industry 120, 122–3
  National Church 111, 113, 114,
    195
  religious schism 111–18
  republicanism 101–2, 152, 156
  revolutions 112, 114, 116, 117
Vauseresse (valley) 62–5, 206
Vevey xv, 29, 87–9, 112, 132–3
  trade/industries 86, 88, 141, 198
Vienna, treaty of 110–11, 117, 118
Villars 171
Viret, Pierre 40

Wahlen plan 193
wars
  Alsace 27–8
  Bern–Burgundy 29–30
  cold 195, 196
  First World xii, 180–9, 190–1,
    213–14
  Franco-German 177
  Napoleonic 101, 104–6, 108–10
  with Ormont 30
  Second World xii, 179–80, 190,
    191–4, 214
  Swiss civil (1847) 116–18, 152,
    209
  Thirty Years 87
watch industry 141–2
water supply: to Lausanne 165
wax industry 130–1
weddings: after Reformation 46
weights and measures 94–5
Werner, Robert 147, 204–5, 211
whey cheeses 74
Wilhelm, Kaiser 191
Wille, Ulrich 190–1
William of Corbière 15
William of Gruyère 15
wine/winemaking 88–9, 154
winter sports 169–71
Wirczburg, Henry 16
witchcraft 29–30, 49–51
women/girls 145, 184–5, 193–4
  and education 143–5, 148, 185
wood crafts 139–40
woods *see* forestry
World War I xii, 180–9, 190–1,
  213–14
World War II xii, 179–80, 190,
  191–4, 214

Zähringen family 13
Zschokke, Henri 117
Zürich 22, 117, 118
  army (1490) 25–6
Zwingli, Huldreich xi, 39, 41